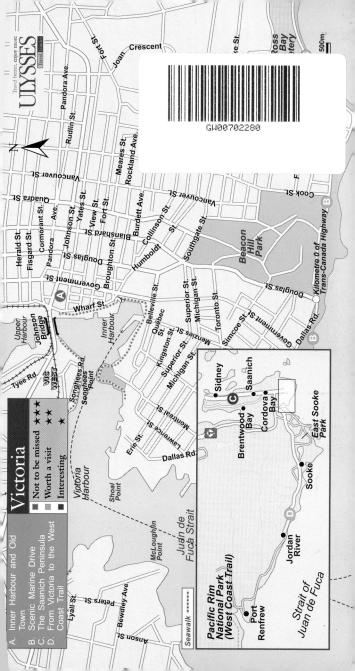

Travel better, enjoy more

ULYSSES
Travel Books

GW00702280

Victoria

Not to be missed ★★★
Worth a visit ★★
Interesting ★

A. Inner Harbour and Old Town
B. Scenic Marine Drive
C. The Saanich Peninsula
D. From Victoria to the West Coast Trail

Seawalk ·······

Upper Harbour

Johnson Bridge

Tyee Rd.

VIC WEST

Songhees Rd.
Songhees Point

Inner Harbour

Wharf St.

Victoria Harbour

Shoal Point

McLoughlin Point

Juan de Fuca Strait

Peters St.
Bewdley Ave.
Anson St.
Lyall St.
Dallas Rd.
Erie St.
Lawrence St.
Montreal St.
Superior St.
Michigan St.
Kingston St.
Québec St.
Belleville St.
Menzies St.

Government St.
Broughton St.
Douglas St.
Pandora St.
Johnson St.
Yates St.
View St.
Fort St.
Blanshard St.
Humboldt
Collinson St.
Burdett Ave.
Southgate St.
Superior St.
Michigan St.
Toronto St.
Simcoe St.
Government St.
Dallas Rd.

Cormorant Ave.
Pandora Ave.
Herald St.
Fisgard St.
Quadra St.
Quadra Ave.

Rudlin St.
Pandora Ave.
Meares St.
Rockland Ave.
Vancouver St.
Vancouver St.
Cook St.

Joan Crescent
Fort St.

Ross Bay Cemetery

Beacon Hill Park

Douglas St.

Kilometre 0 of Trans-Canada Highway

500 m.

(inset map)

Pacific Rim National Park (West Coast Trail)

Port Renfrew

Jordan River

Sooke

East Sooke Park

Brentwood Bay

Cordova Bay

Saanich

Sidney

Strait of Juan de Fuca

The totem poles in Vancouver's Stanley Park are reminders of the First Nations heritage of the B.C. coast. - *Tibor Bognàr*.

Come nightfall, the city is reflected in the waters of Vancouver's Coal Harbour. - *Tibor Bognàr*

6 £1-00
7/23

Vancouver and Victoria

Fourth Edition

Travel better, enjoy more

ULYSSES

Travel Guides

Offices

CANADA: Ulysses Travel Guides, 4176 St. Denis Street, Montréal, Québec, H2W 2M5, ☎(514) 843-9447 or 1-877-542-7247, ⇄(514) 843-9448, info@ulysses.ca, www.ulyssesguides.com

EUROPE: Les Guides de Voyage Ulysse SARL, 127 rue Amelot, 75011 Paris, France, ☎01 43 38 89 50, ⇄01 43 38 89 52, voyage@ulysse.ca, www.ulyssesguides.com

U.S.A.: Ulysses Travel Guides, 305 Madison Avenue, Suite 1166, New York, NY 10165, ☎1-877-542-7247, info@ulysses.ca, www.ulyssesguides.com

Distributors

U.S.A.: BHB Distribution (a division of Weatherhill), 41 Monroe Turnpike, Trumbull, CT 06611, ☎1-800-437-7840 or (203) 459-5090, Fax: 1-800-557-5601 or (203) 459-5095

CANADA: Ulysses Travel Guides, 4176 St. Denis Street, Montréal, Québec, H2W 2M5, ☎(514) 843-9882, ext.2232, 800-748-9171, Fax: 514-843-9448, info@ulysses.ca, www.ulyssesguides.com

GREAT BRITAIN AND IRELAND: Roundhouse Publishing, Millstone, Limers Lane, Northam, North Devon, EX39 2RG, ☎ 1 202 66 54 32, Fax: 1 202 66 62 19, roundhouse.group@ukgateway.net

SWITZERLAND: OLF, P.O. Box 1061, CH-1701 Fribourg, ☎(026) 467.51.11, Fax: (026) 467.54.66

OTHER COUNTRIES: Ulysses Travel Guides, 4176 St. Denis Street, Montréal, Québec, H2W 2M5, ☎(514) 843-9882, ext.2232, ☎800-748-9171, Fax: 514-843-9448, info@ulysses.ca, www.ulyssesguides.com

Canadian Cataloguing-in-Publication Data (see p 4)
© December 2002, Ulysses Travel Guides.
All rights reserved. Printed in Canada
ISBN 2-89464-517-1

*"It has the combined excellence of Nature's gift
and man's handiwork."*

Stephen Leacock on Vancouver
in *My Discovery of the West* (1937)

Writing and research
Pierre Longnus
Jacqueline Grekin
François Rémillard
Paul-Éric Dumontier

Editor
Jacqueline Grekin
Editing assistance
Cindy Garayt
Danielle Gauthier

Publisher
André Duchesne

Page layout
Isabelle Lalonde
Julie Brodeur

Cartographer
Isabelle Lalonde

Illustrations
Vincent
Desruisseaux
Myriam Gagné
Lorette Pierson

Photography
Cover page
Al Harvey
Inside pages
Walter Bibikow
(Reflexion)
Tibor Bognàr
(Reflexion)
P. Brunet
(Megapress Images)
C. Moreno
(Megapress Images)
Sheila Naiman
(Reflexion)
Sean O'Neill
(Reflexion)

Artistic director
Patrick Farei (Atoll)

Acknowledgements

Thanks to Tourism Vancouver, Tourism Victoria, Stephen M. Darling and Karen Karp.

We gratefully acknowledge the financial support of the Government of Canada through the Book Publishing Industry Development Program (BPIDP) for our publishing activities. We would also like to thank the government of Québec for its SODEC income tax program for book publication.

Canadian Cataloguing-in-Publication Data

Main entry under title:

Vancouver and Victoria

4th ed.

(Ulysses travel guide)
Translation of: Vancouver et Victoria.
Includes an index.

ISBN 2-89464-517-1

1. Vancouver (B.C.) - Guidebooks. 2. Victoria (B.C.) - Guidebooks. I. Series.

FC3847.18.V35513 2002   917.11'33044   C2002-941739-2
F1089.5.V22V35513 2002

Table of Contents

Write to Us

We value your comments, corrections and suggestions, as they allow us to keep each guide up to date. The best contributions will be rewarded with a free book from Ulysses Travel Guides. All you have to do is write us at the following address and indicate which title you would be interested in receiving (see the list at the end of the guide).

Ulysses Travel Guides

4176 St. Denis Street
Montréal, Québec
Canada H2W 2M5

305 Madison Avenue
Suite 1166, New York
NY 10165

www.ulyssesguides.com
E-mail: text@ulysses.ca

Map Symbols

✈	Airport	▲	Mountain
🚌	Bus station	🚫	Beach
📱	Train station	----⊙----	SkyTrain
H	Hospital	🏌	Golf course
?	Tourist information	🚗	Car ferry
✉	Post office		

List of Maps

Symbols

≡	Air conditioning
bkfst incl.	Breakfast included
⇌	Fax number
☉	Fitness centre
K	Kitchenette
🐕	Pets allowed
≈	Pool
ℜ	Restaurant
ℝ	Refrigerator
⌂	Sauna
sb	Shared bathroom
pb/sb	Private bathrooms and shared bathrooms *N.B. all lodgings have private bathrooms unless otherwise indicated.*
✺	Spa
☎	Telephone number
⊚	Whirlpool
🚣	Ulysses's favourite

Attraction Classification

★	Interesting
★★	Worth a visit
★★★	Not to be missed

Hotel Classification

$	$50 or less
$$	$51 to $100
$$$	$101 to $150
$$$$	$151 to $200
$$$$$	$201 to $250
$$$$$$	more than $250

Unless otherwise indicated, the prices in the guide are
for one standard room, double occupancy in high season.

Restaurant Classification

$	$10 or less
$$	$11 to $20
$$$	$21 to $30
$$$$	more than $30

Unless otherwise indicated, the prices in the guide are for a
three-course meal for one person, not including drinks and tip.

All prices in this guide are in Canadian dollars.

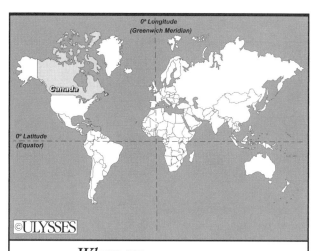

*Where are
Vancouver,
Victoria and
Whistler?*

British Columbia

Capital: Victoria
Population: 4,100,000 inhab.
Area: 950,000km²
Currency: Canadian dollar

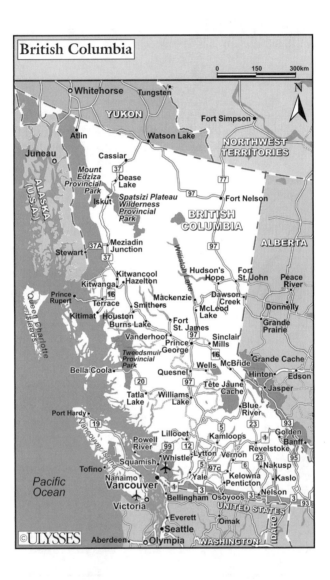

Portrait

Vancouver is truly a new city. But its tall glass towers seem almost dwarfed by the mighty mountains and sea that surround them.

Once one of the most isolated reaches on the planet, over the last century the city has developed close ties with the nations of the largest ocean on Earth and is fast becoming the multi-cultural metropolis of the Pacific Rim.

Although its history is tied to the development of British Columbia's natural resources, most residents were lured here by the magnificent setting and the climate, which is remarkably mild in a country known for its bitter winters and stifling summers. Vancouver, where Asia meets America, is a city well worth discovering.

No trip to Vancouver, however, would be complete without a side trip to Victoria (or vice versa!).

If Vancouver is the "city of glass" (as Vancouver writer Douglas Coupland calls it), then Victoria most certainly deserves its moniker "city of gardens." However, visitors might be tempted to call it the "city of scones." Its British character is legendary, from its afternoon teas, to its tartan shops to its wax museum—home to many a royal family, or reasonable facsimile. But British Columbia's capital city can lay claim to an identity all its own: a magnificent seaside location, a mild, sunny climate, a well-preserved Old Town and Inner Harbour, more than its fair share of handsome Victorian buildings, and a very manageable size that makes sightseeing a sheer pleasure.

To complete your triumvirate of B.C. must-sees, head 120km north from Vancouver to the ski mecca of Whistler, known worldwide for its fashionable restaurants and first-class lodgings, in addition to great skiing. Its permanent resident population may be less than 10,000, but its 900,000 winter visitors and 1.2 million summer visitors support some 115 hotels and over 200 restaurants—not bad for a town that had no road, electricity or sewer system 35 years ago! While skiing is undoubtedly its major draw today, the fabulously scenic trip there along the Sea to Ski Highway is an attraction in itself.

Geography

Canada's West Coast, bounded by the 49th parallel to the south and the Alaskan border to the north, is dominated by the Coast Mountains, a chain of peaks west of the Rockies that form an almost unbroken barrier between the Pacific and the hinterland. The vast delta of the Fraser River does break it and thus proves suitable for human habitation; Vancouver was founded in this favourable location. The city is now the third largest in Canada, with a population of nearly two million in the metropolitan area. It is also the only major city in the country whose eyes are decidedly turned toward the Pacific.

Pacific-minded though it is, Vancouver does not actually face right onto the ocean, but is separated from the sea by Vancouver Island where Victoria, the capital of British Columbia, is located. Vancouver, the province's economic hub, lies on the Strait of Georgia, an arm of the sea separating Vancouver Island from the mainland. Its population is scattered across two peninsulas formed by Burrard

Inlet to the north and False Creek to the south.

Point Grey, the larger and more southerly end, is home to the University of British Columbia and sprawling residential neighbourhoods. On the smaller point to the north, visitors will discover a striking contrast between the east end, with its cluster of downtown skyscrapers, and the west end, which is occupied by the lovely, unspoiled woodlands of Stanley Park. The city's location, surrounded by water and connected to the rest of the country by bridges and ferries, has led to a steady increase in the price of land in the centre and to major traffic problems for commuters from the city's suburbs and satellite towns. Finally, it is worth noting that Vancouver is only about 30km from the U.S. border (and less than 200km north of Seattle).

Vancouver boasts an exceptionally mild climate, with average temperatures of 3°C in January and 17°C in July. Compare these averages to those of Toronto, which experiences a daily mean temperature of -4.5°C

in January and 22°C in July. There is very little snow, though there is a lot of rain (annual average: 1,167mm over 164 days of precipitation, compared to 819mm over 139 days in Toronto) and the summers are temperate and sunny (see the boxes entitled "Average Daily Highs and Lows" in this chapter). Clouds that form over the ocean are blown inland by westerly winds. When they hit the Coast Mountains, they precipitate and cause generally grey weather.

While daily mean temperatures in Victoria are almost identical to those in Vancouver, the capital city receives significantly less precipitation (153 days) and boasts more annual hours of sunshine (2,082) than Vancouver (1919). Victoria is, in fact, the sunniest spot in the province.

Plants thrive in this wet climate. The wide variety of trees and flowers make Vancouver and Victoria vast, luxuriant gardens where everything seems to grow bigger and greener than anywhere else in Canada. Not only are there species indigenous to the temperate rain forest (the northern counterpart of the tropical forest) like enormous Douglas firs, red cedars, giant thuyas, and western hemlocks, but over the decades countless European and Asian plants have been imported to satisfy the local residents' passion for gardening. The numerous private and public ornamental gardens in and around Vancouver and Victoria are thus adorned with North American, European and Asian species, to name but a few. Victoria is, in fact, known as the "city of gardens" and the "garden capital of Canada."

History and Economic Development

Aboriginal Peoples

Over 10,000 years ago, a number of tribes travelled across the Bering Strait from Asia and scattered across North America (their history all but disappeared along with the ice that once covered a large part of the northern hemisphere). They formed the numerous Aboriginal nations and pre-Columbian civilizations of this continent. There is some doubt, however, as to whether or not Aboriginal civilization on the West Coast originated with these

vast waves of immigration. According to one theory, the ancestors of the West Coast First Nations arrived more recently (around 3000 BC) from islands in the Pacific. Proponents of this hypothesis base their argument on the Aboriginal peoples' art, traditions and spoken languages, which are similar to those of the indigenous peoples of the Pacific islands. When the first Europeans arrived here in the late 18th century, the region that would become Vancouver was inhabited by the Salish (the other Aboriginal language families on the Pacific coast are Haida, Tsimshian, Tlingit, Nootka-Kwakiutl and Bellacoola). Like the other First Nations, the Salish favoured this region for its remarkably mild climate and abundance of orcas, salmon, seals, fruit and other resources. This beneficial environment, combined with the barrier formed by the nearby mountains, enabled the coastal communities to thrive. Not only were their populations quite large, but they were also significantly denser than that of other Aboriginal nations in central and eastern Canada.

In 1820, there were some 25,000 Salish living on the shores of the Fraser River, from its mouth south of Vancouver all the way up into the Rockies. Like other

First Nations, the Salish were sedentary and lived in villages of red cedar longhouses. They traded with other nations along the coast during potlatches, festive ceremonies lasting weeks on end and marked by the exchange of gifts.

Belated Exploration

The 18th century saw an increase in exploration and colonization all over the world as European sea powers scoured the planet for natural riches and new territories. The African shores were well charted, and no stone had been left unturned on the east coast of North America. There was, however, an immense area that still seemed inaccessible: the far-off and mysterious Pacific Ocean. Some of the many peoples inhabiting its shores were completely unknown to French, Spanish and English navigators. The Panama Canal had not yet been dug, and sailing ships had to cover incredible distances, their crews braving starvation just to reach the largest of the Earth's oceans.

The voyages of French navigator

Louis Antoine de Bougainville and English explorer James Cook removed some of the mystery surrounding these distant lands. After Australia (1770) and New Zealand (1771), Cook explored the coast of British Columbia (1778). He did not, however, venture as far as the Strait of Georgia, where Vancouver now lies.

In 1792, Cook's compatriot George Vancouver (1757-1798) became the first European to trod upon the soil that would give rise to the future city. He was on a mission to take possession of the territory for the King of England, and by so doing put an end to any plans the Russians and Spaniards had of laying claim to the region. The former would have liked to extend their empire southward from Alaska, while the latter were looking northward. From California, Spanish explorers had even made a brief trip into Burrard Inlet in the 16th century. This far-flung region was not coveted enough to cause any bloody wars, however, and was left undeveloped for years to come.

The Vancouver region was not only hard to reach by sea, but also by land with the Rocky Mountains blocking the way. Imagine setting out across the immense North American continent from Montréal, following the lakes and rivers of the Canadian Shield, and exhausting yourself crossing the endless Prairies, only to end up barred from the Pacific by a wall of rock several-thousand-metres high. In 1908, the fabulously wealthy fur merchant and adventurer Simon Fraser became the first person to reach the site of Vancouver overland. This belated breakthrough had little impact on the region, though, since Fraser was unable to reach any trade agreements with the coastal Aboriginal communities and quickly withdrew to his trading posts in the Rockies.

The Salish First Nation thus continued to lead a peaceful existence here for many more years before being disrupted by European settlers. In 1808, except for sporadic visits by Russians, Spaniards and Englishmen looking to trade pelts for fabrics and objects from the Orient, the Aboriginal peoples were still living according to the traditions handed down to them by their ancestors. In fact, European influence on their lifestyle remained negligible until the mid-19th century, at which point colonization of the territory slowly began.

Development of Natural Resources

In 1818, Great Britain and the United States created the condominium of Oregon, a vast fur-trading zone along the Pacific bounded by California to the south and Alaska to the north. In so doing, these two countries excluded the Russians and the Spanish from this region once and for all. The employees of the North West Company, founded in Montréal in 1784, combed the valley of the Fraser River in search of furs. Not only did they encounter the coastal Aboriginal communities, whose precious resources they were depleting, but they also had to adapt to the tumultuous waterways of the Rockies, which made travelling by canoe nearly impossible. In 1827, after the Hudson's Bay Company took over the North West Company, a large fur-trading post was founded in Fort Langley on the shores of the Fraser River some 90km east of the present site of Vancouver, which would remain untouched for several more decades.

The 49th parallel was designated the border between the United States and British

North America in 1846, cutting the hunting territories in half and thereby putting a damper on the Hudson's Bay Company's activities in the region. It wasn't until the gold rush of 1858 that the region experienced another era of prosperity. When nuggets of the precious metal were discovered in the bed of the Fraser upriver from Fort Langley, a frenzy broke out. In the space of two years, the valley of the golden river attracted thousands of prospectors, and makeshift wooden villages went up overnight. Some came from eastern Canada, but most, including a large number of Chinese Americans, were from California.

In the end, however, it was contemporary industrialists' growing interest in the region's cedar and fir trees that led to the actual founding of Vancouver. In 1862, Sewell Prescott Moody, originally from Maine (U.S.A.), opened the region's first sawmill at the far end of Burrard Inlet and ensured its success by creating an entire town, known as Moodyville, around it. A second sawmill, called Hastings Mills, opened east of present-day Chinatown in 1865. Two years later, innkeeper Gassy Jack Deighton arrived in the area and set up a saloon near Hastings Mills, providing a place for sawmill workers to slake their thirst. Before long, various service establishments sprang up around the saloon, thus marking the birth of Gastown, Vancouver's first neighbourhood.

In 1870, the colonial government of British Columbia renamed the nascent town Granville, after the Duke of Granville. The area continued to develop, and the city of Vancouver was officially founded in April 1886. It was renamed in honour of Captain George Vancouver, who made the first hydrographic surveys of the shores of the Strait of Georgia. Unfortunately, a few weeks later, a forest fire swept through the new town, wiping out everything in its way. In barely 20 minutes, Vancouver was reduced to ashes. In those difficult years, local residents were still cut off from the rest of the world, so the town was reconstructed with an eye on the long term. From that point on, Vancouver's buildings, whether of wood or brick, were made to last.

Portrait

The Umbilical Cord

The end of the gold rush in 1865 led to a number of economic problems for the colony of British Columbia. Due to American protectionism, local industrialists and merchants could not distribute their products in California, while Montréal was too far away and too hard to reach to be a lucrative market. The only favourable outlets, therefore, were the other British colonies on the Pacific, which paved the way for Vancouver's present prosperity. In 1871, British Columbia agreed to join the Canadian Confederation on the condition that a railway line linking it to the eastern part of the country be built.

Recognizing the potential of this gateway to the Pacific, a group of Montréal businessmen set out to build a transcontinental railway in 1879. Angus, Allan, McIntyre, Strathcona (Smith), Stephen and the other men who joined forces under the Canadian Pacific banner were not thinking small; they wanted to transform Canada, theretofore only a nation in the political sense of the word, into an economically unified power. Canadian Pacific chose Port Moody (formerly Moodyville) as the western terminus of the railway. On July 4, 1886, the first train from Montréal reached Port Moody after a tortuous 139-hour, 4,600km journey. British Columbia was no longer cut off from the rest of the world; from that point on, it was regularly supplied with goods from Europe, Québec and Ontario, and could export its own raw materials to more lucrative markets.

Later, the tracks were extended 20km to Vancouver in order to link the transcontinental railway to the new port and thereby allow greater access to the Asian market. The first transcontinental train arrived in Vancouver in 1887. This change proved momentous for the city, whose population exploded from 2,500 inhabitants in 1886 to over 120,000 in 1911! Many of the Chinese who had come to North America to help build (and be exploited by) the railway settled in Vancouver when the project was finished, generating a certain degree of resentment among White residents, who found the new immigrants a little too exotic for their liking. Nevertheless, the Chinese who had worked for Canadian Pacific and the gold mines in the Rockies were soon joined by Asians from Canton, Japan and Tonkin. The city's Chinatown, which grew up between Gastown and Hastings Mills, eventually became the second-largest in North America after San Francisco's.

At the beginning of the 20th century, the city's economic activity gradually shifted from Gastown to the Canadian Pacific Railway yards, located around Granville Street. Within a few years, lovely stone buildings housing banks and department stores sprang up in this area. Nevertheless, most local residents still earned their livelihood from the lumber and fishing industries and lived in makeshift camps on the outskirts of town. In those days, therefore, downtown Vancouver's rapid development was to some extent artificial, based on visions of prosperity that would not be realized for some time

yet. In 1913, the city was much like a gangling adolescent in the midst of a growth spurt. It was then that a major economic crisis occurred, putting an end to local optimism for a while. The opening of the Panama Canal (1914) and the end of World War I enabled Vancouver to emerge from this morass, only to sink right back into it during the crash of 1929. During World War II, residents of Japanese descent were interned and their possessions confiscated. Paranoia prevailed over reason, and these second- and sometimes even third-generation Vancouverites were viewed as potential spies.

Victoria: Capital City

When Europeans began arriving on Vancouver Island in the mid-19th century, three Aboriginal groups, the Songhees, the Klallam and the Saanich, were already living here. In 1842, the Hudson's Bay Company established a fur-trading post near Victoria's harbour. One year later, aided by the Aboriginal people, who were given a blanket for every 40 wooden stakes they cut, the company's adventurers built Fort Victoria alongside the seaport.

The fur trade attracted new workers, and with the gold rush of 1858, Victoria developed into a large town, welcoming thousands of miners on their way inland. The city flourished, and its port bustled with activity. In 1862, Victoria was officially incorporated; shortly thereafter, the fort was demolished, making way for real-estate development. The site is now known as Bastion Square, and the former warehouses of the fort have been transformed into commercial space.

For all those years, Victoria was a colony in its own right, just like British Columbia. The two were united in 1866, and it wasn't until a couple of years later that Victoria became the capital of British Columbia.

The whistle blown by Engine 374 as it pulled the first transcontinental train into Vancouver in 1887 signalled the end of Victoria's reign as the dominant urban centre in the province. Vancouver consequently took over as the province's commercial and manufacturing centre, while Victoria developed as a centre of government. Accordingly, the civil service occupies an important place in the local economy, as does tourism.

The New Metropolis of the Pacific

As a result of the Canadian Pacific Railway company's strong presence on the West Coast, Vancouverites turned their attention away from the ocean stretched out before them and concentrated instead on their ties with central and eastern Canada. Nevertheless, the city's dual role as a gateway to the Pacific for North Americans and a gateway to America for Asians was already well established. This was shown by the massive influx of Chinese immigrants from the 19th century onwards and the numerous import-export businesses dealing in silk, tea and porcelain. The name Vancouver has thus been familiar throughout the Pacific zone for over a century. Starting in 1960, a decline in rail transport to the east prompted the city to shift its attention outward and concentrate on its role as a Pacific metropolis.

With the explosive economic growth of Japan, Hong Kong, Taiwan, Singapore, the Philippines, Malaysia and Thailand, especially in regards to exportation, Vancouver's port expanded at lightning speed. Since 1980, it has been the busiest one in the country. Vancouver's pleasant climate and stunning scenery attract large numbers of eastern Canadians looking to improve their quality of life as well as Asians seeking a new place to live and invest their money. For example, many affluent residents of Hong Kong, anxious about what would happen when their protectorate returned to China in 1997, chose to relocate here.

Thanks to all this new blood, Vancouver (especially the downtown core) has enjoyed continued growth since the late 1960s. Even more than San Francisco or Los Angeles, Vancouver has a strong, positive image throughout the Pacific. It is viewed as a neutral territory offering a good yield on investments and a comfortable standard of living.

The holding of the Asia-Pacific Economic (APEC) summit in Vancouver in November 1997 solidified Vancouver's position as a key player on the Pacific Rim. APEC is a regional consultative body aimed at promoting open trade and economic cooperation between member countries, which include Australia, Brunei, Canada, Chile, China, Hong Kong, Indonesia, Japan, South Korea, Malaysia, Mexico, New Zealand, Papua New Guinea, Philippines, Singapore, Taiwan, Thailand and the United States.

Contemporary Politics

British Columbia has long been a province of political polarity. Over the past 30 years, a pattern of alternation between left- and right-wing governments has been established. The province was led by the left-leaning New Democratic Party (NDP) throughout the 1990s, but in 2001, a Liberal government swept into power. During its first year in power, facing a $2 billion deficit, the Liberals cut personal income tax, announced drastic cuts to the provincial government workforce, slashed spending on health and social services and made no friends in the labour movement by making teacher strikes illegal.

The right-wing agenda of the provincial government was counter-balanced by the election of a left-leaning municipal government in Vancouver in 2002. Larry Campbell was elected mayor of Vancouver by a margin of nearly two to one over his opponent. His party, the Committee of Progressive Electors (COPE), also won control of city council, as well as the school and parks boards, in its first-ever election win since its inception in the 1960s. The Non-Partisan Association (NPA) had dominated city politics for more than 60 years.

Campbell, a former chief coroner and Royal Canadian Mounted Police (RCMP) officer, was the inspiration for the crusading coroner in the Canadian Broadcasting Corporation's (CBC) TV series *Da Vinci's Inquest*. In addition to vowing to improve the city's transit system, reviving city schools, and getting Vancouverites more involved in city government, Campbell has committed himself to improving the lives of Downtown Eastside residents. For example, he promotes the introduction of safe-injection sites, where addicts can shoot up in a clean, safe, supervised setting. If he gets his way, Vancouver will have the first such program in the country. Previous mayor Philip Owen also supported safe-injection sites and championed the cause of the residents of the Downtown Eastside, but for his efforts, he was ousted by his party, the NPA.

Economy

British Columbia's wealth has always been based on its natural resources: lumber, fish and minerals. In the early 1980s, British Columbia was the second-richest province in Canada (on a per capital basis), surpassed only by oil-rich Alberta. But times, and fortunes, have changed. While Alberta continues to lead the pack, British Columbia is now outperformed by both Ontario and Saskatchewan. In fact, by 1998, British Columbia's GDP per person had tumbled below the Canadian average—British Columbia is now a "have-not" province. Analysts point to the prolonged recession in Japan, an important export market; to provincial policies in the 1990s that alienated business leaders; and to the decline in demand and prices for B.C.'s commodities. And the future for commodities does not look good: in 2002, the United States Commerce Department slapped a 29% duty on softwood-lumber imports from Canada to make up for what it considers Canadian subsidization of lumber production and unfair pricing.

Real estate and financial services, fuelled by Asian immigration, supported the province until the mid-1990s. Today, the province's economy depends on oil and gas as well as the tourism, film and high-technology manufacturing industries. Vancouver is now known as "Hollywood North" due to the many American films that are shot in the city. In fact, according to the British Columbia Film Commission, B.C. is the third-largest film and TV production centre in North America, after New York and Los Angeles. In 2001, there were nearly 200 productions in the province, accounting for revenues totaling $1.1 billion, of which foreign productions accounted for $857 million.

Population

Vancouver has always been considered the "end of the line" in Canada, the final destination for those looking for a better world. From the era of the steamship, to the transcontinental railroad to the jumbo jet, the city has continued to attract adventurers eager to line their pockets as well as more philosophical souls looking for peace and a sense of well-being. Located at the edge of a continent that developed from east to west, Vancouver was shrouded in mystery for many years, a sort of Eldorado tinged with Confucianism from the far reaches of the world. These two visions of Vancouver sometimes lead to confrontations between people concerned primarily with economics and developing natural resources and those more interested in ecology. In the end, though, everyone agrees and revels in Vancouver's west-coast way of life.

In 1989, there were nearly 1.5 million people living in Greater Vancouver; today, there are an estimated 2 million. The population has thus grown 35% in just over a decade, illustrating the city's economic vitality and the continued attraction it holds for newcomers. Even early on, Vancouver had a multi-ethnic population. In the wake of the colonial era, however, residents of British descent still formed a large majority. A number of Americans arrived during the gold rush. Soon after, the first wave of Chinese immigrants established the city's Chinatown, which grew considerably after the completion of the Canadian Pacific Railway (1886), much of which was built by Asian labourers. Before long, a Japanese community was born, further diversifying the city's "Pacific" profile. Today,

Vancouver has a Chinese population of around 280,000, a Japanese population of 22,000, and substantial Korean, Filipino and Southeast Asian populations.

The city's cultural mosaic became that much richer in the 20th century, when immigrants from Europe (especially Germany, Poland, Italy and Greece) began arriving. In 1989, Vancouverites of British descent made up only about 30% of the total population. The French Canadian population, which has always been small in British Columbia, stands at about 30,000 in Vancouver (60,000 province-wide), while Vancouver's Aboriginal population is around 139,000 (1996).

For its part, Victoria still has a large population of British origin. Its mild, sunny climate has attracted a great many retirees; it now has the highest proportion of residents over 65 than anywhere else in Canada.

Like the Europeans and the Aboriginals, the Chinese played an important role in the city's development. They came here by the thousands to help build the railroad and settled in the northern part of town. The local Chinatown thus bears the stamp of authenticity, as

it bears witness to a not so distant past.

Victoria is the home town of painter Emily Carr, who left her mark on the early 20th century with her scenes of native life on the west coast.

Architecture

Vancouver was founded during an era of eager westward expansion. Within a few months in 1865, scores of wooden buildings sprang up here, providing the employees of the area's newly opened sawmills with places to sleep, purchase goods and entertain themselves. The vast majority of these makeshift structures fell victim either to the wear and tear of time or the devastating fire of 1886 that destroyed a large part of the young city. You can see one of the few buildings that has survived from that era in Pioneer Park (see p 141).

In the years following the fire, the centre of town, located in what is now Gastown, was rebuilt out of brick to prevent destruction of the growing city by another blaze. The earliest buildings of that era were modelled after the Italianate architecture that had enjoyed such great popularity on the east coast two decades prior (prominent cornices, small pediments over doors and windows). But Vancouver caught up quickly, adopting the Richardson Romanesque style, as had cities all over North America. This style, inspired by French Romanesque art, was reinterpreted by Boston architect Henry Hobson Richardson who designed massive, robust-looking structures with large, arched openings. Other late 19th-century buildings have more in common with the vernacular architecture of San Francisco (multi-level oriel windows overhanging sidewalks, projecting cornices) that are evidence of Vancouver's close ties with the rest of the West Coast.

At the beginning of the 20th century, Vancouver experienced a growth spurt. Entire neighbourhoods sprang up in a single summer. In most residential areas, wood was the material of choice, since it was inexpensive and available in large quantities. The risks of fire, furthermore, were minimal as the houses were almost all free-standing. Space was not a problem, so San Francisco's Queen Anne style, characterized by numerous gables and turrets, was used for these homes. Downtown, brick slowly gave way to stone, a richer material, since proud Vancouverites were eager

to show the rest of the world that they were dynamic and urbane. It is for that reason that the largest skyscraper in the British Empire (see Sun Tower, p 86) was built in Vancouver, rather than in Toronto or London, in 1912. Next, Canadian Pacific introduced the Château style to Vancouver, along with the Beaux-Arts style and its offshoots, neoclassical and Baroque Revival, which are all well represented here. The Chinese community also made a significant contribution to the city's architecture, building narrow commercial buildings with deep loggias and parapets on top, reflecting an interesting blend of North American and Asian styles.

Starting in 1913, Vancouver experienced a growth slump from which it did not truly recover until after the Second World War. Consequently, few new buildings went up in the twenties and thirties. You will nevertheless find a few examples of the Art Deco style here, including the Marine Building, which faces straight down West Hastings Street (see p 103). It is viewed as one of the landmarks of the business district.

As Vancouver is a thriving young city, its architecture is predominantly modern and postmodern. Thanks to talented architects who are open to experimentation and a cultural climate that combines innovative Californian influences with the traditional building techniques of China, Japan and even some of British Columbia's Aboriginal communities, the city has developed an exceptional and modern architectural heritage since the 1940s.

From the glass and steel skyscrapers downtown to the houses clinging to mountainsides in North and West Vancouver, with their simple post-and-beam construction, the accent is usually on purity of line. This sober, sophisticated style contrasts sharply with the ostentation of the early part of the 20th century—and to a certain extent that of late 20th-century architecture as well. Indeed, since the emergence of post-modernism, there has been a shift back to the lavish forms of the past. Many recent immigrants favour columns and decorated pediments. In some areas, furthermore, houses built in the 1950s and '60s are being replaced by what Vancouverites have termed "monster-houses": giant structures that take up almost their entire plot of land, usurping space once occupied by trees and gardens.

Housing prices in Vancouver are notoriously high. Prospective first-time buyers are finding themselves excluded from the market and are heading to suburbs like Surrey, Abbotsford, Langley, Maple Ridge and Coquitlam.

While the overriding image of Vancouver's architecture is one of glass-and-concrete towers (Vancouver author Douglas Coupland refers to it as the "city of glass"), Victoria's downtown architecture is striking in a completely different way. Although the city has plenty of handsome post-war buildings, visitors are charmed by the many elegant, well-preserved Victorian edifices lining its Inner Harbour. Many of these were designed in the Château or Beaux-Arts style by Francis Mawson Rattenbury around the end of the 19th and the beginning of the 20th century.

Rattenbury was chief architect for the Canadian Pacific Railway's western division and designed a great many hotels across Western Canada, including Victoria's Fairmont Empress Hotel. He was also responsible for the design of the Provincial Legislative Buildings (1893), whose design incorporated High Victorian Gothic, Italianate and Richardson Romanesque styles. The rotunda, common in government buildings in the United States at the time, was the first of its kind in Canada. Rattenbury, then 25-years old, won the contract by means of a competition.

Rattenbury left his mark all over the province. Other Victoria buildings that bear his mark include the Château-style Bank of Montreal building on Government Street, which broke from the more conservative neoclassical style normally used on financial buildings across Canada; the Crystal Garden (with an associate); the revised Beaux-Arts CPR Steamship Terminal, which now houses the Royal London Wax Museum; and several hospitals, schools and private homes in Victoria. Rattenbury was also the architect behind Vancouver's Roedde House (see p 112) and the former courthouse, now the Vancouver Art Gallery (see p 107).

Visitors from Québec will likely feel right at home among the Inner Harbour's Second Empire–style buildings, such as the old city hall (corner Pandora Ave. and Douglas St.) and the Dominion Custom House (1002 Wharf St.). Characterized by its mansard roof, often covered in patterned shingles, and dormers, this style is commonly seen in city halls and other important buildings in Québec, but is extremely rare in British Columbia.

Culture

Vancouver's reputation has long been one of a very laid-back city whose beautiful landscape is linked to the "coolness" of its inhabitants living in communion with nature. Starting in 1920, the Polar Bear Swim, an annual dip in the cold waters of English Bay on New Year's Day, became one of the rare "cultural" events. At the time, skiing, hiking and boating were a part of everyday life and cultural life was practically nonexistent. People living in small communities in the area reserved their Sundays for hockey or baseball.

Sports are now at the heart of some very outstanding events in Vancouver. Fans devote particular energy to the cause. Spectators at state-of-the-art GM Place stadium and patrons of bars with giant television screens drink beer and munch on spicy chicken wings. When the Vancouver Canucks took part in the Stanley Cup finals in 1994, 70,000 people flooded Robson Street and a riot ensued.

With an economy based primarily on lumber and

Portrait

fishing, the city lived essentially self-sufficiently until Expo 86 took place there in 1986 and had a significant effect on Vancouver's economy and reputation. Previously unknown on the world stage, the city started to attract tourists and investors, especially from Asia. In response to this economic revival, sky-scrapers started popping up that competed in height with the magnificent Art Deco–style Marine Building and the majestic Hotel Vancouver, built around the same time. Consequently, Vancouver has put a lot of emphasis on architecture. One of its most recent additions, Library Square, is highly characteristic of the work of its designer, Moshe Safdi. In shape and colour, it is reminiscent of the Roman Coliseum ruins. Tourism has also increased since Expo 86 and has become an important source of revenue for Vancouver. Cruises to Alaska are one successful example of the city's efforts to develop its tourist industry.

Vancouver's gay community—the largest in Canada—has grown over the years and its vibrancy contributes greatly to making the city more exciting. Many groups have been founded for the purpose of promoting human rights. In terms of culture, the gay community here is very active and heavily involved in the fields of classical music, singing and visual arts.

Because of its geographic location, Vancouver has always been an inspiration to artists. But artistic and cultural activity here only really started to develop in the last two decades and is slowly becoming more established. Victoria-born Emily Carr (1871-1945), with her relentless desire to depict the natural environment of this isolated area at a time when there were no means of transportation, was the most striking and encouraging role model for artists who followed. Her paintings, many of them stunning, can be seen at the Vancouver Art Gallery as well as at Victoria's Royal British Columbia Museum and the Art Gallery of Greater Victoria. There are also works by members of the Group of Seven, who made landscapes throughout Canada famous.

Aboriginal art is highly prominent in the area and its two most important representatives are Robert Davidson and, especially, the great sculptor, Bill Reid (1920-1998).

The intermingling of people of various ethnic backgrounds gives Vancouver a distinctive character. Asian immigration in particular brings considerable cultural and economic dynamism. Communities from mainland China, Hong Kong and Taiwan bring with them cultures that are rich in symbols and events. The Dragon Boat Festival and Chinese New Year are the biggest events during which Vancouver becomes immersed in Chinese culture for many days.

Cinema has always been a part of daily life in Vancouver. A day doesn't go by when there isn't a film crew on one of Vancouver's streets. Studios have been established in North Vancouver and it's no longer surprising to run into Hollywood stars on the streets or in the shops. Every autumn, the Vancouver International Film Festival offers close to 150 quality foreign films, much to the pleasure of film buffs. Since 1997, the film festivals have been multiplying. The largest ones are devoted to European countries, such as France. Vancouver has a fertile film industry and there's always an excellent selection of French, Italian and Japanese movies. British Columbian producers and local talents are also starting to emerge.

Theatre, music and dance are experiencing excep-

tional growth. Vancouver's theatre scene is booming of late, with dynamic young theatre companies producing highly original, often interdisciplinary works. Internationally reputed artists, such as Pavarotti, Céline Dion and Cher, perform here regularly.

Visual artists here are increasingly coming to the fore, while the Vancouver Art Gallery exhibits are becoming more avant-garde every year. All levels of society support the visual arts, and schools and libraries exhibit local artists' work. The arts in Vancouver are a reflection of the cultural diversity of its population and the West Coast spirit.

The multicultural influence is striking, and each culture expresses itself and blossoms in this environment. The city of Vancouver also offers an impressive array of cultural attractions: a traditional Chinese garden, Greek, Chinese and Japanese cultural festivals, a classical ballet, a Chinese opera, Sumo shows, a Welsh choir, a baroque orchestra, jazz and blues as well as Aboriginal sculpture.

Vancouver is also favoured among writers for the annual Vancouver International Writers Festival which organizes literary event each October.

The city is also slowly starting to gain recognition for its many fine restaurants, which are often influenced by various types of international cuisine and offer the added touch of friendly service. Viticulture, or wine growing, is in full bloom. Wine festivals abound, with consumers' tastes becoming more refined. This cultural explosion, reaching beyond the borders of British Columbia and even Canada, has been so successful that important summits, such as one between Clinton and Yeltsin and the APEC summit have taken place here in recent years.

Famous British Columbians

British Columbia boasts an increasing number of world-famous personalities, particularly in the world of film. Its climate and natural environment, and fiscal conditions attractive to American producers, have contributed to making such Canadian actors as **Cameron Bancroft, Margot Kidder, Michael J. Fox, Bruce Greenwood** and **Cynthia Stevenson** known to the public. American stars such as **Christopher Reeve**, who starred in *Superman*, **Mel Gibson**, featured in *Bird On A Wire*, which was shot in the streets of Gastown, and **Jackie Chan**, who shook the downtown area in *Rumble in the Bronx*, have also been captivated by Vancouver's charm. The list hardly ends here. **Robert DeNiro, Goldie Hawn, Charlton Heston, Antonio Banderas** and many others who have shot movies on the streets of Vancouver. Moreover, popular American TV drama *The X Files* was filmed in Vancouver from 1993 to 1999. Another anecdote: blond bombshell **Pamela Anderson** is also from Vancouver.

Bryan Adams

This rock superstar has sold over 45 million records throughout the world. He comes from West Vancouver, where he still has a house. He returns occasionally to record songs and sign autographs.

David Suzuki

Environmentalist David Suzuki was born in Vancouver in 1936. Like all Japanese-Canadians living on the West Coast, he and his family spent the war years at an internment camp in British Columbia. Upon their release, the family left for Ontario. Suzuki obtained a Ph.D. in zoology from the University of Chicago and went on to lecture in zoology at UBC. He has hosted *The Nature of Things*, a much-respected Canadian Broadcasting Corporation program that explores environmental issues, since the 1970s. He is also president of the David Suzuki Foundation, a Canadian charity that explores environmental issues such as global warming and the conservation of rainforests on B.C.'s northwest coast. Internationally known and respected, he has received many honours and awards. He is a member of the Royal Society of Canada and the Order of Canada, as well as the author of 28 books, many on genetics. He lives in Vancouver.

Diana Krall

Born in 1964 in Nanaimo, north of Victoria, pianist and singer Diana Krall has become a jazz superstar. Her captivating vocals give new life to jazz standards and have won her many fans who were not familiar with the genre. She won three Juno Awards (the Canadian version of the American Grammy Awards) in 2002 for *The Look of Love*, and a Grammy Award for best jazz vocal performance in 1999 for *When I Look in Your Eyes*.

Joe Average

Joe Average is a contemporary figurative artist, using bright colours in his work. His posters can be seen throughout the city; one of these was used as an official promotion for the International Conference on AIDS. He decided to dedicate his art to the cause of AIDS upon being diagnosed HIV positive.

Squire Barnes

Squire Barnes was a sports commentator (especially for hockey) on CBC television for more than 10 years. The province's best known, popular and lively announcer, he's a down-to-earth, straightforward guy who performs his job with precision and a sense of humour. He now appears on the 6pm Global television newscast and writes for sports magazines. In 1998, he received the Orange prize, awarded to the liveliest person on television.

Dave Barr

This Vancouver golfer has been participating in international tournaments for 20 years. Born in Kelowna, in the Okanagan Valley, he began his career in 1974 and has represented Canada many times at the World Cup, winning it twice.

Niels Bendtsen

Another famous Vancouverite, Niels Bendtsen is a furniture designer whose art has transcended national boundaries. His work is on permanent display at the New York Museum of Modern Art, and his output extends all the way to Europe. Closer to home, he designed the interior layout of the Starbucks coffee shops.

George Bowering

This major literary personality was born in Penticton, B.C. and educated in Vancouver. He became famous in the 1960s as the founder and editor in chief of *Tish* magazine. His reputation has been growing ever since. An English professor at SFU, he has written and published over 40 books of poetry, fiction and history, and has been awarded the Governor General's Award on three occasions.

Jay Brazeau

This Vancouver actor attracted notice in the well-known television series *We're No Angels* and *The X Files*. He has also worked in radio and received three Jessie Awards. Leading

actor in the film *Kissed* (1996), he remains part of the current film scene.

Kim Campbell

Born in Port Alberni, north of Victoria, Kim Campbell became Canada's first female Prime Minister (1993), when she became leader of the Progressive Conservative party, which was then in power. Her party was practically wiped out in the next federal election. In 1996, she was named Consul-General of Canada in Los Angeles and is currently Visiting Professor at Harvard University.

James Cheng

A very wealthy architect born in Hong Kong, James Cheng has become the darling of Vancouver. He is currently focusing on the construction of large buildings, giving precedence to quality of life and the environment.

Douglas Coupland

The writer and visual artist who coined the term "Generation X" is another famous Vancouverite. He maintain that Vancouver's geography alone distinguishes it tremendously from the rest of Canada, and that it is developing an identity quite apart from the

Douglas Coupland

Vancouver can be proud of its native son, Douglas Coupland, who, in 1991, at the age of 30, published his first novel, *Generation X*. His work coined a new catchphrase that is now used by everyone from sociologists to ad agencies to describe this young, educated and underemployed generation.

Coupland's novel *Microserfs* (1995), is just as sociologically relevant, but this time he turns his attention to the world of young computer whizzes, which he describes, with sweeping, ironic generalizations about American popular culture mixed with a dash of admiration. Coupland's observations truck a chord with many Canadians, who have mixed feelings about their giant neighbour to the south.

Life After God (1995) explores spirituality in a modern world and the impact of a generation raised without religion. *Girlfriend in a Coma* (1997) criticizes society's "progress" through a woman who wakes up from an 18-year coma to find out nothing has changed for the better. Coupland's other works include *Polaroids From the Dead* (1996) and *Shampoo Planet* (1993). His most recent novel is *Miss Wyoming* (2000).

Coupland has recently shifted focus somewhat, having taken to photography and writing about his city and his country. In *City of Glass*, published in 2000, Coupland writes with typical humour and irony about his home town and accompanies his texts with his own photographs. Coupland's most recent work, *Souvenir of Canada* (2002), marries textual observations and memories with images of Canadian icons.

other major Canadian cities (see the box on previous page).

Sarah McLachlan

Born in Halifax, Nova Scotia, singer and songwriter Sarah McLachlan nevertheless considers herself a Vancouver artist. It may have something to do with the fact that her record label is the Vancouver-based Nettwerk. Fans appreciate her ethereal voice and emotional and forthright songs. Lilith Fair, the all-female musical tour led by McLachlan, which ended in 1999, made her one of the best-known female performers in North America.

Jason Priestley

This young actor from U.S. television and film is Vancouver's darling child. His success in *Beverly Hills 90210* quickly made him a celebrity. He is often invited to major events in the province that are occasions for him to come home and visit his family.

Bill Reid

Born in Victoria and established in Vancouver, this skilled sculptor, jeweller, carver and storyteller revived the art of his Haida ancestors from the 1940s until his death in 1998. His sculptures can be seen all over the city as well as at the UBC Museum of Anthropology and the Vancouver Art Gallery. Two of his works not be missed are at the Vancouver Aquarium and the Vancouver International Airport.

Paul Watson

Co-founder of Greenpeace, Paul Watson is now president of the Sea Shepherd Conservation Society, which is dedicated to protecting the environment and, particularly the waters and their fauna. He has often come under criticism, with some comparing his methods to those of an "eco-terrorist."

Practical Information

Information in this chapter will help visitors better plan their trip to Vancouver, Victoria and Whistler.

It contains important details on entrance formalities and other procedures, as well as general information for visitors from other countries. We also explain how this guide works. Bon voyage in British Columbia!

The area code in Vancouver and Whistler is **604**. Note that you must dial this code for every call you make, even from within Vancouver and Whistler. The area code in Victoria is **250**.

Entrance Formalities

Passport and Visa

A valid passport is usually sufficient for most visitors planning to stay less than three months in Canada. U.S. citizens do not need a passport, but it is, however,

a good form of identification. U.S. citizens and citizens of Western Europe do not need a visa. For a complete list of countries whose citizens require a visa, see the **Canadian Citizenship and Immigration** Web site *(www.cic.gc.ca)* or contact the Canadian embassy or consulate nearest you.

Extended Visits

Visitors must submit a request to extend their visit in writing before the expiration of the first visa (the date is usually written in your passport) to an Immigration Canada office. To make a request you must have a valid passport, a return ticket, proof of sufficient funds to cover the stay, as well as the $75 nonrefundable filing fee. In some cases (work, study), however, the request must be made **before** arriving in Canada. Fir more information, contact Canadian Citizenship and immigration (see above).

Customs

If you are bringing gifts into Canada, remember that certain restrictions apply:

Smokers can bring in a maximum of 200 cigarettes, 50 cigars, 200g of tobacco, and 200 tobacco sticks. Note that the legal age for purchasing tobacco products in British Columbia is 19.

For **wine,** the limit is 1.5 litres; for **liquor,** 1.14

litres. The limit for beer is 24 355ml cans or 341ml bottles. The minimum drinking age in British Columbia is 19 years.

For more information on Canadian customs regulations, contact the **Canada Customs and Revenue Agency** *(☎800-461-9999 within Canada, ☎204-983-3500 or 506-636-5067 outside Canada, www.ccra-adrc.gc. ca)*.

There are very strict rules regarding the importation of **plants**, **flowers**, and other **vegetation**; it is therefore not advisable to bring any of these types of products into the country.

If you are travelling with your **pet**, you will need a rabies-vaccination certificate. For more information on travelling with animals, plants or food, contact the **Canadian Food Inspection Agency** *(www.cfia-acia.agr. ca)* or the Canadian embassy or consulate nearest you before your departure for Canada.

Finally, visitors from out of the country may be reimbursed for certain taxes paid on purchases in Canada (see p 66).

Embassies and Consulates

Canadian Embassies and Consulates Abroad

DENMARK
Canadian Embassy
Kr. Bernikowsgade 1,
1105 Copenhagen K
☎*(45) 33.48.32.00*
⇌*(45) 33.48.32.20/21*

GERMANY
Canadian Consulate General
Internationales Handelszentrum
Friedrichstrasse 95, 12th floor
10117 Berlin
☎*(30) 20.31.20*
⇌*(30) 20.31.24.57*

GREAT BRITAIN
Canada High Commission
Canada House
Trafalgar Square
London, SW1Y 5BJ
☎*(20) 7258-6600*
⇌*(20) 7258-6533*

NETHERLANDS
Canadian Embassy
Sophialann 7,
2500GV, The Hague
☎*(70) 311-1611*
⇌*(70) 311-1620*

SWEDEN
Canadian Embassy
Tegelbacken 4, 7th floor, Stockholm
☎*(8) 453-3000*
⇌*(8) 453-3016*

UNITED STATES
Canadian Embassy
501 Pennsylvania Ave. NW
Washington, DC, 20001
☎*(202) 682-1740*
⇌*(202) 682-7726*

Canadian Consulates General:

1175 Peachtree St. NE
100 Colony Square, Suite 1700,
Atlanta, Georgia, 30361-6205
☎*(404) 532-2000*
⇌*(404) 532-2050*

Three Copley Place, Suite 400
Boston, Massachusetts, 02116
☎*(617) 262-3760*
⇌*(617) 262-3415*

Two Prudential Plaza, 180 N
Stetson Ave., Suite 2400, Chicago,
Illinois, 60601
☎*(312) 616-1860*
⇌*(312) 616-1877*

St. Paul Place, Suite 1700,
750 N. St. Paul St., Dallas, Texas,
75201-3247
☎*(214) 922-9806*
⇌*(214) 922-9815*

600 Renaissance Center, Suite 1100
Detroit, Michigan, 48243-1798
☎*(313) 567-2085*
⇌*(313) 567-2164*

550 South Hope St., 9th floor
Los Angeles, California, 90071-2327
☎*(213) 346-2700*
⇌*(213) 620-8827*

Suite 900, 701 Fourth Ave. S
Minneapolis, Minnesota, 55415-1899
☎*(612) 333-4641*
⇌*(612) 332-4061*

Practical Information

1251 Avenue of the Americas,
Concourse Level, New York,
NY 10020-1175
☎(212) 596-1628
≠(212) 596-1666/1790

412 Plaza 600,
Sixth Ave. and Stewart St.,
Seattle, Washington 98101-1286
☎(206) 442-1777
≠(206) 443-9662

Foreign Consulates in Vancouver

DENMARK
755-777 Hornby St.
Vancouver, B.C. V6Z 1S4
☎(604) 684-5171
≠(604) 682-8054

GERMANY
World Trade Centre, 999 Canada
Place, Suite 704, V6C 3E1
☎(604) 684-8377
☎(604) 218-1390 (24hrs)

GREAT BRITAIN
111 Melville St., Suite 800, V6E 3V6
☎(604) 683-4421
≠(604) 681-0693

NETHERLANDS
475 Howe St., Suite 821, V6C 2B3
☎(604) 684-6448/49
☎(604) 880-4641 (24 hrs)

SWEDEN
1188 Georgia St. W., Suite 1100
V6E 4E9
☎(604) 683-5838
≠(604) 685-5285/7304

UNITED STATES
1095 West Pender St. 21st Floor,
V6E 2M6
☎(604) 685-4311

Tourist Information

Super, Natural British Columbia
Box 9830, Station Province-
Government, Victoria, V8W 9W5
☎800-HELLOBC
www.hellobc.com

Vancouver

Vancouver Tourist InfoCentre
*May to Sep, every day 8am to
6pm; Sep to May, Mon-Fri
8:30am to 5pm, Sat 9am to
5pm*
Plaza Level, Waterfront Centre
200 Burrard St., V6C 3L6
☎(604) 683-2000
≠(604) 682-6839
www.tourism-vancouver.org
Vancouver Tourist
InfoCentre provides bro-
chures and information on
sights and accommodations
for the city as well as for
the province.

Vancouver Parks & Recreation
☎(604) 257-8400
www.parks.vancouver.bc.ca
Provides all information on
sports and recreation activities.

Calendar of Sports and Cultural Events
24hrs/day
☎(604) 661-7373

Victoria

**Tourism Victoria Visitor
Information Centre**
every day 9am to nightfall
812 Wharf St., V8W 1T3
☎*(250) 953-2033*

**Saanich Peninsula Chamber of
Commerce**
9768 3rd St., Sidney
☎*(250) 656-0525*

**Sidney Visitor Information
Centre**
A-2295 Ocean Rd.
☎*(250) 656-3260*

Whistler

Whistler Travel InfoCentre
2097 Lake Placid Rd.
☎*(604) 932-5528*

**Whistler Activity and
Information Centre**
☎*(604) 932-2394*

Tourism Whistler
4010 Whistler Way, Whistler,
BC, V0N 1B4
☎*800-944-7853 (Canada &
U.S.A.)*
☎*(604) 664-5625 (outside North
America)*
www.mywhistler.com

Getting There

Vancouver

By Plane

From Europe

There are two possibilities:
direct flights or flights with
a stopover in Montreal,
Toronto or Calgary. Direct
flights are of course much
more attractive since they
are considerably faster than
flights with a stopover (for
example expect about 9hrs
from Amsterdam for a direct
flight compared to 13hrs).
In some cases, however,
particularly if you have a lot
of time, it can be advantageous to combine a charter
flight from Europe with one
of the many charter flights
within Canada from either
Montreal or Toronto. Prices
for this option can vary
considerably depending on
whether you are travelling
during high or low season.

At press time, the following
airlines offered direct flights
from Europe to Vancouver:

Air Canada offers daily direct
flights during the summer
from Paris to Vancouver
and from London to Van-
couver. Air Canada also
flies twice a week from
Frankfurt to Vancouver.

KLM offers a direct flight from Amsterdam to Vancouver three times a week.

Lufthansa offers a daily flight in partnership with Air Canada from Frankfurt to Vancouver.

British Airways offers daily non-stop service from London to Vancouver.

From the United States

Travellers arriving from the southern or southeastern United States may want to consider **American Airlines** which flies into Vancouver through Dallas.

Delta Airlines offers direct flights from Los Angeles to Vancouver. Travellers from the eastern United States go through Salt Lake City.

Northwest Airlines flies into Vancouver via Minneapolis.

From Asia

Air Canada offers direct flights between Vancouver and Hong Kong.

From elsewhere in Canada

Daily flights to Vancouver are offered from all the major cities in the country. Flights from Eastern Canada often have stopovers in Montreal or Toronto. The following airlines offer regular flights to Vancouver from within Canada:

Air Canada
☎*888-247-2262 or 800-361-8620*
www.aircanada.ca

Tango (Air Canada's no-frills carrier)
☎*800-315-1390*
www.flytango.ca

WestJet
☎*888-937-8538 or 800-538-5696*
www.westjet.ca

Jetsgo
☎*866-440-0441*
www.jetsgo.net

During the high season, the aforementioned flights are complemented by many others offered by the charter company **Air Transat** (☎*866-847-1919, www.airtransat.ca)*. These flights are subject to change with respect to availability and fares.

Air Canada Jazz (☎*888-247-2262, www.flyjazz.ca)*, Air Canada's regional partner, offers flights within British Columbia on Air BC.

Vancouver International Airport

Vancouver International Airport (☎*604-276-6101)* is served by flights from across Canada, the United States, Europe and Asia. The airport is located 15km south

Airline Telephone Numbers (information and reservations)

Air Canada:	☎888-247-2262
Air China:	☎800-685-0921
Air France:	☎800-667-2747
American Airlines:	☎800-433-7300
British Airways:	☎800-247-9297
Cathay Pacific Airways:	☎(604) 214-1180
Continental Airlines:	☎800-231-0856
Delta Airlines:	☎800-221-1212
Harbour Air:	☎(604) 688-1277 or 800-665-0212
Horizon Air:	☎800-547-9308
Japan Airlines:	☎800-525-3663
Jetsgo:	☎866-440-0441
KLM Royal Dutch:	☎800-447-4747
Korean Air:	☎800-438-5000
Lufthansa German Airline:	☎800-563-5954
Quantas Airways:	☎(604) 279-6611
Singapore Airlines:	☎(604) 689-1223
WestJet:	☎800-538-5696
Whistler Air Services:	☎888-806-2299

Practical Information

of downtown. Don't miss the display of Northwest Coast art, including *The Spirit of Haida Gwaii, the Jade Canoe*, by artist Bill Reid, located in the international terminal.

It takes about 30min to get downtown by car or bus. A taxi or limousine will cost you about $25-$30, or you can take the **Airporter** bus (☎604-946-8866) which offers shuttle service to the major downtown hotels and the bus depot. The cost is $12 one-way or $18 return for adults. Call for schedules, as they vary by season and route. During low-season, note that the schedule is rather limited. To reach downtown by public transit take bus 100 for downtown and points east, and bus

404 or 406 for Richmond, Delta and points south. The fare ranges from $1.75 and $3.50, depending on the time of day and destination.

Air Limo
☎(604) 273-1331

Another alternative is to take a limousine to the airport: $32, 20 to 40min journey time.

Like many other airports, Vancouver International Airport charges every departing passenger an **Airport Improvement Fee** (AIF). The fee is $5 for flights within B.C. and to the Yukon, $10 for flights elsewhere in North America, and $15 for overseas flights; credit cards are accepted, and in-transit passengers are generally exempted.

Besides the regular airport services (duty-free shops, cafeterias, restaurants), you will also find an exchange office. Several car rental companies also have offices in the airport (see p 52).

By Train

Travellers with a lot of time may want to consider the train, one of the most pleasant and impressive ways to discover Western Canada and reach Vancouver. **VIA Rail** is the only company that offers train travel between the Canadian provinces. This mode of transportation can be combined with air travel or on its own from big cities in Eastern Canada like Toronto or Montreal. This option requires a lot of time: it takes a minimum of five days to get from Montreal to Vancouver.

The **CanRailpass** is another particularly interesting option. Besides the advantageous price, you only need to purchase one ticket for travel throughout Canada. The ticket allows 12 days of unlimited travel in a 30-day period. At press-time the CanRailpass was $678 ($610 for children, seniors and students) in the high season and $423 ($381 for children, seniors and students) in the low season. CanRailpass holders are also entitled to special rates for car rentals.

VIA Rail offers several discounts on tickets.

Reductions for certain days of the week, during the off-season and on reservations made at least five days in advance: up to 40% off depending on the destination;

Discount for full-time students with an ISIC card and those 24 years of age or less: 10% throughout the year in first class and 35% in economy class if the reservation is made at least five days in advance, except during the holidays;

People aged 60 and over are entitled to a 10% discount; children two to 11 travel for half-price in economy class and are entitled to a 25% discount in first class; children under two accompanied by an adult travel free, provided they do not occupy a seat.

Finally, take note that first-class service is quite exceptional, including a meal, wine, and alcoholic beverages free of charge.

For further information on VIA trains:

In Canada
☎*888-842-7245*
www.viarail.ca

In the Netherlands:
Incento B.V.
☎*(035) 69 55 111*
⇆*(035) 69 55 155*
www.incentro.nl

In the United Kingdom:
Leisurail
☎*0870 7500222*
⇆*0870 7500333*
www.leisurail.co.uk

Airsavers
☎*0141-303-0308*
⇆*041-303-0306*

In the United States:
Amtrak
☎*800-872-7245*
www.amtrak.com

Trains from the United States and eastern Canada arrive at the intermodal **Pacific Central Station** *(Via Rail Canada, 1150 Station St.,* ☎*800-561-8630)* where you can also connect to buses or the surface public transportation system known as the **SkyTrain**. The cross-country Via train, *The Canadian*, arrives in Vancouver three times a week from Toronto. The trip from Edmonton to Vancouver is a spectacular trip through the mountains along the rivers and valleys. Those in a rush should keep in mind that the trip takes 24hrs, and is more of a tourist excursion than a means of transportation. It costs less than $200 one-way; check with VIA, however, about seasonal rates.

BC Rail
1311 West First St., North Vancouver
☎*(604) 984-5246*
☎*800-663-8238*
BC Rail trains travel the northwest west coast. Schedules vary depending on the season.

During the summer, the **Great Canadian Railtour Company Ltd.** offers **Rocky Mountaineer Railtours** *($729 per person double occupancy;* ☎*604-606-7245 or*

800-665-7245,
www.rockymountaineer.com)
between Calgary and Van-
couver. Passing through the
Rockies, it's an extraordinary experience.

Amtrak US Rail
☎ *800-USA-RAIL*
☎ *800-872-7245 (toll-free in*
North America)
There is daily service
aboard **Amtrak's Mount Baker**
International from Seattle,
Washington; the trip takes
3hrs and follows a scenic
route.

Royal Hudson
1311 West First St., North Vancouver
☎ *(604) 631-3500*
The steam locomotive is
very well-known in Van-
couver tourist circles. Dating from the beginning of
the 20th century, but re-
stored, it takes passengers
from its station in North
Vancouver to Squamish,
65km away. The journey
allows passengers to dis-
cover the splendid **Howe**
Sound fjord, as the railway
skirts the shore.

By Bus

Pacific Central Station was
opened in 1993 in the old
VIA Station to allow travellers to connect between
bus, train and public transportation in one place.

Buses provide several links
with the main cities in the
province.

Greyhound Lines of Canada
Pacific Central Station
1150 Station St.
☎ *(604) 482-8747 or 800-661-8747*
Greyhound links Vancouver
to Nanaimo.

Pacific Coach Lines
☎ *(604) 662-8074 or 800-661-1725*
www.pacificcoach.com
Pacific Coach Lines offers
service to Victoria.

Vancouver Main Bus Station
☎ *(604) 683-8133*

By Car

Vancouver is accessible by
the **Trans-Canada Highway 1**
which runs east-west. This
national highway links all of
the major Canadian cities. It
has no tolls and passes
through some spectacular
scenery. Coming from
Alberta, you will pass
through the Rocky Moun-
tains, desert regions and a
breathtaking canyon.

The city is generally
reached from the east by
taking the "Downtown" exit
from the Trans-Canada. If
you are coming from the
United States or from Victoria by ferry, you will enter
the city on Highway
99 North; in this case expect it to take about 30min
to reach downtown.

Table of distances (km)

Via the shortest route

	Calgary (Alberta)	Edmonton (Alberta)	Jasper (Alberta)	Kamloops (B.C.)	Penticton (B.C.)	Prince Rupert (B.C.)	Seattle (Washington)	Vancouver (B.C.)	Victoria (B.C.)	Whistler (B.C.)
Banff (Alberta)	128	412	287	492	542	1385	956	852	885	967
Calgary (Alberta)		286	412	620	670	1513	1085	976	1013	1095
Edmonton (Alberta)			363	800	964	1461	1264	1155	1193	1245
Jasper (Alberta)				439	670	1100	1016	794	832	914
Kamloops (B.C.)					231	1246	464	355	393	473
Penticton (B.C.)						1429	500	395	433	515
Prince Rupert (B.C.)							1616	1502	1693	1621
Seattle (Washington)								227	247	350
Vancouver (B.C.)									69	124
Victoria (B.C.)										192

Example: The distance between Edmonton and Vancouver is 1155 km.

© ULYSSES

By Ferry

Two ferry ports serve the greater Vancouver area for travellers coming from other regions in the province. Horseshoe Bay, to the northwest, is the terminal for ferries to Nanaimo (crossing time 90min), Bowen Island and the Sunshine Coast. Tsawwassen, to the south, is the terminal for ferries to Victoria (Swartz Bay) (crossing time 95min), Nanaimo (crossing time 2hrs) and the southern Gulf Islands. Both terminals are about 30min from downtown. For information on these routes, contact **BC Ferries** *(☎250-386-3431 or 888-BCFERRY, www.bcferries.bc.ca)*.

Victoria

By Plane

Victoria International Airport *(☎250-953-7500)* is located north of Victoria on the Saanich Peninsula, a half-hour's drive from downtown on Highway 17.

Airporter Bus *(☎250-386-2525)* transports passengers between Victoria International Airport and the downtown hotels.

Air Canada/Air BC Connector *(☎888-247-2262, www.aircanada.ca)* offers 16 flights a day between Vancouver and Victoria airports, as well as 11 flights a day on a seaplane between the ports of Victoria and Vancouver.

Helijet Airways *($200-$275 return; Victoria ☎250-382-6222, Vancouver ☎604-273-4688 or 800-665-4354, www.helijet.com)* provides frequent, scheduled helicopter service between the ports of Vancouver and Victoria, as well as between Seattle and Victoria.

Harbour Air Seaplanes
950 Wharf St.
☎(604) 274-1277 from Vancouver
☎800-665-0212
This company provides frequent service via seaplane between Vancouver and Victoria *($198 return)*.

West Coast Air
1000 Wharf St.
☎(250) 388-4521
☎800-347-2222
West Coast Air provides twin otter service between Vancouver and Victoria *($198 return)*.

Pacific Coastal Airlines
114-1640 Electra Blvd., Sidney
☎(604) 273-8666
☎800-663-2872
This company flies between Victoria and Vancouver and offers special advance-purchase fares.

Kenmore Air (☎800-543-9595, or in Seattle, U.S.A. ☎425-486-1257, www.kenmoreair.com) shuttles back and forth between the ports of Seattle and Victoria in a seaplane.

By Bus

Pacific Coach Lines (☎250-385-4411 or 800-661-1725, www.pacificcoach.com) shuttles back and forth between Vancouver and Victoria eight times a day (16 times a day during summer). Bus passengers board the ferry and rejoin the bus after the crossing. A hassle free option.

Laidlaw Coach Lines ($18 one way; ☎250-385-4411) runs between Victoria and Nanaimo with stops in the major towns along the way. From Nanaimo, two other routes serve the north up to Part Hardy and the West Coast up to Tofino.

By Car/Ferry

You can reach Victoria by car by taking a BC Ferry from Tsawwassen, located south of Vancouver on the coast. This ferry (BC Ferries; in the summer, every day on the hour from 7am to 10pm; in the winter, every day every other hour from 7am to 9pm; ☎888-223-3779 in B.C. or 250-386-3431 from outside the province, www.bcferries.com)

will drop you off at the Sydney terminal in Swartz Bay. From there, take Highway 17 South to Victoria.

BC Ferries also offers transportation to Victoria from the east coast of Vancouver Island. The ferry sets out from the Horseshoe Bay terminal, northwest of Vancouver, and takes passengers to Nanaimo. From there, follow the signs for the Trans-Canada Highway 1 South, which leads to Victoria, 113km away.

Visitors setting out from Seattle, Washington can take the **Victoria Clipper** (year-round; Victoria ☎250-382-8100, Seattle ☎206-448-5000 or 800-888-2535, www.victoriaclipper.com), a sea ferry for pedestrians only, which takes passengers directly to the port of Victoria.

Black Ball Ferry
From Victoria to Port Angeles, Washington, U.S.A.
☎(250) 386-2202

Scenic Gulf Island Ferry Tours Ltd.
2550 Beacon Ave., Sidney
☎(250) 655-4465

Victoria-San Juan Cruises
From Bellingham, Washington U.S.A. to Victoria
☎800-443-4552

Whistler

By Train

From North Vancouver, a train skirts northward around Howe Sound, passing through Squamish and Whistler along the way and offering passengers a chance to contemplate the landscape.

BC Rail *(☎604-984-5246 or 800-663-8238, www.bcrail.com)* serves the towns in the northern part of the province by way of the Whistler resort area. The *Caribou Prospector* departs North Vancouver daily at 7am and at 9:35am and departs Whistler at 7:05pm, arriving in North Vancouver at 9:30pm ($79).

By Bus

Greyhound Lines of Canada
Pacific Central Station, 1150 Station St., Vancouver
☎*(604) 932-5031*
☎*800-661-8747*
Greyhound provides daily service to Whistler ($42 return).

Perimeter's Whistler Express
☎*(604) 266-5386 (in Vancouver)*
☎*(604) 205-0041 (in Whistler)*
☎*877-317-7788 (elsewhere in North America)*
If you're in a hurry to get on the slopes, Perimeter's will whisk you directly from Vancouver International Airport to Whistler ($110).

Maverick Coach Lines
Pacific Central Station, 1150 Station St., Vancouver
☎*(604) 662-8051*
Maverick caters mainly to skiers going to Whistler for the day, but also serves other towns along Highway 99.

By Car

Whistler is located about 120km north of Vancouver, via the spectacular **Sea to Sky Highway** (Hwy. 99). Simply cross Lions Gate Bridge and follow the signs for Whistler. It's a scenic, 2hr trip.

Driving in British Columbia

Rules of the Road

Driver's licenses from Western European countries are valid in Canada and the United States. While North American travellers won't have any trouble adapting to the rules of the road in western Canada, European travellers may need a bit more time to get used to things. Here are a few hints:

Drivers in western Canada are particularly courteous when it comes to **pedestrians**. They willingly stop to give them the right of way even in big cities, so as a driver keep an eye out for pedestrians. Pedestrian crosswalks are usually indicated by a white sign.

Turning **right on a red light** when the way is clear is permitted in British Columbia.

When a **school bus** (usually yellow in colour) has stopped and has its signals flashing, you must come to a complete stop, no matter what direction you are travelling in. Failing to stop at the flashing signals is considered an extremely serious offense, and carries a heavy penalty.

Wearing of **seatbelts** in the front and back seats is mandatory at all times.

Almost all highways in western Canada are toll-free, and just a few bridges have tolls. The **speed limit** on highways is 100 km/h. The speed limit on secondary highways is 90 km/h, and 50 km/h in urban areas. Note that the speed limit on the Sea to Sky Highway (between Vancouver and Whistler) is 80km/h.

Because Canada produces its own crude oil, **gasoline** (petrol) prices are much less expensive than in Europe, and only slightly more

than in the United States. Some gas stations (especially in the downtown areas) might ask for payment in advance as a security measure, especially after 11pm.

Accidents and Emergencies

In case of serious accident, fire or other emergency dial ☎**911** or **0**. Parts of the interior and Vancouver Island do not have 911.

If you run into trouble on the highway, pull onto the shoulder of the road and turn the hazard lights on. If it is a rental car, contact the rental company as soon as possible. Always file an accident report. If a disagreement arises over who was at fault in an accident, ask for police help.

Finding Your Way Around

Vancouver

By Car

Getting around Vancouver by car is easy. Despite its rather confusing geography (for more on this see the box "Knowing Your West End From Your West Side," in the Vancouver chapter), all you really need to do is memorize a handful of street names and orientations, and the rest will be a breeze. Remember that Burrard, Granville and Cambie streets are main commercial thoroughfares heading south from downtown as far as the Fraser River (in the case of the latter two), across eponymous bridges. Once you've committed those to mem-

ory, try adding Main Street, further east. Next, you absolutely must remember the main downtown artery, Robson Street; Georgia Street, north of Robson, leads into Stanley Park and onto the Lions Gate Bridge to North Vancouver (and eventually Whistler). In the West Side (the area south of False Creek), numbered avenues head from east to west.

Parking in Vancouver

If you decide to explore Vancouver by car, sooner or later you will face the problem of parking. Most major hotels offer parking for a fee. Otherwise, there is no shortage of public parking lots. You can pay as little as $2 to park near the north end of the Granville Bridge, or as much as $14 to park next to the Waterfront SkyTrain station at Granville and Cordova streets. You can typically park near Burrard and Robson for $7.50 or less. There are more than 50 city-run EasyPark lots, most of

which are "pay and display," charging between $5 and $13 (at the Pacific Centre) a day, and $3 to $5 evenings from 6pm to 6am (which may entail getting up early and depositing another $1.50 every hour after 6am). Most of these lots are unattended, a factor which is important to consider in a city where car break-ins (rather than car theft) are common. Do not under any circumstances leave any valuables (not even spare change) anywhere in your parked car.

Vancouverites are bewilderingly patient and courteous drivers. Nevertheless, they do tend to complain about the low skill level of drivers in their city, all of which makes perfect sense: any city with bad drivers has to have its fair share of patient ones! Furthermore, pedestrians are quite civilized; jaywalking is very rare in the city centre—so much so that crossing a street on a red light (even when no cars are in the vicinity) is a telltale sign of a tourist.

Take note that the government has decided not to build any expressways through downtown which is exceptional for a city of two million people; as a result, rush-hour traffic can be quite heavy. If you have the time, by all means explore the city on foot.

Car Rental

Packages including air travel, hotel and car rental (or just hotel and car rental) are often less expensive than car rental alone. It is best to shop around. Remember also that some companies offer corporate rates and discounts to auto-club members. Some travel agencies work with major car rental companies (Avis, Budget, Hertz, etc.) and offer good values; contracts often include added

bonuses (reduced ticket prices for shows, etc.).

When renting a car, find out if the contract includes unlimited kilometres, and if the insurance provides full coverage (accident, property damage, hospital costs for you and passengers, theft).

Certain credit cards, gold cards for example, cover the collision and theft insurance. Check with your credit card company before renting.

To rent a car, you must be at least 21 years of age and have had a driver's license for **at least** one year. If you are between 21 and 25, certain companies (for example Avis, Thrifty, Budget) will ask for a $500 deposit, and in some cases they will also charge an extra sum for each day you rent the car. These conditions do not apply for those over 25 years of age.

A credit card is extremely useful for the deposit to avoid tying up large sums of money.

Most rental cars come with an automatic transmission; however you can request a car with a manual shift.

Child safety seats cost extra.

Practical Information

Car Rental Companies

You can rent a car at the airport or in the city.

National Car Rental
1130 W. Georgia St.
(604) 685-6111
800-CAR-RENT
airport
273-3121

Budget
450 West Georgia St. and at the airport
(604) 668-7000
800-268-8900 (from Canada)
800-527-0700 (from the U.S.)

Thrifty
1400 Robson St.
(604) 681-4869
airport
(604) 606-1655

Avis
757 Hornby St.
(604) 606-2868
airport
(604) 606-2847

By Taxi

Hailing a taxi in Vancouver is not a problem, especially near big downtown hotels and along main arteries such as Robson Street and Georgia Street. The main taxi companies are:

Yellow Cab
(604) 681-1111

McLure's
(604) 731-9211

Black Top
(604) 731-1111
(604) 871-1111 (wheelchair accessible taxis)

Vancouver Limousine Service
(604) 421-5585 or 888-515-5565

Public Transportation

BC Transit bus route maps are available from the Vancouver Tourist InfoCentre (see p 38) or from the BC Transit offices in Surrey *(13401 108th Ave., fifth floor, Surrey, 604-953-3333/3000)*. BC Transit also claims that timetables and route maps are available at local convenience stores; in reality, they prove to be somewhat elusive. Better to download them from *www.translink.bc.ca* or call them with specific questions. Service is extremely polite and helpful.

BC Transit also includes a rail transit system and a marine bus. The **SkyTrain** runs east from the downtown area to Burnaby, New Westminster and Surrey. These automatic trains run from 5am to 1am all week, except Sundays when they start at 9am. The **SeaBus** shuttles frequently between Burrard Inlet and North Vancouver.

Tickets and passes are available for **BC Transit**, including the SkyTrain and

SeaBus, from the coin-operated machines at some stops, in some convenience stores or you can call ☎604-521-0400.

The fares are the same whether you are travelling on a BC Transit bus, the SkyTrain or the SeaBus. A single ticket generally costs $2 for adults and $1.50 for seniors, children and students (must have BC Transit GoCard), except at peak hours *(Mon-Fri before 9:30am and 3pm to 6:30pm)* when the system is divided into three zones. It then costs $2 for travel within one zone, $3 within two zones and $4 within three zones.

**BC Transit
lost and found**
☎*(604) 682-7887*

Blue Bus
☎*(604) 985-7777*
Serves West Vancouver

Car & Van Pooling
☎*(604) 879-RIDE*

Transportation for People with Disabilities

HandyDART
300-3200 East 54th St.
☎*(604) 430-2742/2692*
This company provides public transportation for people who use wheelchairs. You must reserve your seat in advance.

Vancouver Taxis
2205 Main St.
☎*(604) 255-5111*
☎*(604) 874-5111*
Vancouver Taxis offers transportation for wheelchair users.

By Ferry

Little put-put ferries ply the waters of False Creek, linking Granville Island, the Maritime Museum in Vanier Park, Stamp's Landing and Science World on one side, with the Aquatic Centre, Yaletown and Hornby Street on the other. Rides take all of five or 10 minutes and cost little more than the bus. For information, contact **False Creek Ferries** *(☎604-684-7781)* or **Aquabus Ferries** *(☎604-689-5858)*.

On Foot

The best way to truly appreciate the many facets of any city is generally by foot. This guide outlines nine walking tours in different neighbourhoods of Vancouver. Don't forget your walking shoes!

Drivers in Vancouver are particularly courteous when it comes to **pedestrians**, and willingly stop to give them the right of way, so be careful when and where you step off the curb. Pedestrian crosswalks are

Practical Information

usually indicated by a white sign. When driving, pay special attention that nobody is about to cross near these signs.

Victoria

Car Rentals

If you plan on renting a car, make the necessary arrangements once you arrive in Victoria; this will spare you the expense of bringing the car over on the ferry.

Avis Rent A Car
1001 Douglas St.
☎*(250) 386-8468*

Budget Car and Truck Rental
757 Douglas St.
☎*(250) 953-5300*

National Car and Truck Rentals
767 Douglas St.
☎*(250) 386-1213*

Roadside Assistance

Totem Towing
day or night
☎*(250) 475-3211*

Public Transportation

You can pick up bus schedules and a map of the public-transportation system at **Tourism Victoria** *(812 Wharf St.,* ☎*250-953-2033).*

Public transportation in the greater Victoria area is provided by **BC Transit** *(*☎*250-382-6161, www.bctransit.com).*

By Taxi

Blue Bird Cabs
☎*(250) 382-4235*

Empress Taxi
☎*(250) 381-2222*

Victoria Taxi
☎*(250) 383-7111*

By Scooter

If you like to do things a little differently, why not explore Victoria on a little scooter (49 cc) from **Harbour Rentals** *(811 Wharf St.,* ☎*250-995-1661)* or **Cycle BC** *(747 Douglas St.,* ☎*250-385-2453).* Maps provided. Driver's license required.

By Cycle Rickshaw

An original way to see Victoria is at the back of a three-wheeled cycle rickshaw. The energetic and entertaining guides pedaling **Kabuki Kabs** *($1/minute;* ☎*250-385-4243)* can take you where you want to go or offer guided tours. With prices by the minute, however, you might want to ask about the estimated time of arrival before hopping aboard.

Whistler

Public Transportation

Whistler Transit System
☎*(604) 932-4020*

Guided Tours

Guided tours of all sorts are available to help you discover every facet of Vancouver and Victoria.

Architectural Institute of British Columbia
440 Cambie St.,
☎*(604) 683-8588*
☎*800-667-0753*
The AIBC offers student-led guided tours of Vancouver and Victoria (Jun-Aug). Tours are free but participants must call to register beforehand. Call for schedules.

Vancouver

Gray Line of Vancouver
255 First Ave. E.
☎*(604) 879-3363*
☎*800-667-0882*
Gray Line offers city tours year-round aboard comfortable buses. The tour lasts 3.5hrs and costs $42 ($30 for children). In the summer, they also offer a shorter double-decker tour. You can get on and off as you please; the cost for a two-day pass is $24 ($14 for children). The route is posted in the lobbies of most downtown hotels and the entire tour takes about 2hrs. You must purchase your ticket ahead of time, either by calling the above numbers or by visiting the agent in the lobby of the Fairmont Hotel Vancouver (see p 176). Gray Line also offers excursions to Victoria and Whistler.

The Vancouver Trolley Company Ltd.
875 Terminal Ave.
☎*(604) 801-5515*
☎*888-451-5581*
The Vancouver Trolly Company toots around town in old-fashioned trolleys, picking up and dropping off passengers as they wish at 16 different stops, and providing narration the whole way.

Harbour Cruises Ltd.
☎*(604) 688-7246*
☎*800-663-1500*
Harbour Cruises organizes narrated boat tours that last about 90min and depart three times daily at 11:30am, 1pm and 2:30pm.

Practical Information

The cost is $18 for adults and $6 for children. They also offer sunset dinner cruises which feature a buffet meal and a trip out to English Bay and False Creek. This is a great way to experience this city set between sea and mountains.

Stanley Park Horse Drawn Tours
☎(604) 681-5115
Stanley Park Horse Drawn Tours offers 1hr-long jaunts through beautiful Stanley Park. Your carriage awaits at the information booth at the Coal Harbour parking lot every day from mid-March to November. There are departures every 20 to 30min and the cost is $18.65 ($11.20 for children).

West Coast City and Nature Sightseeing Tours
$24-$129
3945 Myrtle St., Burnaby, BC
☎(604) 451-1600
This Company has multilingual guides and offers minibus tours year round. Destinations include Whistler, Victoria, Capilano and Butchart Gardens.

Victoria

Victoria Harbour Ferry Co.
☎(250) 708-0201
In addition to offering harbour tours, this company also offers transportation to various places along the Inner Harbour (Mar to Oct).

Gray Line of Victoria
☎(250) 388-9461
Gray Line offers 1.5hr city tours (around $20), 3hr Butchart Gardens tours (around $45) and harbour tours aboard amphibious crafts (around $25). Frequent departures (Mar through Nov).

Tally Ho Horse Drawn Tours
(☎250-383-5067), **Victoria Carriage Tours** (☎250-383-2207) and **Black Beauty Carriage Tours** (☎250-361-1220) offer horsedrawn trolley city tours (around $14) as well as considerably more expensive horsedrawn carriage tours ($60 to $150) to various destinations around the city.

Insurance

Cancellation

Your travel agent will usually offer you cancellation insurance when you buy your airline ticket or vacation package. This insurance allows you to be reimbursed for the ticket or package deal if you must cancel your trip due to serious illness or death.

Theft

Most residential insurance policies protect some of your goods from theft even if it occurs in a foreign country. To make a claim, you must fill out a police report. It may not be necessary to take out further insurance, depending on the amount covered by your current home policy. As policies vary considerably, you are advised to check with your insurance company. European visitors should take out baggage insurance.

Health

This is the most useful kind of insurance for travellers, and should be purchased before your departure. Your insurance plan should be as complete as possible because health care costs add up quickly.

When buying insurance, make sure it covers all types of medical costs such as hospitalization, nursing services and doctor's fees. Make sure your limit is high enough, as these expenses can be costly. A repatriation clause is also vital in case the required care is not available on site. Furthermore, since you may have to pay immediately, check your policy to see what provisions it includes for such situations. To avoid any problems during your vacation, always keep proof of your insurance policy on your person.

Health

General Information

Vaccinations are not necessary for people coming from Europe, the United States, Australia and New Zealand. On the other hand, it is strongly suggested, particularly for medium or long-term stays, that visitors take out health and accident insurance. There are different types so it is best to shop around. Bring along all medication, especially prescription medicine. Unless otherwise stated, the water is drinkable throughout British Columbia.

During the summer, always protect yourself against sunburn. It is often hard to feel your skin getting burned by the sun on windy days. Do not forget to bring sunscreen!

Canadians from outside British Columbia should take note that in general your province's health care system will only reimburse you for the cost of any hospital fees or procedures at the going rate in your province. For this reason, it is a good idea to get additional private insurance. In case of accident or illness, make sure to keep your receipts in order to be reimbursed by your province's health care system.

Emergencies

In case of emergency (police, fire department, ambulance), dial ☎*911*.

Vancouver

Hospitals

Children's Hospital
4480 Oak St.
☎*(604) 875-2345*

Vancouver General Hospital
855 W. 12th Ave.
☎*(604) 875-4111*

Burnaby Hospital
☎*(604) 434-4211*

Lions Gate Hospital
231 15th Ave., North Vancouver
☎*(604) 988-3131*

St. Paul's Hospital
1081 Burrard St.
☎*(604) 682-2344*

UBC Hospital
2211 Westbrook Mall
☎*(604) 822-7121*

Pharmacies

There are two **Shoppers Drug Mart** branches that are open 24hrs:

1125 Davie St.
☎*(604) 669-2424*
2302 W. Fourth Ave.
☎*(604) 738-3138*

Victoria

Victoria Police Station
850 Caledonia Ave.
☎*(250) 995-7654*

Victoria General Hospital
35 Helmcken Rd.
☎*(250) 727-4212*

Emergency Dental Service of British Columbia
☎*(250) 361-8901*

Poison Control Centre
☎*800-567-8911*

Need Crisis & Information Line
☎*(250) 386-6323*

Air and Sea Rescue
☎*800-567-5111*

Pharmacies

McGill & Orme
649 Fort St.
☎*(250) 384-1195*

Shoppers Drug Mart
corner of Yates and Douglas
☎*(250) 381-4321*
☎*(250) 384-0544*

Emergency Phone Numbers

Police, Firefighters and Ambulance: ☎*911*

Hospital Emergency: ☎*(604) 875-4995*
To consult a family doctor, contact one of the many clinics, often open from 9am to 10pm, 7 days a week (leaf through the yellow pages or call directory assistance at ☎*411*).

Dental Emergency: ☎*(604) 736-3621* (College of Dental Surgeons). Or call a dental clinic (consult the yellow pages or call ☎*411*).

Poison Centre: ☎*(604) 682-2344*

Crisis Centre (in case of emotional trauma)**:** ☎*(604) 872-3311*

Vancouver Veterinary Emergency Clinic (24 hours/day): ☎*(604) 734-5104*

Help for Women: ☎*(604) 872-8212*

Legal Aid: ☎*(604) 687-4680*. 24hr information service on laws in effect in British Columbia.

Roadside Assistance: ☎*(604) 293-2222* Vancouver and surroundings (BCAA). Rest of British Columbia: ☎*800-CAA-HELP*

Whistler

Whistler Health Care Centre
Lorimer Rd.
☎*(604) 932-4911*

Pharmacies

Pharmasave
4212 Village Square
☎*(604) 932-4251*
4360 Lorimer Rd.
☎*(604) 932-2303*

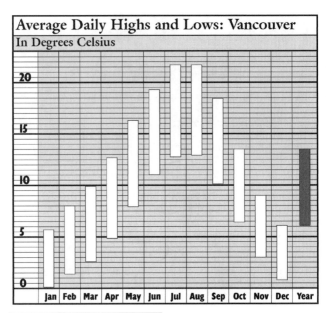

Average Daily Highs and Lows: Vancouver
In Degrees Celsius

| | Jan | Feb | Mar | Apr | May | Jun | Jul | Aug | Sep | Oct | Nov | Dec | Year |

Safety

By taking the normal precautions, there is no need to worry about your personal security. If trouble should arise, dial ☎*911*.

Climate

The climate of Canada varies widely from one region to another. The Vancouver area benefits from a sort of micro-climate thanks to its geographic location between the Pacific Ocean and the mountains. Temperatures in Vancouver vary between 0°C and 15°C in the winter and are much warmer in the summer. Average temperatures in July and August approach 22°C in Vancouver and Victoria. See boxes on average temperatures in Vancouver and Victoria, in this chapter.

Weather
Environment Canada
☎*(604) 664-9010*

Winter

Vancouver has a particularly wet winter so don't forget your raincoat. In southern British Columbia, the mercury rarely falls

Average Daily Highs and Lows: Victoria
In Degrees Celsius

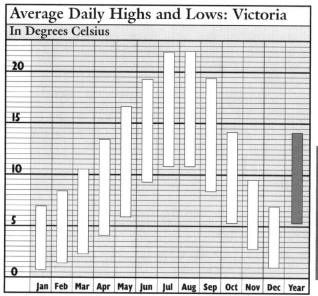

| | Jan | Feb | Mar | Apr | May | Jun | Jul | Aug | Sep | Oct | Nov | Dec | Year |

below 0°C. December to March remains the ideal season for winter-sports enthusiasts who can enjoy many activities not far from the city (skiing, skating, etc.). During this season, it's essential to wear warm clothing (coat, scarf, hat, gloves, wool sweaters and boots) if you plan on visiting the mountains.

Spring and Fall

In Vancouver, spring and fall, and winter too for that matter, are hardly discernable. Spring is short (end of March to end of May), and conditions are generally rainy. Warmer temperatures encourage a beautiful blossoming of flowers. Fall is often cool and wet. A sweater, scarf, gloves, windbreaker and of course an umbrella are recommended for these seasons.

Summer

Summer lasts from May to the end of August. Bring along T-shirts, lightweight shirts and pants, shorts and sunglasses; a sweater or light jacket is a good idea for evenings. If you plan on doing any hiking, remember that temperatures are cooler at higher altitudes.

Luggage

The maximum luggage weight allowed into an airplane varies from one airline to the next. On chartered flights, it is restricted to a minimum, and charges are applied for excess weight. Remember that you are usually only allowed one piece of hand luggage on the plane, and it must fit under the front seat.

Be sure to securely fasten all bags and suitcases and to carefully wrap all packages, since they could get damaged by the trolley's mechanism as they go into or come out of the baggage hold. Some airlines and airports supply sturdy plastic bags for backpacks, boxes and other pieces of luggage.

Before boarding the plane, you might be asked whether or not you left your luggage unattended, or if you packed it yourself. The reason for this is to prevent strangers from slipping illegal merchandise into your bags, which you would then unknowingly carry with you.

You are not allowed to bring dangerous objects, such as knives and pocket knives, into the plane; these items can, however, be kept in luggage that will be put in the baggage hold. Outdoor enthusiasts should note that oxygen tanks cannot be carried into airplanes and that bicycle tires must be deflated. If you are travelling with unusual items, it is best to inquire with the airline before packing.

Jet Lag and Travel Sickness

The discomfort caused by major jet lag is unavoidable. There are tricks to help reduce its effects, but the best way to recover from jet lag is to give your body the time to let itself adapt. You can slowly adjust your daily schedule before your departure and once you have boarded the plane. Eat well and drink plenty of water. As soon as you arrive, it is strongly advised that you force yourself to abide by the local time. In other words, stay awake if it's the morning or go to bed if it's night. This way it will be easier for your body to get accustomed to the change.

To minimize travel sickness, avoid strong jolts as much as possible and keep your eyes locked on the horizon (for example, sit in the middle of a boat or in front of a car or bus). Eat light meals only and avoid overeating before and during the journey. Various accessories and medications can help reduce symptoms such as nausea. A piece of good advice: try to relax and keep your mind on something else.

Money and Banking

Currency

The monetary unit in Canada is the dollar ($), which is divided into cents (¢). One dollar=100 cents.

Bills come in 5-, 10-, 20-, 50-, 100-, 500- and 1000-dollar denominations, and coins come in 1- (pennies), 5- (nickels), 10- (dimes) and 25-cent pieces (quarters), and in 1-dollar (loonies) and 2-dollar (twoonies) coins.

Exchange

Most banks readily exchange American and European currencies but almost every one of these will charge a **commission**. There are, however, exchange offices that do not charge commissions and keep longer hours. Just remember to **ask about fees** and to **compare rates**.

Vancouver

Custom House Currency Exchange
375 Water St.
☎*(604) 482-6007*

International Securities Exchange
1169 Robson St.
☎*(604) 683-9666*

Thomas Cook
777 Dunsmuir St.
☎*(604) 687-6111*

Money Services Money Mart
24 hrs/day
☎*(604) 606-9522 or 606-9612*

Victoria

Califorex International
724 Douglas St.
☎*(250) 384-6631*

Custom House Currency Exchange
815 Wharf St.
☎*(250) 389-6007*

Money Mart
1720 Douglas St.
☎*(250) 386-3535*

Whistler

Custom House Currency Exchange
4268 Mountain Square (Westbrook Hotel)
☎*(604) 938-1051*

4557 Blackcomb Way
☎*(604) 938-2876*

Exchange Rates*

CAD$1	= USD$0.63	USD$1	= CAD$1.59
CAD$1	= £0.40	£1	= CAD$2.50
CAD$1	= 0.63 € (euro)	1 € (euro)	= CAD$1.59
CAD$1	= 4.67 DKK	1 DKK	= CAD$0.21

*Samples only—rates fluctuate

4227 Village Stroll (Crystal Lodge)
☎ *(604) 938-6658*

4433 Sundial Place
☎ *(604) 938-0858*

Toronto Dominion Bank
4370 Lorimer Rd.
☎ *(604) 905-5500*

Traveller's Cheques

Traveller's cheques are accepted in most large stores and hotels. However it is easier and to your advantage to change your cheques at an exchange office. For a better exchange rate, buy your traveller's cheques in Canadian dollars.

Credit Cards

Most major credit cards are accepted at stores, restaurants and hotels. While the main advantage of credit cards is that they allow visitors to avoid carrying large sums of money, using a credit card also makes leaving a deposit for car rental much easier. Some cards, gold cards for example, automatically insure you when you rent a car (check with your credit card company to see what coverage it provides). In addition, the exchange rate with a credit card is generally better. The most commonly accepted credit cards are Visa, MasterCard, and to a lesser extent, American Express.

Banks

Banks can be found almost everywhere and most offer the standard services to tourists.

Vancouver

Royal Bank
1025 W. Georgia St.
☎*(604) 665-6991*
982 Howe St.
☎*(604)665-5138*
685 W. Hastings St.
☎*(604) 665-6766*

Scotiabank
1205 Robson St.
☎*(604) 668-2070*

TD Canada Trust
700 W. Georgia St.
☎*(604) 654-3665*
1055 Dunsmuir St.
☎*(604) 659-2070*

Victoria

American Express Travel Choice
1213 Douglas St.
☎*(250) 385-8731*
☎*800-669-3636*

Scotiabank
702 Yates St.
☎*(250) 953-5400*

Canadian Imperial Bank of Commerce
1175 Douglas St.
☎*(250) 356-4211*

TD Canada Trust
1080 Douglas St.
☎*(250) 356-4000*

Royal Bank
1079 Douglas St.
☎*(250) 356-4500*

Automated Teller Machines (ATMs)

Many banks have ATMs that allow you to make cash withdrawals. Most are members of the Cirrus and Plus networks, which allow visitors to make direct withdrawals from their personal accounts. You can use your card as you do normally—you'll be given Canadian dollars with a receipt, and the equivalent amount will be debited from your account. All this will take no more time that it would at your own bank! That said, the network can sometimes experience communication problems that will prevent you from obtaining money. If your transaction is refused by the ATM at one bank, try another bank where you might have better luck. In any case, take precautions so that you do not find yourself empty-handed.

Practical Information

Taxes

The ticket price on items generally **does not include tax**. There are two taxes, the GST or federal Goods and Services Tax, of 7% and the PST or Provincial Sales Tax of 7.5%. They are not cumulative and must be added to the price of most items and to restaurant bills. For hotel taxes, see p 67.

There are some exceptions to this taxation system, such as books, which are only taxed with the GST and food (except for ready made meals), which is not taxed at all.

There is no provincial sales tax on restaurant meals in British Columbia.

The provincial tax is not charged on items you purchase that are directly mailed to you at an address outside British Columbia.

Tax Refunds for Non-Residents

Non-residents can obtain refunds for the GST paid on purchases. To obtain a refund, it is important to keep your receipts. Note that the total of your purchase amounts (before taxes) for eligible goods and accommodation must be at least $200 and that each individual receipt for eligible goods must indicate a minimum total purchase amount (before taxes) of $50. Refunds are obtained by filling in and mailing a special form to Revenue Canada. Forms are available at airports, duty-free shops, and other locations.

For information, call:
☎ *800-66-VISIT*,
☎ *800-668-4748 in Canada*
☎ *(902) 432-5608 from outside Canada*
www.ccra-adrc.gc.ca/visitors.

Tipping

In general, tipping applies to all table service: restaurants, bars and night-clubs (therefore no tipping in fast-food restaurants). Tips are also given in taxis and in hair salons.

The tip is usually about 15% of the bill before taxes, but varies of course, depending on the quality of service.

Exploring

Each chapter in this guidebook leads you on tours through Vancouver, Victoria and Whistler. Major tourist attractions are described and classified according to a star-rating system, so you don't miss the must-sees if your time is limited.

★   Interesting
★★   Worth a visit
★★★   Not to be missed

The name of each attraction is followed by its address and phone number in parentheses. The price of admission for one adult is also provided. Most establishments offer discounts for children, students, senior citizens and families. Opening hours are indicated within these same parentheses. Note that attractions in tourist areas may open only during tourist season. Even in the off-season, however, some of these places welcome visitors, particularly groups, upon request.

Accommodations

A wide choice of accommodation is available in Vancouver, Victoria and Whistler. Rooms do not, however, come cheap, particularly in Vancouver and Whistler. Nevertheless, we recommend something for every budget. In high season, you will be hard-pressed to find a decent hotel room in Vancouver for less than $150; the same goes for Whistler. Rates in Victoria are more affordable. Remember that the more services the establishment offers, the more you will pay. Keep your needs in mind when you book, so as to avoid paying for services you don't need. Remember to add the 17% tax, which includes the GST, PST and a 2 or 3% hotel tax. The GST is refundable for non-residents in certain cases (see p 66). A credit card will make reserving a room much easier, since payment for the first night is required in most cases.

Many hotels offer corporate discounts as well as discounts for automobile club (CAA, AAA) members. Be sure to ask about these special rates as they are generally very easy to obtain. Furthermore, check in the travel brochures given out at tourist offices, since there are often coupons inside.

Prices and Symbols

All the prices mentioned in this guide apply to a **standard room for two people in peak season**. The actual cost to guests is often lower than the prices quoted here, particularly for travel during the off-peak season. Prices are indicated with the following symbols:

$	$50 or less
$$	$51 to $100
$$$	$101 to $150
$$$$	$151 to $200
$$$$$	$201 to $250
$$$$$$	more than $250

The various services offered by each establishment are indicated with a small symbol, which is explained in the legend in the opening pages of this guidebook. By no means is this an exhaustive list of what the establishment offers, but rather

Practical Information

the services we consider to be the most important.

Please note that the presence of a symbol does not mean that all the rooms have this service; you sometimes have to pay extra to get, for example, a whirlpool tub. And likewise, if the symbol is not attached to an establishment, it means that the establishment cannot offer you this service. Please note that unless otherwise indicated, all lodgings in this guide offer private bathrooms.

The Ulysses Boat

The Ulysses boat pictogram is awarded to our favourite accommodations. While every establishment recommended in this guide was included because of its high quality and/or uniqueness, as well as its good value, every once in a while we come across an establishment that absolutely wows us. These, our favourite establishments, are awarded a Ulysses boat. You'll find boats in all price categories: next to exclusive, high-price establishments, as well as budget ones. Regardless of the price, each of these establishments offers the most for your money. Look for them first!

Hotels

Hotels rooms abound, and range from modest to luxurious. There are many internationally reputed hotels in Vancouver, Victoria and Whistler.

Inns

Often set up in beautiful historic houses, inns offer quality lodging. These establishments are usually more charming and picturesque than hotels. Many are decorated with beautiful period furniture. Breakfast is often provided.

Bed and Breakfasts

There are many bed and breakfasts in Vancouver. Besides the obvious price advantage, the unique atmosphere of these establishments and the personalized service is a plus. Credit cards are not always accepted in bed and breakfasts.

The following B&B associations can help you plan a stay in a bed and breakfast by providing addresses and occasionally making reservations for you:

**Western Canada Bed and
Breakfast Innkeepers
Association**
P.O. Box 74534, 2803 W. Fourth Ave.,
Vancouver, B.C. V6K 4P4
www.webbia.com

**Beachside Bed & Breakfast
Registry**
4208 Evergreen Ave.
West Vancouver, V7H 1H1
☎(604) 922-7773
☎800-563-3311
≈(604) 926-8073
www.beach.bc.ca

**Old English Bed & Breakfast
Registry**
1226 Silverwood Cr.
North Vancouver, V7P 1J3
☎(604) 986-5069
≈(604) 986-8810
www.oldenglishbandb.bc.ca

**Best Canadian Bed & Breakfast
Network**
1064 Balfour Ave.
Vancouver, V6H 1X1
☎(604) 738-7207

Motels

There are many motels on
the main access roads into
these cities. Though they
tend to be cheaper, they
often lack atmosphere.
These are particularly useful
when you are pressed for
time.

University Residences

Due to certain restrictions,
this can be a complicated
alternative. Residences are
generally only available
during the summer (mid-
May to mid-August). Reservations must be made sev-
eral months in advance,
usually by paying for the
first night with a credit card.

This type of accommoda-
tion, however, is less costly
than the "traditional" alter-
natives, and making the
effort to reserve early can
be worthwhile. Visitors with
valid student cards can expect to pay approximately
$25 plus tax. Bedding is
included in the price, and
there is usually a cafeteria
in the building (meals are
not included in the rate).

Restaurants

Excellent restaurants are
easy to find in Vancouver,
Victoria and Whistler. Expect to be able to satisfy
your every craving. A strong
Asian presence and the
proximity of the sea have a
considerable effect of the
types of cuisine offered.
You'll also find restaurants
in every budget range, from
fast-food to fine dining.
Prices in this guide are for a
meal (appetizer, main
course and dessert, where
applicable) for one person,
excluding drinks and tip.

**Practical
Information**

Prices and Symbols

$	less than $10
$$	$11 to $20
$$$	$21 to $30
$$$$	more than $30

Note that a 10% tax is charged on alcoholic beverages.

The Ulysses Boat

The Ulysses boat pictogram is awarded to our favourite restaurants. To find out more about it, see p 68.

Entertainment

Bars and Nightclubs

In most cases there is no cover charge, aside from the occasional mandatory coat-check. However, expect to pay a few dollars to get into discos on weekends. The legal drinking age in British Columbia is 19; if you're close to that age, expect to be asked for proof.

Wine, Beer and Alcohol

The legal drinking age is 19. Beer, wine and alcohol can only be purchased in liquor stores (closed on Sun) run by the provincial government. Stores specializing in beer and wine are also scattered across these cities.

Shopping

In general, prices indicated on price tags for all goods do not include the sales tax (see p 65).

What to Buy

Salmon: You'll find this fish on sale, fresh from the sea and packed for travel, throughout Vancouver. Smoked salmon is a particularly coveted delicacy. "Indian Candy," a sweetened version of smoked salmon, is not to be missed.

Local crafts: Paintings, sculptures, woodworking items, ceramics, copper-based enamels, weaving, and other items are widely available.

Aboriginal Arts & Crafts: Beautiful sculptures and masks made from different types of stone, wood and even animal bone are available, though they are generally quite expensive. Make sure the sculpture is authentic by asking for a certificate of authenticity issued by the Canadian government. Silver and gold jewellery, carved by

First Nations artists with totemic animals like ravens and bears, are beautiful souvenirs. Quality varies, however, so look around before making your choice. Limited edition prints are also available in galleries and can be rather affordable.

Responsible Travel

The adventure of travelling will probably be an enriching experience for you. But will it be the same for your hosts? The question of whether or not tourism is good for a host country is controversial. On one hand, tourism brings many advantages, such as economic development, the promotion and rejuvenation of a culture and inter-cultural exchange; on the other hand, tourism can have negative impacts: an increase in crime, deepening of inequalities, environmental destruction, etc. But one thing is for sure: your journey will have an impact on your destination.

This is rather obvious when we speak of the environment. You should be as careful not to pollute the environment of your host country, just as you wouldn't do at home. We hear it often enough: we all live on the same planet! But when it comes to social, cultural

and even economic aspects, it can be more difficult to evaluate the impact of our travels. Be aware of the reality around you, and ask yourself what the repercussions will be before acting. Remember that you may make an impression that is much different than the one you wish to give.

Regardless of the type of travelling we choose, it is up to each and every one of us to develop a social conscience and to assume responsibility for our actions in a foreign country. Common sense, respect, altruism, and a hint of modesty are useful tools that will go a long way.

Travelling with Children

Travelling with children, however young they may be, can be a pleasant experience. A few precautions and ample preparation are the keys to a fun trip.

Aboard the Airplane

A good reclining stroller will allow you to bring an infant or small child everywhere you go and will also be great for naps, if needed. In the airport, it will be easy to carry with you, especially since you are allowed to bring the stroller up to plane's gates.

Travellers with children can board the plane first, avoiding long line-ups. If your child is under the age of two, remember to ask for seats at the front of the plane when reserving your tickets since they offer more room and are more comfortable for long flights, especially if you've got a toddler on your lap. Some airlines even offer baby cribs.

If you are travelling with an infant, be sure to prepare the necessary food for the flight, as well as an extra meal in case of a delay. Remember to bring enough diapers and moist towels, and a few toys might not be a bad idea!

For older kids who might get bored once the thrill of taking off has faded, books and activities such as drawing material and games will probably do the trick.

When taking off and landing, changes in air pressure may cause some discomfort. In this case, some say that the nipple of a bottle can soothe infants, while a piece of chewing gum will have the same effect for older children.

In Hotels

Many hotels are well equipped for children, and there is usually no extra fee for travelling with an infant. Many hotels and bed and breakfasts have cribs; ask for one when reserving your room. You may have to pay extra for children, however, but the supplement is generally low.

Car Rentals

Most car rental agencies rent car seats for children. They are usually not very expensive.

The Sun

Needless to say, a child's skin requires high protection against the sun; in fact, it is actually preferable not to expose toddlers to its harsh rays. Before going to the beach, remember to apply sunscreen (SPF 25 for children, 35 for infants). If you think your child will spend a long time under the sun, you should consider purchasing a sunscreen with SPF 60.

Children of all ages should wear a hat that provides good coverage for the head throughout the day.

Swimming

Children usually get quite excited about playing in the waves and can do so for hours on end. However, parents must be very careful and watch them constantly; accidents can happen in a matter of seconds. Ideally, an adult should accompany children into the water, especially the younger ones, and stand farther out in the water so that the kids can play between the beach and the supervising adult. This way, he or she can quickly intervene in case of an emergency.

For infants and toddlers, some diapers are especially designed for swimming, such as Little Swimmers by Huggies. These are quite useful when having fun in the water!

Pets

Vancouver, in particular, is a dog-friendly city. A good many hotels welcome dogs, usually for an additional charge. Note that in this guide, the following pictograph 🐕 appears with the description of accommodations in which pets are permitted. In some cases, there is a small extra charge or restrictions apply on the size of the animal.

For the safety of your pet and that of those to follow you, make sure that your pet is treated for fleas with a reliable product (available from your veterinarian) before bringing it to any commercial lodging.

City parks are open to leashed dogs, and some have off-leash areas and scheduled periods (morning and evening).

Mail

Canada Post provides efficient (depending on who you talk to) mail service across the country. At press time, it cost $0.48 to send a letter elsewhere in Canada, $0.65 to the United States and $1.25 overseas. Stamps can be purchased at post offices and in many pharmacies and convenience stores.

Canada Post
General Information
☎*800-267-1177*

Postal Codes
☎*900-565-4362*

Post Offices

Vancouver
757 West Hastings

Victoria
905 Gordon St., Downtown

Telecommunications

The area code in Vancouver and Whistler is **604**; in Victoria, it is **250**. Remember that in Vancouver and Whistler, you must dial the area code before the number, even for local calls.

Long distance charges are cheaper than in Europe, but more expensive than in the U.S. Pay phones can be found everywhere, often in the entrances of larger department stores and in restaurants. They are easy to use and most accept credit cards. Local calls to the surrounding areas cost $0.25 for unlimited time. Have a lot of quarters on hand if you are making a long distance call. It is less expensive to call from a private residence. **Note that telephone numbers beginning with 800, 888, 877 and 876 are toll-free. Simply add 1 before dialing.** These numbers are generally operational only in Canada and the United States

TELUS sells phone cards in various denominations for placing local and long distance calls in pay phones.

Holidays

The following is a list of public holidays in the prov-

ince of British Columbia. Most administrative offices and banks are closed on these days.

New Year's Day:
January 1

Easter Monday and/or Good Friday

Victoria Day:
third Monday in May

Canada Day:
July 1

Civic holiday:
first Monday in August

Labour Day:
first Monday in September

Thanksgiving:
second Monday in October

Remembrance Day:
November 11 (only banks and federal government services are closed)

Christmas Day:
December 25

Boxing Day:
December 26

Business Hours

Stores

Stores generally remain open the following hours:

Monday to Wednesday
10am to 6pm
(some stores are open later)

Thursday and Friday
10am to 9pm

Saturday
9am or 10am to 5pm

Sunday
noon to 5pm

Well-stocked convenience stores are plentiful and are sometimes open 24hrs a day.

Banks

Banks are open Monday to Friday from 10am to 4pm. Some are open on Thursdays and Fridays until 6pm or even 8pm and on weekends. Automatic teller machines are widely available and are open night and day.

Post Offices

Large post offices are open Monday to Friday from 9am to 5pm. There are also several smaller post offices located in shopping malls, convenience stores, and even pharmacies; these post offices stay open much later than the larger ones.

Travellers with Disabilities

The BC Coalition of People with Disabilities
204-456 West Broadway
Vancouver, V5Y 1R3
☎(604) 875-0188
For information on wheelchair accessible attractions, banks, churches, parks, restaurants, stores and theatres get a copy of *Accessibility Awareness Vancouver Guide.*

Public transportation in Vancouver is available from HandyDART (see p 53).

Advice for Smokers

Cigarette smoking is considered taboo, and it is being prohibited in more and more public places.

Smoking is prohibited in restaurants in Vancouver, North and West Vancouver, Victoria and several other cities in B.C. Efforts to extend the anti-smoking regulation across the province have, however, met with resistence. Smoking is also prohibited in bars in these cities.

Time Zone

Vancouver is on Pacific Standard Time. It is 3hrs

Practical Information

Weights and Measures

Although the metric system has been in use in Canada for more than 20 years, some people continue to use the Imperial system in casual conversation. Here are some equivalents:

Weights
1 pound (lb) = 454 grams (g)
1 kilogram (kg) = 2.2 pounds (lbs)

Linear Measure
1 inch (in) = 2.54 centimetres (cm)
1 foot (ft) = 30 centimetres (cm)
1 mile (mi) = 1.6 kilometres (km)
1 kilometre (km) = 0.63 miles (mi)
1 metre (m) = 39.37 inches (in)

Land Measure
1 acre = 0.4 hectare (ha)
1 hectare (ha) = 2.471 acres

Volume Measure
1 U.S. gallon (gal) = 3.79 litres
1 U.S. gallon (gal) = 0.8 imperial gallons

Temperature
To convert °F into °C: subtract 32, divide by 9, multiply by 5.
To convert °C into °F: multiply by 9, divide by 5, add 32.

behind Montreal and New York City, 8hrs behind the United Kingdom and 9hrs behind continental Europe.

Daylight Savings Time (+ 1hr) begins the first Sunday in April and ends on the last Sunday in October.

Electricity

Voltage is 110 volts throughout Canada, the same as in the United States. Electricity plugs have two parallel, flat pins, and adaptors are available here.

Illegal Drugs

Recreational drugs are illegal and are not tolerated (even "soft" drugs). Anyone caught with drugs in their possession risks severe consequences.

Laundromats

Laundromats are found almost everywhere in urban areas. In most cases detergent is sold on site. Although change machines are sometimes provided, it is best to bring plenty of quarters ($0.25) with you.

Newspapers

The two principal newspapers in Vancouver are the *Vancouver Sun* and the *Vancouver Province*. The *Georgia Straight* is Vancouver's main entertainment weekly. The *WestEnder* also has useful reviews and listings. Both are published on Thursdays and are widely available.

B.C. Bud

Marijuana, or "B.C. bud," is one of Vancouver's most dynamic growth industries. There are an estimated 9,000 "grow operations" in Vancouver. Many of these operate indoors, powered by mega-watt bulbs running on pirated electricity, in homes and apartments on quiet suburban streets.

In 2002, New York–based *High Times* magazine "honoured" Vancouver by naming it the best place in the world for marijuana smokers, citing the city's tolerance as well as the availability and quality of the herb. Before you light up, however, remember that marijuana is still illegal in Canada.

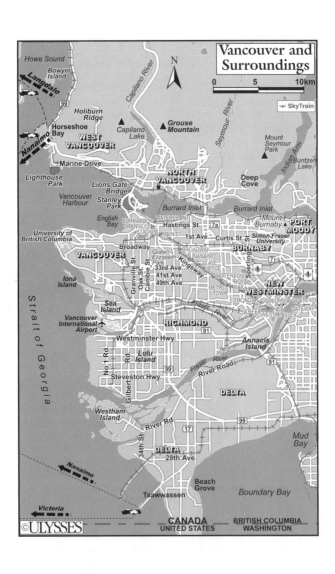

Vancouver and Surroundings

0   5   10km

⊶ SkyTrain

Vancouver

The following 10 tours, each covering a different part of Vancouver, will help you fully enjoy the local sights:

Tour A: Gastown ★

Tour B: Chinatown, Downtown Eastside and East Vancouver ★★

Tour C: Downtown ★★

Tour D: The West End ★

Tour E: Stanley Park ★★★

Tour F: Burrard Inlet ★★

Tour G: False Creek ★

Tour H: West Side ★★★

Tour I: Shaughnessy and Surroundings ★

Tour J: Richmond and Steveston ★

These are primarily walking or cycling tours, although you will need a car or other transport to tour Burrard Inlet (Tour F), parts of The West Side (Tour H) and Shaughnessy and Surroundings (Tour I). Also, to get from Chinatown to East Vancouver (in Tour B) you will need to take the SkyTrain or drive.

The area code in this chapter is **604**, unless otherwise indicated. The area code must be used before each telephone number, even within Vancouver.

Knowing your West End from your West Side

A first glance at any map of Vancouver can be a real brow-wrinkler. Just when you think you've figured out where the West End is, you're confronted with a West Side; then you realize that there's both an Eastside and an East Vancouver—not to mention three bodies of water surrounding the city! So in the interest of smoothing out the wrinkles, here's a brief glance at Vancouver's geography, with the corresponding tours in which they are described in this guidebook.

Gastown (Tour A) is located in the northeastern corner of downtown, beginning at the intersection of Richards, Water and West Cordova streets, and stretching a few blocks east, roughly to Carrall Street. It is bounded to the south by West Cordova Street and to the north by Burrard Inlet.
Chinatown (Tour B) stretches southeast of Gas-

town, from Carrall Street in the west to Gore Street in the east, and from East Pender Street in the north to East Georgia Street in the south.

The **Downtown Eastside** (Tour B) is bounded by Burrard Inlet to the north and Hastings Street to the south, Clark Drive to the east and Main Street to the west.

East Vancouver (Tour B), not to be confused with the **Downtown Eastside**, includes the area east of Ontario Street (south of False Creek) and is centred on Commercial Drive.

Downtown (Tour C) takes over where the West End leaves off and extends east to Main Street, on the north side of False Creek.

The **West End** (Tour D) stretches from Stanley Park in the west to Burrard Street in the east.

Georgia Street is the northern boundary and English Bay the southern boundary. Beyond these areas is Vancouver's downtown.

Stanley Park (Tour E) is bounded by Burrard Inlet everywhere except to the east, where it is bounded by the West End.

Burrard Inlet (Tour F) separates North Vancouver and West Vancouver from the city of Vancouver. Our tour briefly highlights sights of interest lining the south shore of the inlet (technically downtown), where a voyage north by SeaBus will begin, heading into North and West Vancouver.

False Creek (Tour G) separates the downtown area from the West Side, but three bridges—the Burrard, Granville and Cambie—make the separation seem more psychological than geographical. Tour G highlights attractions on both the north side (technically downtown) and south side of False Creek (primarily Granville Island).

The **West Side** (Tour H), not to be confused with the **West End**, is located south of False Creek. It includes everything west of Ontario Street, including the communities of Fairview and Kitsilano, as well as the University Endowment Lands (see Tour I).

Shaughnessy (Tour I) is one of the many neighbourhoods (such as Kitsilano, Mount Pleasant, where the city hall is located, and Fair-view, home to the Vancouver General Hospital) that make up the West Side.

Richmond (Tour J), home to Vancouver International Airport, is located south of the North Arm of the Fraser River, the southern limit of the city of Vancouver. **Steveston** is located at the southwestern limit of Richmond, on the coast of the Gulf of Georgia.

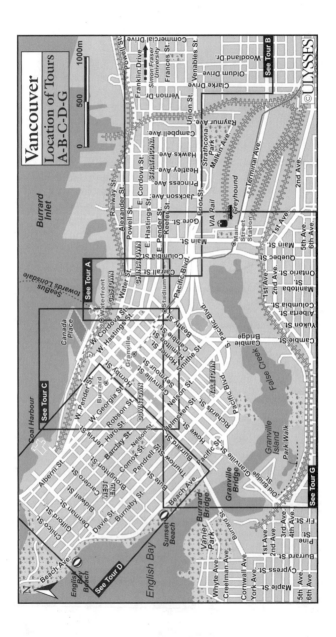

Exploring

Tour A: Gastown

This walking tour can easily be combined with Tour B, Chinatown, Downtown Eastside and East Vancouver.

Long before there were the glass towers housing million-dollar condos on the shores of Burrard Inlet, there was Gastown, the birthplace of the city of Vancouver. The area dates back to 1867 when John Deighton, known as "Gassy" Jack for his talkative nature, opened a saloon for the employees of a neighbouring sawmill, the Hasting Mill (see p 141). Gastown was destroyed by fire in 1886, but this catastrophe did not deter the city's pioneers. They rebuilt from the ashes and started anew the development of their city, this time in brick and stone, rather than wood; the city was incorporated several months later.

By 1887, when the Canadian Pacific Railway reached its new western terminus, Gastown was booming. Like any true Wild West town, its streets surged with hotels, saloons and shops that catered to the sawmill workers, lumberjacks, railway workers, land speculators and other hopefuls.

In the late 19th century, Gastown's economic development was driven by rail transport and the gold rush. The neighbourhood then became an important commercial distribution centre, whose warehouses eventually became so crowded that a second warehouse district was established in Yaletown (see p 129), which eventually supplanted Gastown. Long since abandoned and neglected, the restoration of Gastown began in the mid-1960s and continues to this day.

Located a short walk from downtown and the Cruise Ship Terminal, Gastown is high on the agenda of many sightseers and cruise-ship passengers on a day pass. Today, Gastown is a historic district with many handsome late-19th and early 20th-century Victorian and Edwardian commercial vernacular buildings, which narrowly escaped the wrecker's ball in the late 1960s. Although many of these buildings now house some good restaurants and popular nightspots, the district has somehow managed to retain a whiff of

Vancouver

that "Wild West" atmosphere, as a decidedly seedy feel permeates its rundown hotels and tacky souvenir stores. Gastown is also home to a number of First Nations art galleries, though before making any serious purchases, you'd be well advised to check out Gallery Row, south of the Granville Street Bridge.

Some of Gastown's commercial heritage buildings have been converted to residential use, particularly along Alexander and Water streets, contributing to the viability of local businesses but also creating tensions with long-term, low-income residents.

Despite the caveats, many of our readers will still enjoy a little stroll along its bricked streets lined with gas-lit lanterns.

Start off your tour at the corner of Water and West Cordova streets, at the west edge of Gastown (the eastern limit of downtown), which is accessible from the Waterfront station of the SkyTrain. It can also be reached from downtown by walking north on Richards Street until Water Street.

*Note that if you prefer a guided tour, the **Gastown Business Improvement Society** (131 Water St., ☎683-5650) offers free walking tours of Gastown once a day during the months of*

June, July and August. Tours last about 2hrs.

The **Landing** *(375 Water St.)*, with its brick and stone facade, was a commercial warehouse at the time of its construction in 1905; today it is a fine example of restoration. Since the late 1980s, it has housed offices, shops and restaurants.

Walk east along Water Street.

Like many other 19th-century North American buildings, **Hudson House** *(321 Water St.)* has its back to the water and the natural setting. Erected in 1897 as a warehouse for the Hudson's Bay Company, it was renovated in 1977 in order to accentuate the pure lines of its red brick arches. Today it houses a souvenir shop, an antique shop and a restaurant.

The **Gastown Steam Clock**, at the corner of Cambie Street, uses steam conducted through an underground network of pipes to whistle the hours. The clock is far from historic, however, having been built in 1977. In clear weather, this spot affords a stunning view of the mountains north of the city. It's also a favourite stop for photographs.

The intersection of Water and Carrall streets is one of the liveliest parts of

Gastown Steam Clock

Gastown. Long **Byrnes Block** *(2 Water St.)*, on the southwest corner, was one of the first buildings to be erected after the terrible fire of 1886; it was also one of Vancouver's first brick buildings. It was built on the site of Gassy Jack's second saloon, torn down in 1870; a rather crudely rendered **statue** of the celebrated barkeep graces tiny **Maple Tree Square**, the city's first public gathering place. The thick cornice on the brick building is typical of commercial buildings of the Victorian era. Rising in front is the former **Europe Hotel** *(4 Powell St.)*, a triangular building erected in 1908 by a Canadian hotel-keeper of Italian descent. Its leaded-glass windows bejewel what remains a strikingly elegant

building; it now provides affordable housing.

Head south on Carrall Street.

Nip into **Gaoler's Mews**, a peaceful brick courtyard surrounded by heritage buildings. As its name indicates, Gaoler's Mews was the site of Vancouver's first jail and customs house. The city's first telegraph office and fire station were also located here. The Irish Heather pub (see p 221) backs onto it, as do some offices and a café or two.

Turn right onto West Cordova.

Lonsdale Block *(8-28 West Cordova St.)*, built in 1889, is one of the most remarkable buildings on this street. Its early tenants included the city's first synagogue. Despite the 1974 restoration of its classical-style facade, today it looks pretty run down and is occupied by an Army and Navy Store.

Turn left on Abbott Street.

At the corner of Hastings Street stands the former **Woodwards department store** *(101 West Hasting St.)*, founded in 1892 by Charles Woodward. It closed exactly 100 years later, following the death of the Woodward family patriarch, and now belongs to the provincial government. In the 1990s, the provincial NDP

Vancouver

government had plans to redevelop the building and turn it into 350 affordable housing units. As of 2002, however, the Liberal government had planned to sell it to a private developer. Frustration with the situation led to some 50 homeless people squatting in the building in September of that year.

The south end of Abbott Street is dominated by the **Sun Tower ★** *(100 West Pender St.)*, erected in 1911 for the *Vancouver World* newspaper. It later housed the offices of the local daily, *The Vancouver Sun*, after which it was named. At the time of its construction, the 17-storey Sun Tower was the tallest building in all of the British Empire.

Continue south on Abbott until West Pender Street.

Turn right on West Pender Street and continue to Cambie Street, where you turn right, passing the **Architectural Institute of British Columbia** *(440 Cambie St., ☎683-8588)*, which has a small gallery and offers guided tours of Vancouver during the summer. Opposite is **Victory Square**, in the centre of which

stands **The Cenotaph**, a memorial to those who lost their lives in the two World Wars. It was sculpted by Thornton Sharp in 1924. The square separates the streets of Gastown from those of the modern business district. Facing onto the north side is the elegant **Dominion Building ★** *(207 West Hastings St.)* whose mansard roof is reminiscent of those found on Second Empire buildings along the boulevards of Paris.

Continue north on Cambie Street to return to the Gastown Clock.

On your way, you can turn left on West Cordova, where you'll find several triangular buildings. They're shaped in accordance with the streets, which intersect at different angles. Other

Black-capped Chickadee

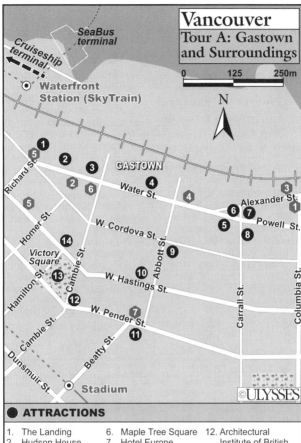

Vancouver
Tour A: Gastown and Surroundings

SeaBus terminal

Cruiseship terminal

Waterfront Station (SkyTrain)

0   125   250m

N

GASTOWN

Richard St.

Water St.

Homer St.

Alexander St.

W. Cordova St.

Powell St.

Victory Square

Abbott St.

W. Hastings St.

Hamilton St.

Cambie St.

Carrall St.

Columbia St.

W. Pender St.

Cambie St.

Beatty St.

Dunsmuir St.

Stadium

©ULYSSES

● ATTRACTIONS

1. The Landing
2. Hudson House
3. Gastown Steam Clock
4. Gaslight Square
5. Byrnes Block
6. Maple Tree Square
7. Hotel Europe
8. Gaoler's Mews
9. Lonsdale Block
10. Woodwards
11. Sun Tower
12. Architectural Institute of British Columbia
13. Victory Square
14. Dominion Building

● RESTAURANTS

1. Incendio
2. India Village
3. Jewel of India
4. Old Spaghetti Factory
5. Steamworks Brewing Co.
6. Water Street Café
7. Wild Rice

buildings, with their series of oriel windows, are reminiscent of San Francisco.

Tour B: Chinatown, Downtown Eastside and East Vancouver

This tour takes in three distinct neighbourhoods, Chinatown and the adjacent Downtown Eastside, as well as East Vancouver, which is further east. Each tour can be enjoyed on foot, but you'll need to drive or take the SkyTrain to get from Chinatown and the Downtown Eastside to East Vancouver.

Also note that Chinatown extends from Gore Street, in the east, to just beyond Carrall Street in the west, and south from East Pender to East Georgia Street. Vancouver's notorious Downtown Eastside is centred just a block beyond, on the corner of East Hastings and Main streets. When wandering around Chinatown, it's quite easy to stumble upon this area, which, though not dangerous to the passer-by, may not be a choice destination for visitors with delicate sensibilities. If this describes you, keep your eyes open and avoid the area altogether.

A good way to get to know Chinatown is by taking part in a **guided walking tour**. Tours last 90min *($6; Jun to Sep every day 10:30am and 2:30pm; Chinese Cultural Centre, 50 E. Pender St, ☎658-8883).*

● ATTRACTIONS

1. Chinatown Millenium Gate
2. Century's Winds of Change mural
3. Shanghai Alley
4. Sam Kee Building
5. Dr. Sun Yat-Sen Classical Chinese Garden
6. Chinese Cultural Centre Museum and Archives
7. Dr. Sun Yat-Sen Park
8. Lee Building
9. CIBC Building
10. Carnegie Centre
11. Vancouver Police Centennial Museum
12. St. James Anglican Church
13. Simon Fraser University

◯ ACCOMMODATIONS

1. Apricot Cat & Black Dog Bed and Breakfast
2. Simon Fraser University

● RESTAURANTS

1. Cannery Seafood Restaurant
2. Gain Wah
3. Havana
4. Hon's Wun-Tun House
5. Joe's Café
6. Kam Gok Yuen
7. La Casa Gelato
8. Nick's Spaghetti House
9. Only Café
10. Park Lock
11. Pink Pearl
12. Sun Sui Wah Seafood Restaurant
13. WaaZuuBee Café

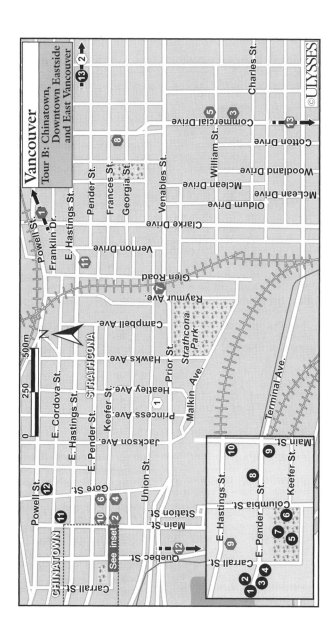

This tour starts on West Pender Street, between Abott and Carrall streets; at Carrall, West Pender becomes East Pender.

On East Pender Street, the scene changes radically. The colour and atmosphere of public markets, plus a strong Chinese presence, bring this street to life. The 1858 Gold Rush in the hinterland drew Chinese from San Francisco and Hong Kong; in 1878, railway construction brought thousands more Chinese to British Columbia. This community resisted many hard blows that might have ended its presence in the province. At the beginning of the 20th century, the Canadian government imposed a heavy tax on new Chinese immigrants, and then banned Chinese immigration altogether from 1923 to 1947. Today, the local Chinese community is growing rapidly due to the massive influx of immigrants from Hong Kong.

But while Vancouver's Chinatown is one of the largest in all of North America, much of Vancouver's Chinese population now lives in Richmond, south of Vancouver.

For an unusual way to experience Chinatown, visit the **Chinatown Night Market** *(Jun to Sep Fri-Sun 6:30pm to 11pm)*, where you can shop for exotic products you just can't find at the grocery store. A festive atmosphere reigns.

The western entrance to Chinatown, at West Pender and Taylor streets, has recently been marked by the addition of the **Chinatown Millenium Gate**. Designed by architect Joe Wai, who is also responsible for the Dr. Sun Yat-Sen Classical Chinese Garden and the Chinese Cultural Centre Museum and Archives, the gate is being funded by three levels of government and the local community in an effort to revitalize the area. The design is based on 19th- and 20th-century tomb and burial ground gates in Beijing, and, following local concern about this being a bad omen, was approved, with minor changes, by a Feng Shui master.

On your left, just past the gate, is the **Century's Winds of Change Mural**, depicting the history of Chinese integration into Canada. Duck into **Shanghai Alley**, just past the gate to your right. In the early 1900s, Chinese merchants moved into this alley, as well as Canton Alley, which ran parallel one block west, as a result of pressure from White merchants on Hastings Street. Most of the buildings, including restaurants, stores, a theatre and several tenements, had double fronts, opening onto both the alley and Carrall Street. They were demolished in the 1940s.

The alley's walkway is made of coloured asphalt imprinted with a template to give it the look of paving stones; its original surface consisted of wood blocks sealed with sap and covered with tar. The walkway leads to **Allan Yap Circle**, site of a replica of the 2,200-year-old Western Han Dynasty bell. This was a gift from the City of Guangzhou, Vancouver's twin city and the place where the original bell was unearthed in 1983. Also in the circle are panels recounting Chinatown's social and architectural history from 1870 to 1940.

On your way into Chinatown, you'll see the strange little **Sam Kee Building** *(8 West Pender St.)*, which occupies a leftover piece of land 1.8m deep. The Sam Kee Company, one of the wealthiest firms in late-18th-century Chinatown, bought a standard-sized lot here in 1903. When the City expropriated 7m from the front of the lot to widen the street, the determined owner vowed to build regardless. This 1.8m-wide building was erected about 10 years later. According to *Ripley's Believe It or Not* and the *Guinness Book of Records*, it is the narrowest commercial building in the world. Its interior space is augmented by the oriel windows overhanging the sidewalk and a basement that extends under the street, which once harboured public baths; sunlight was provided by glass blocks that are still embedded in the sidewalk. Today, the building houses an insurance company and is not open to the public. This area was once home to several famous brothels as well as to a number of opium dens.

Take East Pender Street into the heart of Chinatown.

It is well worth stopping in at the **Dr. Sun Yat-Sen Classical Chinese Garden ★** *($7.50; every* *day early May to mid-Jun 10am to 6pm, mid-Jun to end Aug 9:30am to 7pm, early Sep to end Sep10am to 6pm, early Oct to end Apr 10am to 4:30pm; several tours scheduled daily, call for times; 578 Carrall St., ☎689-7133)* behind the traditional portal of the **Chinese Cultural Centre** *(50 East Pender St.)* Built in 1986 by Chinese artists from Suzhou, this garden is the only example outside Asia of landscape architecture from the Ming Dynasty (1368-1644). This green space is surrounded by high walls that create a virtual oasis of peace in the middle of bustling Chinatown. It is worth noting that Dr. Sun Yat-Sen (1866-1925), considered the father of modern China, visited Vancouver in 1911 in order to raise money for his newly founded Kuomintang ("People's Party").

Those who are unfamiliar with Chinese gardens will appreciate the guided tours; docents provide a wealth of information to help neophytes appreciate and understand the significance of every element. Reflecting the Daoist philosophy of yin and yang, classical Chinese gardens represent a balance of opposing forces: human beings versus nature, heaven versus earth, light versus dark, hard versus soft. Its water and plants represent yin, its covered walkways, yang. Built as private gardens by scholars, such gardens were meant to inspire reflection; the unusually shaped, eroded limestone rocks throughout the garden were referred to as "moon rocks" and displayed as sculptures meant to influence artistic creativity. Note that there is not a nail in the place: all of the structures were built using mortise-and-tenon construction. The water in the pond was intentionally made jade-coloured and opaque by lining the bottom of the pond with clay, in order to increase the water's reflectivity and enhance the mystery of the underwater world, enriching the garden experience. In the summer, water lillies cover the water—symbols of purity, growing from its murky depths. The intricately patterned paving stones beneath your feet were collected from stream beds in China; the white flower designs in the pattern were created with pottery shards. It's a charming spot to contemplate your own place in the world. Call for a schedule of events.

Leaving the garden, turn left onto Keefer Street, and left again onto Columbia Street, where you'll find the **Chinese Cultural Centre Museum and Archives** ★ (*$4; Tue-Sun 11am to 5pm; tours by prior arrangement; 555 Columbia St., ☎658-8880*). On the first floor of this facility, designed in a style that was popular during the Ming Dynasty (1368-1644 CE), there are changing exhibits on such subjects as painting, calligraphy and music, all beautifully presented. The permanent exhibit on the second floor (while you're there, take a peek at the gardens from the observation deck) traces the history of Vancouver's Chinese population from 1788 to modern times. You'll find photographs, including one of a brand-new Sam Kee Building, mounted press clippings and a variety of 19th-century artifacts, such as a wooden abacus handmade by a miner and tiny models of a Chinese funeral procession. Here you'll learn that British Columbia's first Chinese immigrants mined for gold in the Cariboo area of northern British Columbia; the town of Barkerville, where they lived, is today a historic

site. Chinese immigrants were long subjected to discrimination on many fronts; the concentration of Chinese in Chinatowns across North America is itself testament to the hostility they faced. Only in 1947 did the B.C. government allow the Chinese to vote in federal elections. There is also a small military history museum on site, which documents the role played by Chinese Canadians in World War II.

Next to the museum is **Dr. Sun Yat-Sen Park** (*free admission; corner Columbia and Keefer sts.*), which adjoins the garden of the same name. Attractively landscaped, it's a pleasant place for a stroll, but no substitute for the genuine article next door. Chances are good, however, that you might also encounter neighbourhood vagrants, who similarly enjoy the park.

Leaving the park, turn left on Columbia and left again on East Pender.

The architecture of the buildings along East Pender Street reflects the background of Vancouver's first Chinese immigrants, most of whom were Cantonese. Take, for example, the deep, multi-storey loggias on a number of the facades, such as that of the **Lee Building** (*129 East Pender St.*),

Vancouver

Pain and Wastings

The Downtown Eastside is Vancouver's skid row. Considered the poorest neighbourhood in Canada, it is home to a disproportionate number of drug addicts and HIV/AIDS sufferers, and is rife with poverty, prostitution and crime. Over 80% of its households are considered "low income" by Statistics Canada, compared with 31% in Vancouver as a whole (1996 census).

The neighbourhood is defined by Burrard Inlet to the north, East Hastings Street to the south, Clark Drive to the east and Main Street to the west. Its nerve centre is the corner of Main and Hastings, known to residents as "Pain and Wastings." There, in front of the Carnegie Centre (Vancouver's former public library) and in full view of Vancouver Police headquarters on Main Street, is where drug dealers and clients congregate.

Walking through the area, any visitor will be alarmed by its many detox centres, rundown rooming houses and staggering poverty. Its handsome Victorian buildings, however, testify to a once-vibrant neighbourhood. Vancouver's first downtown developed here in the early 20th century, near the nucleus of the growing city. It was home to the municipal courthouse, city hall, the Carnegie Public Library, several theatres and Woodward's department store. It was also the transportation hub of the city, with the streetcar station at Hastings and Carrall streets, and the ferry and pier just north on Burrard Inlet.

The westward shift of downtown and the consequent decline of the Eastside began with the opening of the new courthouse on Georgia Street in 1907 (today the Vancouver Art Gallery), and accelerated in the late 1950s, when the library moved to Burrard and Robson streets, the streetcar service was terminated and the ferry service discontinued (today the SeaBus leaves from the foot of Seymour Street, further west). As a result, some 10,000 fewer people passed through the neighbourhood each day. By the time Woodward's department store closed in 1992, taking with it many other stores and restaurants, the Downtown Eastside had seen better days. As the area declined, housing became increasingly affordable here, attracting those on fixed incomes who could not afford the soaring rents in other parts of the city.

The community's problems were brought to national attention in 1999 with the release of the award-winning documentary *Through a Blue Lens*. A National Film Board production, it was filmed by a number of Vancouver constables who captured the lives of addicts on their Eastside beat for use as an anti-drug educational tool. The film compellingly portrays the squalor, desperation and fear in which these people live. The neighbourhood has made national headlines more than ever lately, as a result of the case of the more than 50 missing women, mostly drug addicts and prostitutes, who have disappeared from the Downtown Eastside since 1983.

A number of community organizations work tirelessly to improve the lot of residents. The Vancouver Agreement, a five-year plan signed by three levels of government in 2000, will address the community's needs by providing a new health program and treatment centre, street clean-ups, improved housing, and stepping up police efforts against drug dealers.

The election in 2002 of a new mayor, for whom the clean-up of the Downtown Eastside is a priority, is another sign that change is on the horizon.

Vancouver

built in 1907. Gutted by fire in 1972, its original facade conceals the completely new structure behind it. This is a fine example of successful private preservation of a heritage building.

To the left of this building is a passageway leading to an inner court surrounded by shops. Many of these buildings feature historical plaques; right across the street from the garden is the oldest building in Chinatown, built in 1889.

During Chinese festivals, the loggias along East Pender Street are packed with onlookers, heightening the lively atmosphere.

Continue along East Pender Street until Main Street.

At the corner of Main Street, to your right, stands a branch of the **CIBC (Canadian Imperial Bank of Commerce)** *(501 Main St.)*, whose architecture was inspired by the English baroque style. Faced with terra cotta, this colossal edifice was designed by architect Victor Horsburgh and erected in 1915.

If you turn left onto Main Street, you will approach East Hastings Street. One of the country's most notorious corners, Main and Hastings is also referred to as "Pain and Wastings" by residents of the area. The nerve centre of Vancouver's Downtown Eastside, the poorest community in Canada, it is alight with panhandlers, drug dealers and prostitutes. The police claim that it is not a dangerous place for tourists (although the same cannot necessarily be said for residents) and that the worst that might happen is being harassed to buy drugs or for spare change. Nevertheless, some may prefer to avoid the area altogether. The drug dealing is concentrated around the Carnegie Library (see below) on the west side of Main Street, in plain view of Vancouver Police headquarters, so if you'd rather not be confronted with it at close hand, cross Main Street at East Pender, and stay on the east side of the street.

Another example of the English baroque revival style is the former **Carnegie Library** *(at the corner of Main and East Hastings)*, now used as a community centre (the Carnegie Centre). This building owes its existence to American philanthropist Andrew Carnegie, who financed the construction of hundreds of neighbourhood libraries in the United States and Canada. If you're not put off by the goings-on outside, enter the building and take a look at the stained-glass portraits of

Shakespeare, Robert Burns and Sir Walter Scott, which illuminate the main stairwell inside.

If you'd rather skip this corner, continue along East Pender Street to Gore Street, one block east of Main Street, and turn left on Gore Street until East Cordova Street. Otherwise, turn right on East Cordova Street, past the Salvation Army, several detox centres and run-down rooming houses.

If the poverty, suffering and addiction you see around here aren't bleak enough for you, head into the **Vancouver Police Centennial Museum ★** *($6; year-round Mon-Fri 9am to 3pm, early May to end Aug also Sat 10am to 3pm)*, (although it bills itself as a place of "mystery, history and intrigue" it's more like "sordid, morbid and graphic"). Located in the former coroner's courtroom and autopsy laboratory, the exhibit begins harmlessly enough with memorabilia tracing the history of the Vancouver Police Department (VPD), punctuated by rather spooky models dressed in historical police uniforms. This exhibit is likely to be of local interest only, and one hopes that this, rather than what comes later, is the focus of the popular tours given to local schoolchildren. Interestingly enough, however, one

learns that in 1912, the first woman constable in the entire British Empire was hired right here in Vancouver.

The exhibit then takes a turn for the gory, with its collection of weapons, many hideously crude, that were seized on the streets of Vancouver. Other "delights" include a re-created murder scene in a Downtown Eastside rooming house, black-and-white photographs of past murder scenes, and a forensic display in the autopsy lab, with mounted organs and autopsies being performed by dummies—definitely not for the squeamish. If you're wondering why there's a portrait of late Hollywood actor and notorious ladies' man Errol Flynn, it's because the actor died in Vancouver in 1959 and his autopsy took place in this very lab. Rumour has it that some of Flynn's genital warts were harvested as souvenirs by lab staff after his death, but promptly stitched back on before his body was sent back home for burial. These days, Hollywood stars such as Brad Pitt, Jack Nicholson and Gwyneth Paltrow make "live" appearances at the former morgue, shooting scenes for films. You can buy your very own VPD paraphernalia at the Cop Shoppe.

Vancouver

Across East Cordova, at the corner of Gore Street, stands **St. James Anglican Church** ★ *(303 East Cordova)*, one of the most unusual buildings erected in Canada between the two World Wars. A tall, massive structure made of exposed reinforced concrete, it was designed by British architect Adrian Gilbert Scott in 1935.

Head south on Gore Street to admire all the exotic products displayed along East Pender Street or enjoy a meal in one of the many Chinese restaurants there.

If you wish to leave no stone unturned in your exploration of Vancouver's ethnic neighbourhoods, take Gore all the way to Keefer, turn right, then take a left on Main Street to reach Pacific Central Station (about a 5min walk). Take the SkyTrain toward Surrey, and get off at the next station (Broadway). If you're driving, head east on Georgia Street, turn onto Prior Street at the viaduct, then take a right on Commercial Drive. When you get off the SkyTrain, head north up Commercial Drive.

The next part of town you'll pass through is known as **Little Italy**, but is also home to Vancouverites of Portuguese, Spanish, Jamaican and South American descent. In the early 20th century, the **Commercial Drive** area became the city's first suburb, with middle-class residents building small, single-family homes with wooden siding here. The first Chinese and Slavic immigrants moved into the neighbourhood during World War I, and another wave of immigrants, chiefly Italian, arrived at the end of World War II. North Americans will feel pleasantly out of their element in the congenial atmosphere of Little Italy's Italian cafés and restaurants.

Today, "The Drive," between Venables and 12th Avenue, is awash with the flavours of Italy, Portugal, Greece, Mexico, India, the Caribbean and Vietnam, to name but a few, with Italian coffee houses and markets, little bars where East Vancouver hipsters converge on patios in dry weather, vegetarian cafés and restaurants galore, and groovy shops of every variety—but not a sushi bar in sight! There aren't any attractions to be visited here per se—it's the street life that warrants a slow-paced afternoon here, ensconced among the locals. The view of Vancouver's skyline, to the west, and the mountains to the north, is indeed grand from **Grandview Park** *(William and Charles sts.)*, especially when the sun is setting.

Marker of Change

To commemorate the killing of 14 women at the École Polytechnique in Montréal in 1989, the Women's Monument Committee erected the Marker of Change on December 6, 1997, the eighth anniversary of the massacre. Designed by Torontonian Beth Alber, it features 14 pink-granite benches, each inscribed with the name of one of the victims, arranged in a circle in Thornton Park in East Vancouver. The monument's dedication to all women killed by men is written in seven languages.

To conclude your tour of East Vancouver, head to the city of Burnaby to visit **Simon Fraser University ★★** (SFU), located about 30min from the centre of Vancouver. If you don't have a car, take bus 135 to the campus. Otherwise, drive east on East Hastings Street, take a right on Sperling Avenue, then a left on Curtis Street, which turns into Gagliardi Way.

Perched atop Burnaby Mountain, SFU looks like a huge spaceship that just arrived here from another galaxy. The campus offers a panoramic view of downtown Vancouver, Burrard Inlet and the towering mountains to the north—a breathtaking sight in clear weather. The main buildings of bare concrete that form the nucleus of the university were designed in 1963 by western Canada's star architect Arthur Erickson and his associate Geoffrey Massey. Their architecture reflects the influence of Japanese temples, European cloisters, Mayan ruins and the Californian practice of leaving large parts of the exterior open. The grouping is laid out around a large courtyard. There is also a mall, half of which is sheltered by a glass and metal structure so that students can enjoy pleasant temperatures winter and summer alike and find shelter from the region's frequent rainfalls.

★★

Tour C: Downtown

On May 23, 1887, Canadian Pacific's first transcontinental train, which set out from Montréal, arrived at the Vancouver terminus. The railway company, which had been granted an area

Vancouver

roughly corresponding to present-day downtown Vancouver, began to develop its property. To say that it played a major role in the development of the city's business district would be an understatement. Canadian Pacific truly built this part of town, laying the streets and erecting many very important buildings. Downtown Vancouver has been developing continually since the 1960s. It's a sign of the city's great economic vitality, which can be attributed to Asian capital and the Canadian population's shift westward to the mild climes of the Pacific coast.

This tour starts at the corner of West Hastings and Seymour streets. This tour can easily be combined with Tour A, which covers Gastown and ends nearby.

Begin your tour at Harbour Centre. Vancouver's tallest building, topped by what looks like a flying saucer hovering above, is hard to miss. The building is home to Simon Fraser University's downtown campus. **The Lookout! at Harbour Centre** *($10; 555 West Hastings St., ☎689-0421),* Vancouver's version of Toronto's CN Tower, offers a "360-degree view" of Vancouver and surroundings. A glassed-in

---

● ATTRACTIONS

1. The Lookout! at Harbour Centre
2. Toronto Dominion Bank
3. CIBC Building
4. Royal Bank
5. Sinclair Centre
6. Crédit Foncier Franco-canadien
7. Vancouver Club
8. Marine Building (R)
9. Canada Place
10. Bentall Centre
11. Royal Centre
12. Christ Church Cathedral
13. Fairmont Hotel Vancouver
14. Cathedral Place
15. Canadian Craft Museum
16. Robson Street
17. B.C. Hydro Building
18. St. Andrew's Wesley United Church
19. First Baptist Church
20. Provincial Law Courts
21. Robson Square
22. Vancouver Art Gallery
23. Granville Mall
24. Pacific Centre
25. The Bay
26. Vancouver Centre
27. Eaton's
28. Commodore Theatre
29. Orpheum Theatre
30. Vogue Theatre
31. Library Square
32. Centre in Vancouver for the Performing Arts
33. Canadian Broadcasting Corporation (CBC)
34. General Post Office
35. Queen Elizabeth Theatre
36. Cathedral of Our Lady of the Rosary

(R) establishment with restaurant (see description)

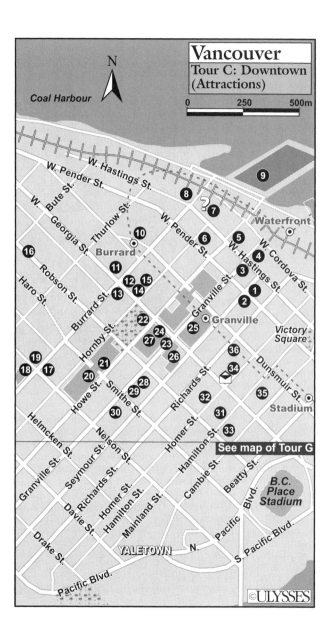

N

Coal Harbour

0   250   500m

W. Hastings St.

W. Pender St.

W. Bute St.

W. Georgia St.

Thurlow St.

W. Pender St.

Waterfront

W. Cordova St.

W. Hastings St.

Granville St.

Robson St.

Burrard

Haro St.

Burrard St.

Hornby St.

Granville

Victory Square

Dunsmuir St.

Howe St.

Smithe St.

Richards St.

Stadium

Helmcken St.

Nelson St.

Homer St.

Hamilton St.

See map of Tour G

Granville St.

Seymour St.

Richards St.

Homer St.

Hamilton St.

Davie St.

Mainland St.

Cambie St.

Beatty St.

B.C. Place Stadium

Drake St.

Pacific Blvd.

Pacific Blvd.

YALETOWN

N.

Pacific Blvd.

S. Pacific Blvd.

©ULYSSES

elevator whisks you to a height of 174m, almost too quickly to enjoy the ride. Those who enjoy observation towers may well not balk at the $9 admission fee, but others might find this a little steep (no pun intended), particularly when, after reluctantly coughing it up and becoming a captive audience, you are bombarded by advertisements for shopping centres, tour companies and various other costly Vancouver attractions. Furthermore, those unfamiliar with the city could use more user-friendly plans indicating the precise location of many of the landmarks or sectors referred to in the panels. Nevertheless, the view of English Bay and the fiords of the North Shore is really quite lovely from the top. To get the most out of your ticket, save it and return later in the evening to see the city lights.

Located opposite Harbour Centre, the former regional headquarters of the **Toronto Dominion Bank** (*580 West Hastings St.*) exemplify the classical elegance of early 20th-century financial banking halls. The bank abandoned this registered heritage building in 1984 for one of the modern skyscrapers along Georgia Street. It is now held by

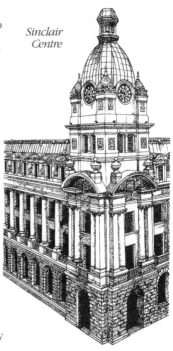

Sinclair Centre

Simon Fraser University. One block west, the former regional headquarters of the **Canadian Bank of Commerce** (*698 West Hastings St.*), a veritable temple of finance, met the same fate and now houses the elegant Henry Birks and Sons shop. Also a heritage building, it was renamed the Birks Building in 1994. With its massive Ionic columns, this building was erected in 1906 according to a design by Darling and Pearson, whose credits include the Sun Life Building in Montréal. Opposite stands the massive **Royal Bank** ★ *(675 West Hastings St.)* building, designed by S. G. Davenport. The Italian Renaissance–style banking hall is stunning and well worth a look.

The **Sinclair Centre** ★ *(701 West Hastings St.)* is a group of government offices. It occupies a former post office, and its annexes are connected to one another by covered passageways lined with shops. The main building, dating from 1909, is considered to be one of the finest examples of the neo-baroque style in Canada.

A little further, at the corner of Hornby Street, is an austere edifice built in 1913 by the **Crédit Foncier Franco-Canadien** *(850 West Hastings St.)*, a financial institution jointly founded by French and Québecois bankers. On the other side of the street, the **Vancouver Club** *(915 West Hasting St.)* is dwarfed by the skyscrapers on either side of it. Founded in 1914, it is a private club for businessmen modelled after similar clubs in London.

Facing you as you head west on West Hastings Street, is the **Marine Building** ★★ *(355 Burrard St.)*, a fine example of the Art Deco style. It's charac-

terized by vertical lines, staggered recesses, geometric ornamentation and the absence of a cornice at the top of the structure. Erected in 1929, the building lives up to its name in part because it is lavishly decorated with nautical motifs, and also because its occupants are ship-owners and shipping companies. Its facade features terra cotta panels depicting the history of shipping and the discovery of the Pacific coast. The interior decor is even more inventive, however. The lights in the lobby are shaped like the prows of ships, and there is a stained-glass window showing the sun setting over the ocean. The elevators will take you up to the mezzanine, which offers an interesting general view of the building.

Turn right on Burrard Street, heading toward the water, and duck into the **Vancouver Tourist Info Centre** *(200 Burrard St., ☎683-2000)* to stock up on any additional information you might need.

Take Burrard Street toward the water to reach **Canada Place** ★★ *(999 Canada Place)*, which occupies one of the piers along the harbour and looks like a giant sailboat ready to set out across the waves. This multi-purpose complex, which served as the Canadian pavilion at Expo 86, is home to the city's Convention Centre, the cruiseship terminal, the luxurious **Pan Pacific Hotel** (see p 176) and an IMAX theatre. Even if you're not setting sail, take a walk on the "deck" and drink in the magnificent panoramic view of Burrard Inlet, the port and the snow-capped mountains.

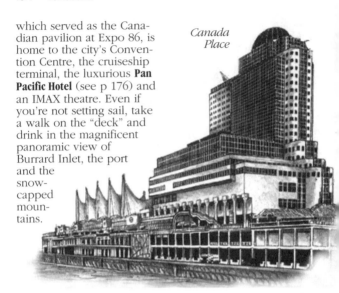

Canada Place

Take Burrard Street back into the centre of town and continue southward to West Georgia Street.

On your way, you'll see the giant **Benttal Centre** *(at the corner of Pender St.)*, made up of three towers designed by architect Frank Masson and erected between 1965 and 1975.

On your right, you'll also see the **Royal Centre** *(1055 W. Georgia St.)*, which includes the 38-storey Royal Bank tower. These skyscrapers have to be "low" and squat in order to withstand the seismic activity in the Pacific Ring of Fire.

On your left, just before West Georgia Street, stands tiny **Christ Church Cathedral** *(690 Burrard St.)*. This Gothic Revival Anglican cathedral was built in 1889, back when Vancouver was no more than a large village. Its skeleton, made of Douglas fir, is visible from inside. What is most interesting about the cathedral, however, is neither its size nor its ornamentation, but simply the fact that it has survived in this part of town, which is continually being rebuilt. It now also functions as a community centre.

Across West Georgia Street and dwarfing the cathedral, stands the imposing, 23-storey **Fairmont Hotel Vancouver ★** *(900 W. Georgia St.)* (see p 176), a veritable monument to the Canadian railway companies that built it between 1928 and 1939. For many years, its high copper roof served as the principal symbol of Vancouver abroad. Like all major Canadian cities, Vancouver had to have a Château-style hotel. Make sure to take a look at the gargoyles near the top and the bas-reliefs at the entrance, which depict an ocean liner and a moving locomotive. Note that this is actually the third Hotel Vancouver built by the Canadian Pacific Railroad, the first one having been built at the corner of Georgia and Granville streets in 1887 and the second near the current hotel, on the site of the Pacific Centre (1916-1949).

Flanking the cathedral to the east are the shops and offices of **Cathedral Place** *(925 West Georgia St.)*, built in 1991. Its pseudo-medieval gargoyles have not managed to make people forget about the Art Deco-style Georgia Medical Building, which once occupied this site, and whose demolition in 1989 prompted a nation-wide outcry. Even with rock singer Bryan Adams's help, a major campaign to save the building proved futile. Cathedral Place is thus a building that is trying to gain acceptance. Its pointed roof was modelled after that of the neighbouring hotel, and is adorned with the stone nurses that once graced the Georgia Medical Building. The **Canadian Craft and Design Museum** *($5; Mon-Sat 10am to 5pm, Sun and holidays noon to 5pm, Thu to 9pm, Sep to May closed Tue; 639 Hornby St., ☎687-8266)* lies behind in a pretty little garden integrated into the project. (You can also get there by turning left on Hornby Street.) This small museum houses a sampling of Canadian handicrafts and a few decorative elements that were part of the Georgia Medical Building. It stages rotating exhibits with eclectic themes, ranging from cookie-cutter design to architectural furniture. On-site craft shop.

Head west on West Georgia Street.

Turn left on Thurlow Street and left again on **Robson Street ★**, which is lined with fashionable boutiques, elaborately decorated restaurants and West Coast-style cafés. People sit at tables outside, enjoying the fine weather and watching the motley crowds stroll by. This activity has become a veritable mania among cof-

Vancouver

fee lovers. American celebrity Bette Midler, passing through Vancouver once marvelled at the number of cafés on Robson Street, going so far as to declare that Vancouverites are addicted to coffee. If this is true, it hasn't changed the tempo of life here, which is known to be quite laid back. In the mid-20th century, a small German community settled around Robson Street, dubbing it Robsonstrasse, a nickname it bears to this day.

Return to Burrard Street, turn right and continue to Nelson Street. Or, turn left on Robson and window shop until you reach Burrard Street.

At the intersection of Thurlow and Robson streets, notice the triumvirate of coffee shops on three of the four corners, two of which are Starbucks! How long can the boutique on the fourth corner withstand the onslaught?

The former **B.C. Hydro Building** ★ *(970 Burrard St.)*, at the corner of Nelson and Burrard streets, was once the head office of the province's hydroelectric company. In 1993, it was converted into a 242-unit co-op and renamed The Electra. Designed in 1955 by local architects Thompson, Berwick and Pratt, it is considered one of the most sophisticated skyscrapers of that era in all of North America. The ground floor is adorned with a mural and a mosaic in shades of grey, blue and green, executed by artist B.C. Binning. Kitty-corner stands **St. Andrew's Wesley United Church**, which was built in 1931 and houses a window created by master glassworker Gabriel Loire of Chartres, France in 1969. The **First Baptist Church** *(969 Burrard St.)*, located opposite, was erected in 1911.

Walk east on Nelson Street.

Turn left on Howe Street to Smithe Street, to view the **Provincial Law Courts** ★ *(800 Smithe St.)*, designed by talented Vancouver architect Arthur Erickson and completed in 1978. The vast interior space, accented in glass and steal, is worth a visit. The courthouse and **Robson Square** *(on the 800 block of Robson St.)*, by the same architect, form a lovely ensemble. Vancouver's luxuriant vegetation (sustained by abundant rainfall and a temperate climate) which is unlike anything else in Canada, is put to maximum use here. Plants are draped along rough concrete walls and in between multiple little stepped ponds over which little waterfalls flow. Shops, restaurants and a skating rink welcome passers-by.

Continue along Howe Street to Robson Street.

The **Vancouver Art Gallery ★** *($12.50; end Apr to mid-Oct every day 10am to 5:30pm, mid-Oct to end Apr closed Mon, year-round Thu until 9pm; 750 Hornby St., ☎662-4700, www.vanartgallery.bc.ca),* located north of Robson Square, occupies the former Provincial Law Courts. This big, sumptuous, neoclassical-style building was erected in 1908 according to a design by British architect Francis Mawson Rattenbury. His other credits include the British Columbia Legislative Assembly and the Empress Hotel, both located in Victoria on Vancouver Island. Later, Rattenbury returned to his native country and was murdered by his wife's lover.

The building was renovated by Arthur Erickson in the 1980s. Make sure to peer up into the rotunda as you climb the stairs. Painted gray and white and ornately decorated with bas-relief, it is quite simply magnificent. The same can be said of the Emily Carr gallery on the fourth floor, decorated in the same style and fondly referred to by the staff as the "wedding cake room." The gallery is home to an important Emily Carr collection of more than 200 works, most of which are paintings. Selections are displayed on a rotating basis. Emily Carr (1871-1945) was a major Canadian painter whose primary subjects were the Aboriginal peoples and landscapes of the West Coast. One look at her magnificent red cedars, vividly rendered with expressive swooshes of blue and green, and you'll immediately understand why her work is so cherished by Westerners. The gallery also hosts very contemporary travelling exhibits, which you'll either like...or you won't. In short, fans of Emily Carr and of contemporary art will not be disappointed. There is a lovely café, with a reasonably priced menu, on site (see p 199).

Continue along Howe Street.

Turn right on West Georgia Street, then right again on the **Granville Mall ★**, the street of cinemas, theatres, nightclubs and retail stores. Its busy sidewalks are hopping 24hrs a day. The black skyscrapers at the corner of West Georgia belong to the **Pacific Centre** *(on either side of Georgia St.),* designed by architects Cesar Pelli and Victor Gruen (1969). Beneath the towers lie the beginnings of an underground city modelled after Montréal's, with 130 shops and restaurants. Opposite stands the Hudson's Bay

Vancouver

Company department store (1913), better known as **The Bay**. The company was founded in London in 1670 in order to carry out fur-trading operations in North America. In 1827, it became one of the first enterprises to set up shop in British Columbia. Across the street stands the **Vancouver Centre** *(650 West Georgia St.)*, which contains Scotia Bank's regional headquarters, and the **Vancouver Block** *(736 Granville St.)*, topped by an elegant clock. Finally, south of the Pacific Centre, you can't miss the massive **Sears Downtown** department store, occupied until 2002 by **Eaton's**, one of a chain of Canadian department stores that started in Toronto in 1869 and went bankrupt in 1999. This branch was one of a handful across the country that held out until 2002.

Stroll along the Granville Mall heading south past Robson Street.

The portion of Granville Street from Georgia to Nelson streets (700 to 900 block) is known as the Theatre Row Entertainment District, as indicated on the banners strung up along the street. The City has so zoned the area in an attempt to concentrate the bars, dance clubs and theatres away from residential districts. Looking for some nightlife? Just stroll along Granville, check out the crowd that invariably gathers in front of these venues and take your pick. The scene is largely made up of college kids—he in baggy pants, she in merciless hiphuggers—but you'll also find a thirtysomething-friendly venue or two. Also attracted here are homeless people asking for change, self-described dope heads politely requesting money for pot, forlorn guitarists stubbornly trying to bring the music of the 1960s to the hip-hopping masses, the occasional flamenco duo and, always, flower vendors. It's a moveable feast of sights and sounds that some may find more interesting than the scene inside the clubs! Inevitably, it's a mob scene at 2am, when the bars close. (For a review of selected venues, see Entertainment, p 223.)

You'll pass the **Commodore Theatre** *(870 Granville St.)* and the **Orpheum Theatre** ★ *(601 Smithe St., free group tour upon reservation ☎665-3050)*. Behind the latter's narrow facade, barely 8m wide, a long corridor opens onto a 2,800-seat Spanish-style Renaissance Revival theatre. Designed by Marcus Priteca, it was the largest and most luxurious movie theatre in Canada when it opened in 1927. After being meticulously restored in 1977, the Orpheum became the concert hall of the Vancouver Symphony Orchestra and stages musical performances of all genres. The theatre turned 75 on November 7, 2002. Further south, you'll see the vertical sign belonging to the **Vogue Theatre** *(918 Granville St.)*, erected in 1941. Today, popular musicals are presented in its Streamlined Art Deco hall.

Retrace your steps along Granville Street, turning right on Robson Street.

At the corner of Robson and Homer streets is a curious building that is more than a little reminiscent of Rome's Coliseum—the **Vancouver Public Library** ★ ★ *(free admission; year-round, Mon-Thu 10am to 8pm, Fri and Sat 10am to 5pm, Sun 1pm to 5pm; free tours can be arranged, ☎331-4041; 350 West Georgia St., ☎331-3603, www.vpl.vancouver.bc.ca)*, known as **Library Square**. This impressive building, completed in 1995, is the work of Montréal architect Moshe Safdie, known for his Habitat '67 in Montréal and the National Art Gallery in Ottawa. The project stirred lively reactions both from local people and from architecture critics. The design was chosen after finally being put to a referendum. The six-storey atrium is positively grandiose.

The somewhat awkwardly named **Centre in Vancouver for the Performing Arts** *(777 Homer St., ☎602-0616)*, formerly known as the **Ford Centre for the Performing Arts**, completed in 1996, lies just opposite on

Library Square

Vancouver

Homer Street, next to the Westin Grand. Also designed by Moshe Safdie, it contains an 1,800-seat theatre whose orchestra seats, balcony and stage are depicted on the facade north of the glass cone that serves as the entryway. The centre closed in 1998 when its original owners went bankrupt and re-opened in the spring of 2002.

Behind the library lies the long, low building belonging to the **Canadian Broadcasting Corporation**. The tubular structures on the facade are actually air ducts.

Continue heading north on Homer Street.

The **General Post Office** *(349 West Georgia St.)*, north of the library, was built in 1953. Hidden behind it to the east is the **Queen Elizabeth Theatre** *(630 Hamilton St.)*, designed chiefly by Montréal architects Ray Affleck and Fred Lebensold. It contains three theatres of different sizes. Its opening in 1959 foreshadowed the construction of similar complexes across North America, including New York's celebrated Lincoln Centre and Montréal's Place des Arts.

Take Homer Street north, then turn left on Dunsmuir Street.

To conclude your tour of downtown Vancouver, stop by the city's Catholic cathedral, the **Cathedral of Our Lady of the Rosary** *(corner of Dunsmuir and Richards sts.)*, erected in 1899. The rusticated stone facing and the wood and metal clock towers are reminiscent of parish churches built around the same time in Québec.

Tour D: The West End

This tour starts at the corner of Thurlow and Davie. Head west on the latter.

The population of the West End is a mixture of students and professionals, many of whom made a fortune on new technologies and the various new therapies now in fashion. The gay community is also well represented here.

This tour starts at **Barclay Heritage Square**, bounded by Barclay, Nicola, Haro and Broughton streets.

There are eight heritage houses on this square, which is actually an Edwardian garden with its very own gazebo, all of which date from the 1890s. One of them has been reborn as a museum showcasing furnishings from the Victorian period. Built in 1893, the

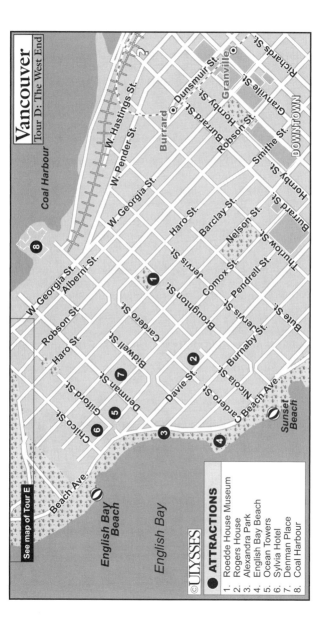

Vancouver
Tour D: The West End

Coal Harbour

W. Hastings St.
W. Pender St.
W. Georgia St.
Dunsmuir St.
Burrard
Granville
Hornby St.
Burrard St.
Robson St.
Richards St.
Granville St.
Smithe St.
DOWNTOWN
Hornby St.
Burrard St.
Thurlow St.
Nelson St.
Haro St.
Barclay St.
Comox St.
Jervis St.
Broughton St.
Pendrell St.
Bute St.
Nicola St.
Jervis St.
Burnaby St.
Cardero St.
Beach Ave.
Davie St.
Bidwell St.
Cardero St.
Robson St.
Alberni St.
W. Georgia St.
Haro St.
Denman St.
Gilford St.
Chilco St.
Beach Ave.

Sunset
Beach

See map of Tour E

English Bay
Beach

English Bay

© ULYSSES

● ATTRACTIONS

1. Roedde House Museum
2. Rogers House
3. Alexandra Park
4. English Bay Beach
5. Ocean Towers
6. Sylvia Hotel
7. Denman Place
8. Coal Harbour

Roedde House Museum ★★
*($4; admission by tour only,
Wed-Fri 2pm to 4pm; 1415
Barclay St.,* ☎*684-7040)* was
the family home of Gustav
and Matilda Roedde and
their family until 1925.
Gustav was the first book
binder and printer in Vancouver, a vocation profit-
able enough to permit the
construction of a comfortable upper-middle-class
home. The house was de-
signed by notable architect
and family friend Francis
Rattenbury, known for his
design of the rather more
grand Empress Hotel and
the Parliament Buildings in
Victoria and the Vancouver
Art Gallery (see p 107). Ten
of the home's 12 rooms are
furnished with period
pieces, most of which were
donated to the museum by
individuals; others are on
loan from the Vancouver
Museum and some are orig-
inal to the house. The attention to detail is astounding
and anyone with an interest
with Victoriana and Art
Nouveau will be delighted
by this charming little museum.

*Leave the square, heading
south on Broughton Street
until Davie Street.*

Vancouver's gay village,
known as **Davie Village**, extends along Davie Street
just east of Broughton Street
and as far east as Thurlow
Street. You can't miss it: just
look for the rainbow ban-
ners strung up along the
street lamps *(turn left from
Broughton Street).* The village
is a pleasantly shabby-look-
ing mix of cafés, diners and
discount stores punctuated
by high-rise apartment
buildings.

Roedde House Museum

Retrace your steps and head west along Davie.

When you get to the corner of Nicola Street, take a look at **Rogers House** *(1531 Davie St.)*, christened "Gabriola" by its owner when it was built in 1900. It was designed by one of the most prolific architects of well-heeled Vancouver society, Samuel Maclure. The house, with its numerous chimneys and circular gazebo, originally belonged to sugar magnate Benjamin Tingley Rogers, a native of New York. At the turn of the 20th century, the West End seemed destined to become an affluent suburb with large houses surrounded by gardens. One street was even given the pretentious name Blue Blood Alley. Things turned out otherwise, however, when the streetcar tracks were laid and a popular public beach on English Bay was opened in 1912. Gabriola is one of the only remaining houses of that era, and has since been converted into a restaurant (Romano's Macaroni Grill).

Head west on Davie Street, then left on Bidwell Street and follow the dogs, human companions in tow, to **Alexandra Park ★** which forms a point south of Burnaby Street. It boasts a pretty wooden bandstand (1914) for outdoor concerts,

as well as a marble fountain adorned with a brass plaque honouring Joe Fortes, who taught several generations of the city's children to swim.

The east end of **English Bay Beach ★★** *(along the shore between Chilco and Bidwell sts.)*, whose fine sands are crowded during the summer, is just opposite the park. Here you'll find an enormous inukshuk created by Alvin Kanak for the Northwest Territories pavilion at Expo 86; it was moved to this site the following year. The apartment high-rises behind the beach give beach-goers the illusion that they are lounging about at a seaside resort like Acapulco, when they are actually just a short distance from the heart of Vancouver. Few cities can boast beaches so close to their downtown core. Fleets of sailboats skim across the magnificent bay, which has recently been cleaned of pollutants. To the west, it is bordered by the verdant expanse of Stanley Park (see p 115).

After dipping your big toe in the Pacific Ocean (it's that close!), head back into town on Morton Avenue where you'll see the **Ocean Towers** *(1835 Morton Ave.)*, a cluster of jazzily shaped apartment buildings dating from 1957 (Rix Reinecke,

Vancouver

architect). The previous year, Vancouver had modified the zoning regulation for the West End so that these high-rises could be built. That provoked a frenzy among real-estate developers and led to the construction of an interesting group of buildings that is as 1950s and "piña colada" as Miami Art Deco is 1930s and "dry martini." The Ocean Towers' neighbour to the west, the **Sylvia Hotel** (see p 178) *(1154 Gilford St.)* is the oldest building on the beach. Its construction in 1912 sounded the death knell of the West End's country atmosphere. It is flanked by two postmodern buildings, **Eugenia Tower** and **Sylvia Tower**, topped in a very amusing fashion.

Head back east to Denman Street.

When they're not out surfing or sailboarding, the local beach bums often hang out around Denman and Davie streets. The numerous restaurants in this area serve gargantuan brunches.

Fans of the recently kiboshed TV series *The X-Files*, filmed for years in Vancouver, may want to make a right turn onto Pendrell Street. **Pendrell Suites** *(1419 Pendrell St., near Broughton St.)*, a handsome, brick Edwardian building, stood in for Agent Scully's Maryland apartment.

Continue north on Denman Street.

Denman Place Mall *(1733 Comox St.)*, at the corner of Comox Street, is a multifunctional complex made of bare concrete. Erected in 1968, it is home to the West End's largest shopping mall, complete with a supermarket, stores and movie theatres. The commercial area is topped by a 32-storey tower containing apartments and a hotel.

Continue to the north end of Denman Street.

Take the path beside 1779 West Georgia Street to the waterfront and lovely **Coal Harbour ★**, which offers some outstanding views of Stanley Park and the mountains across Burrard Inlet. You will also be greeted by a rather strange sight along the docks: a floating village of houseboats. The bay is full of yachts and sailboats, adding to the West End's seaside charm. If you have the urge to hop aboard, you can take a cruise with **Harbour Cruises** *(at the foot of Denman St., ☎688-7246).*

Our tour of the West End finishes here. You can either head downtown (bus no. 19 runs along Georgia Street, two blocks north), or you can begin your tour of Stanley Park (Tour E), which begins a couple of blocks west.

Tour E: Stanley Park

Lord Stanley, for whom the National Hockey League's Stanley Cup was named, founded Stanley Park on a romantic impulse back in the 19th century when he was Canada's Governor General (1888-1893) and dedicated it "to the use and enjoyment of people of all colours, creeds and customs for all time." Like New York's Central Park and Montréal's Mount Royal, Stanley Park was largely designed by Frederick Law Olmsted.

Stanley Park lies on an elevated peninsula stretching into the Georgia Strait, and encompasses 405ha of flowering gardens, dense woodlands and lookouts offering views of the sea and the mountains. Obviously Vancouver's many skyscrapers have not pre-

Lord Stanley sculpture

vented the city from maintaining close ties with the nearby wilderness.

A 9km waterfront promenade known as the **Seawall ★★** runs around the park, enabling pedestrians and cyclists to drink in every bit of the stunning scenery here (see box p 126). The **Stanley Park Scenic Drive** is the equivalent of the Seawall for motorists. This road runs one-way in a counter-clockwise direction. There are numerous parking lots along the road *($1/2hrs, $3/day)* and although parking is inexpensive, traffic is heavy in the park on summer weekends. A good alternative is to take the bus from downtown (nos. 23, 123, 35 or 135) and once in the park, to take advantage of the free **Stanley Park Shuttle Bus**, which provides transportation between 14 of the park's most popular attractions *(every 15min, mid-Jun to mid-Sep, 10am to 6:30pm)*. You can also take the **express bus to Stanley park**, which operates from about a dozen downtown hotels and is free of charge for those heading to the Vancouver Aquar-

Vancouver

ium or the Horse-Drawn Tour. Speaking of which, if a splurge is in order, hop aboard a **Stanley Park Horse-Drawn Tour** *($20.55; mid-Mar to late Oct; ☎681-5115)*, which will take you around in style. Tours last 1hr.

The best way to explore Stanley Park, however, is by bicycle. You can rent one from **Spokes Bicycle Rental** *(corner of West Georgia and Denman sts., ☎688-5141)*. Remember that the path is also one-way for cyclists, counter-clockwise from Coal Harbour to English Bay.

Another way to discover some of the park's hidden treasures is to walk along one of the many footpaths crisscrossing the territory. There are numerous rest areas along the way.

From West Georgia Street, walk along Coal Harbour toward Brockton Point.

You'll be greeted by the sight of scores of gleaming yachts in the Vancouver marina with the downtown skyline in the background. This is the most developed portion of the park, where you'll find the **Malkin Bowl** (inland from the rowing club), where **Theatre Under**

the Stars performs *(about $30; Jul and Aug; ☎687-0174)*.

Near the Malkin Bowl, Stanley Park harbours some lovely **flower gardens ★** that are meticulously tended by a team of gardeners.

Continue along the Seawall.

Follow the footpath to the renowned **Vancouver Aquarium Marine Science Centre ★★★** *($14.95; Jul and Aug, every day 9:30am to 7pm; early Sep to end Jun, every day 10am to 5:30pm; ☎659-3474, www.vanaqua. org)*, appropriately located by the ocean. (Sign indicating the way via the footpaths can be hard to find—ask someone to direct you. Directions by car are well indicated from West Georgia Street.) It displays representatives of the marine animal life of the West Coast and the Pacific as a whole, including magnificent killer whales, belugas, dolphins, seals and exotic fish.

You'll want to leave a couple of hours for the visit. There are shows or feeding

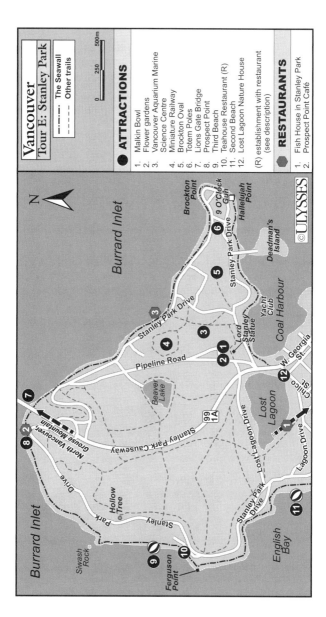

Vancouver
Tour E: Stanley Park

—·—·— The Seawall
— — — Other trails

0   250   500m

● **ATTRACTIONS**

1. Malkin Bowl
2. Flower gardens
3. Vancouver Aquarium Marine
    Science Centre
4. Miniature Railway
5. Brockton Oval
6. Totem Poles
7. Lions Gate Bridge
8. Prospect Point
9. Third Beach
10. Teahouse Restaurant (R)
11. Second Beach
12. Lost Lagoon Nature House

(R) establishment with restaurant
    (see description)

⬡ **RESTAURANTS**

1. Fish House in Stanley Park
2. Prospect Point Café

© ULYSSES

Burrard Inlet

Burrard Inlet

N

Siwash Rock

North Vancouver, Grouse Mountain

Stanley Park Drive

Hollow Tree

Beaver Lake

Pipeline Road

Stanley Park Drive

Ferguson Point

Stanley Park Causeway

99 1A

Stanley Park Drive

Lost Lagoon Drive

Stanley Park Drive

Lost Lagoon Drive

Lagoon Drive

Chilco St.

W. Georgia St.

Lost Lagoon

English Bay

Coal Harbour

Yacht Club

Lord Stanley Statue

Deadman's Island

9 O'Clock Gun

Hallelujah Point

Brockton Point

sessions scheduled every 30min (subject to change), so if you have your heart set on seeing a dolphin-training session or a beluga show, call first. Make sure to visit the outside exhibit, home to harbour seals, Spinnaker the dolphin, sea otters and belugas, all of which face particular challenges that prevent them from being released into the wild. Inside, there are underwater viewing areas for the belugas and dolphins. The Treasures of the B.C. Coast displays representative ecosystems, one tank for each area, complete with interpretive panels. There is a section of the shores of Stanley Park, supplied by seawater piped in from Burrard Inlet. Finally, don't miss the Amazon gallery, where rainforest residents of all kinds make their home, including free-flying Costa Rican butterflies. Take the time to look for the sloths in the trees.

While you're at the aquarium, don't miss the new **BC Hydro Salmon Stream Project**, a salmon run created as a public education project. From the B.C. Forest Headwaters Exhibit, visitors can follow a man-made stream through the park to Coal Harbour, near the Vancouver Rowing Club, where 10,000 hatchery-bred chinook and coho salmon fry were released in 1998. A pheromone was released into the water to help the mature salmon find their way to their home stream, which they began to do in November 2001. This marked the first time in over a century that salmon returned to downtown Vancouver! The salmon hatchery is located in the former bear pit, part of the now defunct **Stanley Park Zoo**, which closed in the early 1990s.

Totem pole

There are several food concessions that actually offer more imaginative fare than hot dogs (although hot dogs are available too) at reasonable prices.

North of the aquarium are the **Miniature Railway**, **farmyard** and **playground**, all a real hit with kids.

From here, you can head south and return to the Seawall or take one of the interior footpaths toward the east, leading to the **Brockton Oval**, where rugby and cricket are played. Further east are the famous **Totem Poles** ★ reminders of a sizeable Aboriginal population on the peninsula barely 150 years ago. Most of these totem poles, however, are fairly modern, having been carved since 1987. Note that one was carved by famed Haida artist Bill Reid and his assistants in 1964.

The **Nine O'Clock Gun** goes off every day at 9pm on Hallelujah Point (it is best not to be too close when it does). This shot used to alert fishermen that it was time to come in.

Continue along the Seawall, passing Brockton Point and some lovely landscapes to photograph. About 2.5km further, you will pass beneath **Lions Gate Bridge** ★★, an elegant suspension bridge built in 1938. Measuring 1,527m long and 111m high, it spans the First Narrows, linking the affluent suburb of West Vancouver to the centre of town. At the entrance to the bridge, artist Charles Marega sculpted two immense lion heads. The bridge was rehabilitated between 1999 and 2002, following extensive study by the government, which examined and finally rejected proposals that the bridge be widened or replaced. It remains an enduring symbol of the city. **Prospect Point** ★★★, to the west, offers a general view of the bridge, whose steel pillars stand 135m high.

The **Seawall Promenade** runs along the edge of the park, and after rounding a 45-degree bend, offers a panoramic view of the Georgia Strait, with Cypress Park and Bowen Island visible in the distance on clear days. Next, it passes **Third Beach** ★, one of the most pleasant beaches in the region. The numerous cargo ships and ocean liners waiting to enter the port complement the setting. From here, stairs lead up to the **Third Beach Café**, where snacks can be purchased.

We recommend stopping at the **Teahouse Restaurant** ★ (see p 207), located between Third Beach and

Second Beach ★. In the 1850s, the British government, fearing an American invasion (the U.S. border is less than 30km from Vancouver), considered building artillery batteries on this site. The risk of such a conflict had diminished by the early 20th century, so a charming tearoom was erected here instead. The Swiss-chalet-style building, surrounded by greenery, dates from 1911.

At Second Beach, you'll find the new **Second Beach Pool** (mid-May to early Sep, ☎257-8370) and another concession stand with—this being the West Coast—capuccino and herbal teas to accompany your fish and chips.

From Second Beach, complete the loop by following the signs to Georgia Street/Seawall, which will take you past **Lost Lagoon** ★, which was once part of Coal Harbour but was partially filled in during the construction of Lions Gate Bridge. It is now a bird sanctuary where large numbers of

Mallard ducks

barnacle geese, mallards and swans can be seen frolicking about.

On your way out of the park you'll see signs indicating the **Lost Lagoon Nature House**, home to the Stanley Park Ecology Society (Jul to Sep Mon-Fri noon to 7pm, Sat and Sun 11am to 7 pm, fall and spring Fri-Sun 11am to 5 pm, Dec to Feb Sat and Sun 9 am to 4 pm, ☎257-8544), which has a small nature display and organizes thematic walks through the park ($5; call for schedule).

Tour F: Burrard Inlet

Burrard Inlet is the long and very wide arm of the sea on which the Vancouver harbour—Canada's most important port for over 20 years now—is located. The Atlantic was once a favourite trading route, but the dramatic economic growth of the American West Coast (California, Oregon, Washington) and even more importantly, the Far East (Japan, Hong Kong, Taiwan, China, Singapore, Thailand, etc.), has crowned the Pacific lord and master of shipping.

Beyond the port lie the mountainside suburbs of North and West Vancouver, which offer some spectacular views of the city below. Along their steep, winding roads, visitors can admire some of the finest examples of modern residential architecture in North America. These luxurious houses, often constructed of posts and beams made of local wood, are usually surrounded by lofty British Columbian firs and a luxuriant blend of plants imported from Europe and Asia.

There are two ways to take this tour. The first is by foot: hop aboard the SeaBus, the ferry that shuttles back and forth between downtown Vancouver and the north shore of Burrard Inlet, enjoy the open air and take in some exceptional views of both the city and the mountains. The other option is to drive across Lions Gate Bridge, take Marine Drive east to Third Street and head south on Lonsdale Avenue. The following descriptions refer to the walking tour, unless otherwise indicated.

Start off your tour in front of the neoclassical facade of the former **Canadian Pacific Station** ★ (*601 West Cordova St.*), which dates from 1912 and was designed by

Montréal architects Barrott, Blackader and Webster.

This station, Canadian Pacific's third in Vancouver, occupies a special place in the city's history. Before ships arriving from the west took over, trains arriving from the east fuelled the area's prosperous economy. In keeping with the times, the station no longer welcomes trains, but provides access to the Granville terminal of the SeaBus. It also provides indirect access to the Waterfront terminal of the SkyTrain (at the far end of Howe Street), but that's somewhat of a meagre consolation prize. Above the latter terminal is tiny **Portal Park** and its azaleas. **Granville Square**, the skyscraper immediately to the west, is the only completed portion of a major real-estate development project (1971) which was to include the demolition of the train station.

Follow the signs for the **SeaBus**. The crossing (*$1.75*) to **North Vancouver** ★★ takes barely 15min, though you'll wish it were longer. The ferry lands at its northern terminal near the pleasant **Lonsdale Quay Market** ★, built on a quay stretching out into Burrard Inlet. The cafés surrounding the market offer an unimpeded view of Vancouver and the mountains as well as all the activity at the nearby port, with the colourful tugboat dock flanking the market to the east. Built in 1986, Lonsdale Quay Market was the brainchild of architects Hotson and Bakker, who wanted to satisfy every basic human need here: food (ground floor), clothing (second floor) and lodging. From here, Vancouver really looks like a Manhattan in the making.

The market is the main urban attraction in North Vancouver, a city of more than 41,000 people sandwiched between Burrard Inlet and mountains over 1,500m high. The urbanization of the north shore of the inlet began in the second half of the 19th century. Some businessmen from New Westminster decided to make capital of the firs, hemlock, spruce and red cedars in the surrounding forest. It was Maine (U.S.) native Sewell Prescott Moody, however, who made British Columbia's timber known around the world. Ferry service between Gastown (see p 83) and "his" town, Moodyville, was introduced in 1866. At the beginning of the 20th century, most of the property in North and West Vancouver was transferred to British interests who began developing the areas as residential suburbs. The old banks and public buildings bear witness to the prosperous past of the wood industry. Leave the market from the north end and head to your left, by the water. You will find yourself on part of the Trans Canada Trail,

● ATTRACTIONS

1. Canadian Pacific Station	11. Mount Seymour Provincial Park
2. Granville Square	12. Deep Cove
3. Lonsdale Quay Market	13. Baden Powell Trail
4. Waterfront Park	14. Ambleside Park
5. Mission Indian Reserve	15. Pratt House
6. St. Paul Catholic Church	16. Berwick House
7. Capilano Suspension Bridge and Park	17. British Properties
8. Capilano Salmon Hatchery	18. Lighthouse Park
9. Cleveland Dam Park	19. Gordon Smith House
10. Grouse Mountain	20. Cypress Provincial Park

◯ ACCOMMODATIONS

1. Canyon Court Inn and Suite	4. Horseshoe Bay Motel
2. Capilano Bed & Breakfast	5. Lonsdale Quay Hotel
3. Grouse Inn	6. Palms Guest House

● RESTAURANTS

1. Beach Side Café	4. Bread Garden
2. Bean Around The World	5. Bridge House Restaurant
3. Boathouse Restaurant	6. Salmon House

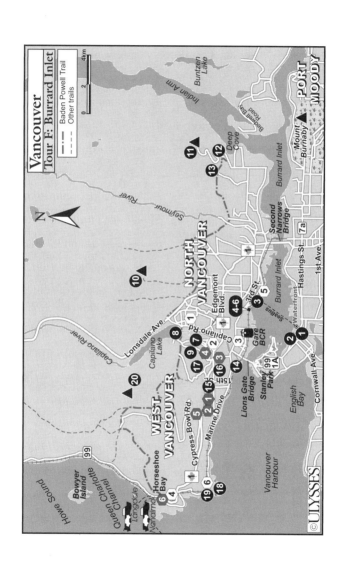

which leads to **Waterfront Park**, where you can take in a breath of sea air, a good view and a pleasant stroll.

On either side of the market, the east shore is scattered with tiny Aboriginal reserves, some barely two blocks across. One of these is the **Mission Indian Reserve**, centred around Mission Road and stretching north of the waterfront, beyond the park. The reserve is home to Squamish Indians, a group of Coast Salish people. It is so named because a Catholic mission was founded here in the 1860s.

Mission Road leads to West Esplanade, where you will find **St. Paul's Catholic Church** (*424 W. Esplanade*), erected between 1884 and 1909 by Oblate missionaries from Québec. The interior is decorated with stained-glass windows and polychrome statues.

If you are travelling by car, return to Marine Drive heading west and go up Capilano Road until you reach the **Capilano Suspension Bridge and Park** (*$13.95; mid-May to early Sep 8:30am to 8pm, reduced hours the rest of the year, call first; 3735 Capilano Rd., ☎985-7474*). If you are on foot at Lonsdale Quay Market, take bus number 236, which stops across the street from the entrance. Buses depart every half hour, on the quarter hour. Paths lead to this metal-cabled bridge, suspended 70m above the Capilano River, which replaced the original bridge of rope and wood built in 1899.

This heavily advertised, privately owned attraction draws some 800,000 visitors a year, each of whom pays a small fortune for the not-so-thrilling opportunity to walk across a shaky suspension bridge for all of two minutes. The admission fee is outrageous and the place is clearly a tourist trap. Its only redeeming feature, although just barely, are its planked walkways through the forest—negligible for hikers, but for seniors, or those with physical limitations, they do provide readily accessible exposure to the forest. That said, however, the shaky bridge itself is probably not suitable for anyone who is unsteady on their feet. Save your money and take a lovely walk (free!) through Stanley Park instead. But if you insist on visiting, make sure to walk down to the lookout to the right of the bridge, for a good view of it from below. And if you actually found the experience thrilling, visit the gift shop, where you can purchase your very own "I survived" T-shirt.

A good alternative, though substantially more physically challenging because it actually involves a hike, is the suspension bridge at Lynn Canyon Park (see p 156).

Three kilometres to the north is the **Capilano Fish Hatchery** ★ *(free; 4500 Capilano Park Rd., ☎666-1790)*, the first salmon hatchery in British Columbia. This well laid-out spot provides visitors with an introduction to the life cycle of the salmon. In the summer, Pacific salmon wear themselves out as they make their way up the Capilano River to reach their spawning grounds, making for an exceptional spectacle for visitors.

The upper part of Upper Capilano Road was re-named Nancy Greene Way after the Canadian skier who won the gold medal for the giant slalom at the 1968 Olympics in Grenoble, France. On the left, a road leads to **Cleveland Dam Park** ★★ on the shores of Lake Capilano. The construction in 1954 of the impressive 100m-high dam at the centre of the park led to the creation of the lake, Vancouver's main source of drinking water. Spectacular views of the neighbouring mountains surround the park.

At the north end of Nancy Greene Way, there is a **cable car** *($21.95; $5 down only; if you arrive here by city bus, no. 236, present your transfer for a 20% discount; every day 9am to 10pm; ☎980-9311)* that carries passengers to the top of **Grouse Mountain** ★★★, for a small fortune. At an altitude of 1,250m, skiers and hikers can contemplate the entire Vancouver area as well as Washington State (in clear weather) to the south. At this price, make sure you head up on a clear day! The view is particularly beautiful at the end of the day. Wilderness trails lead out from the various viewing areas. During summer, Grouse Mountain is also a popular spot for hang-gliding.

It's a popular sport (and a popular way to avoid the rather steep cable-car charge) to climb the mountain (see p 156) instead. Remember that this is primarily a ski mountain, so during the winter, be prepared for crowds with ski equipment to jostle you about in the cable car. While you're up there, head into the Theatre in the Sky (in the chalet) to view the rather decent film *Born to Fly* (which provides a bird's-eye view of B.C.), shown hourly (free admission). But don't bother with the very-brief tractor-driven

Vancouver

The Seaside Bicycle Route

Of Vancouver's many bike paths, the most interesting one for visitors is undoubtedly the Seaside Bicycle Route. From it, visitors can take in some spectacular scenery along Burrard Inlet, Stanley Park, English Bay and False Creek.

Cyclists can pick up the trail on Burrard Inlet as far west as Thurlow Street, west of the Pan Pacific Hotel, and travel in a counter-clockwise direction to Stanley Park, where they pick up the Stanley Park Seawall path. (Those renting bicycles will probably want to start at the foot of Denman Street, close to the bicycle rental shops.) After riding the 9km Seawall, passing the totem poles, Lions Gate Bridge and several beaches, cyclists will continue along English Bay to the shores of False Creek all the way to Science World. The route continues to Granville Island and along the shore of English Bay through to Vanier Park, Kitsilano Park and several beaches, ending at Spanish Bank West. Shortcuts can be taken from the north shore of False Creek to the south shore via the Cambie or Burrard bridges (the latter a good bet for making a beeline to Granville Island). The entire route is about 30km long and is also part of the Trans Canada Trail. It's a fabulous way to experience Vancouver!

sleigh ride (departure from chalet in the winter), which, though free, isn't worth your five minutes (plus waiting time).

To return to Vancouver, get on the bus again, then take the SeaBus back the other way.

Among the other sights in North Vancouver that are

accessible by car and worth mentioning is **Mount Seymour Provincial Park ★★** (see p 156).

Deep Cove, at the eastern edge of North Vancouver on the shore of Indian Arm, makes a nice outing (30min drive from Vancouver), with cafés and a splendid view; its also a fine spot for canoeing and kayaking.

The Burrard Inlet walking tour ends at Grouse Mountain.

Motorists can continue exploring the area by heading to **West Vancouver ★★** *(go back down Upper Capilano Rd., then turn right on Marine Dr.)*, a fashionable residential suburb located on a mountainside. Many talented architects have helped enrich the city's modern heritage.

Marine Drive leads past two large shopping centres. On Marine Drive between 24th and 25th streets is another charming shopping area called Dundarave. **Ambleside Park ★**, located to the west, is worth a stop for some lovely views of Stanley Park and Lions Gate Bridge. Near the water, landscape architect Don Vaughan created the **Waterside Fountain** out of cubes of granite in 1989. West of the park, an attractive promenade leads along the water to 24th Street.

Turn right on 15th Street, then right again on Lawson Avenue, where you'll find **Pratt House** *(1460 Lawson Ave.; not open to the public)*, designed by architect C.E. Pratt in 1948 for his own use. Pratt was a great promoter of this style of wooden house, which is open on the outside and blends into the natural environment. Although designed to withstand earthquakes and resist rotting due to the heavy rainfall here (wide-edged roofs, cedar construction), these houses might appear fragile to Europeans more accustomed to stone and brick buildings.

The nearby **Berwick House** *(1650 Mathers Ave.; not open to the public)*, designed by the same architect, dates back to 1939. It was thus a forerunner of this type of construction. Since the 1930s, Canadian architects working on the West Coast have been greatly influenced both by the Californian buildings of the Greene brothers and Richard Neutra as well as by much older Japanese designs dating from the time of the *shoguns*.

Head north on 15th Street, which becomes Cross Creek Road, and then Eyremount Drive.

Vancouver

Next, you'll reach **British Properties** ★ *(on either side of the road starting at Highland Dr.)*, where untouched woodlands and suburbia overlap. British Pacific Properties Limited, owned by London's famous Guinness family, stout-brewing, began developing this mountainous area in 1932. The overall design was the work of the Olmsted Brothers, the worthy successors of Frederick Law Olmsted, whose credits include Montréal's Mount Royal Park, New York's Central Park and Vancouver's Stanley Park. Author Douglas Coupland (see p 32), who grew up here, refers to it as "a hillside Pacific Palisades/Glendale-ish suburb."

Return to Marine Drive.

Turn right on Marine Drive and continue to **Lighthouse Park** ★ *(entrance on Beacon Lane)*; located on a point that stretches out into the Strait of Georgia, it has a lighthouse on its southern tip. Strolling around this peaceful place truly evokes a feeling of infinite space. The nearby **Gordon Smith House** *(The Byway via Howe Sound Lane; not open to the public)* is a West Coast version of the glass houses of Mies van der Rohe and Philip Jonson. Designed by Erickson and Massey, it was built in 1965.

Like the Trans-Canada Highway, Marine Drive ends at the port of the village of **Horseshoe Bay** ★, home of the Vancouver Island ferry terminal. To return to Vancouver, head east on the Trans-Canada Highway, then follow the signs for Lions Gate Bridge. On the way, there is an exit for **Cypress Bowl Road**, a scenic road whose steep hills are ill-suited to cars with weak engines. It leads to **Cypress Park** ★★★ and **Cypress Mountain** itself, a mountain where skiers can enjoy a 900m vertical drop and breathtaking views of the Strait of Georgia.

Tour G: False Creek

False Creek is located south of downtown Vancouver and, like Burrard Inlet, stretches far inland.

The presence of both water and a railroad induced a large number of sawmills to set up shop in this area in the early 20th century. These mills gradually filled a portion of False Creek, leaving only a narrow channel to provide them with the water that is needed for sawing. Over the years, two thirds of False Creek, as explorer George Vancouver had known it in 1790, disappeared under asphalt.

Stanley Park is proof positive that despite Vancouver's many
skyscrapers, the city maintains close ties with the nearby wilderness.
- *Sheila Naiman*

Due to the massive influx of Asian immigrants, Vancouver's Chinatown has become one of the largest in North America.
- *P. Brunet*

English Bay Beach, whose fine sands are a short distance from the heart of Vancouver, is a hit with urban beach-goers.
- *Tibor Bognàr*

By the early 1980s, the saw-mills and other industries had disappeared and a century's worth of industrial pollution had left the area a mess. The City purchased the site, quickly cleaned it up, and during the summer of 1986 hosted Expo 86, a world's fair that attracted several-million visitors in the space of a few months. The vast stretch of unused land along the north shore of False Creek was occupied by dozens of showy pavilions with visitors crowding around them.

The City then rezoned the land for residential and commercial use and sold it to a Hong Kong tycoon for $145 million.

Our tour of the False Creek area begins in Yaletown, southeast of downtown and bordering on False Creek. From downtown, take Robson street east until Homer and turn right.

Yaletown ★ stretches between Homer to the west, Pacific Boulevard to the east, Nelson to the north and Drake to the south, but the two blocks of Mainland and Hamilton streets between Davie and Nelson are probably the most interesting for visitors.

Originally, Yaletown was located just south of its

current location, on Drake Street between Granville Street and Pacific Boulevard; in fact, even before that, "Yaletown" was actually the town of Yale, in the Fraser River Canyon. It was there that the western terminus of the Canadian Pacific Railway (CPR) was located until 1886, when Vancouver took over that role. The CPR then moved its facilities from Yale to Yaletown, where a community of railway workers grew. The **Yale Hotel** *(1300 Granville St., near Drake St.),* today a popular blues venue, was originally the Colonial Hotel, a rooming house for these workers. Built in 1890, it is one of the oldest buildings in Vancouver. In the early 1900s, the City erected a warehouse district next to the original community, in the area commonly considered Yaletown today. Its warehouses were built with loading docks at the rear, sheltered by permanent canopies, where goods from the boxcars could be directly loaded and unloaded.

The growth of the trucking industry shifted business away from Yaletown's big warehouses and the area declined. The train tracks were removed in the 1980s, around the time "loft livers"

Vancouver

discovered the area. The loading docks of Hamilton and Mainland streets have since been transformed into outdoor cafés and restaurants and a new group of tenants now occupies the old brick warehouses; designers, architects, film production companies and business people in general have brought this area back to life. Trendy cafés and restaurants have followed suit.

After exploring Yaletown's historic buildings, boutiques and restaurants, take Homer Street down to False Creek and you'll find yourself in **David Lam Park**, a pleasant spot for dog walkers, cyclists, soccer players and stone skippers, equipped with plenty of spots to sit and witness it all.

Here, you will have unwittingly found yourself in the midst of the largest planned community in North America, **Concord Pacific Place**, located on the former Expo 86 site. This 83ha site is about halfway through its 20-year plan to develop 9,200 condominiums, divided into six "neighbourhoods," providing housing for more than 15,000 people. It will also provide 175,000m^2 of commercial space stretching from the

● ATTRACTIONS

1. David Lam Park
2. Concord Pacific Place
3. Concord Pacific Place Presentation Centre
4. CPR Roundhouse
5. Engine 374
6. BC Place Stadium
7. GM Place
8. Plaza of Nations
9. Science World
10. Pacific Central Station
11. Granville Island Public Market
12. Emily Carr College of Art and Design
13. Granville Island Brewing Company
14. Granville Island Museums
15. False Creek Development
16. Charleson Park

◯ ACCOMMODATIONS

1. Granville Island Hotel
2. Opus Hotel

● RESTAURANTS

1. Blue Water Café and Raw Bar
2. Bridges Bistro
3. Brix
4. C Restaurant
5. Capone's
6. Château Madrid - La Bodega
7. Dix Barbecue and Brewery
8. Dockside Brewing Company
9. Il Giardino
10. Keg Steakhouse
11. Kettle of Fish
12. La Baguette et l'Échalotte
13. Maverick's
14. Monk McQueen's
15. Pacific Institute of Culinary Arts
16. Panama Jacks Bar & Grill
17. Provence Marinaside
18. Rodney's Oyster House
19. Urban Fare
20. Yaletown Brewing Co.

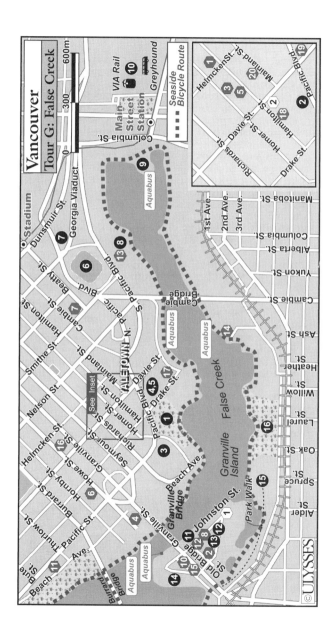

Granville Bridge to Science World, at the end of False Creek. As part of the deal, the City extracted some $250 million from the developers for public housing and amenities, including 1,300 units of social housing, with rents subsidized by the provincial government, and 20ha of parks, schools, community facilities, and a waterfront walkway and bicycle route. The high-rises, whose architecture resembles that of Battery Park City in New York, appear from a distance to be built of nothing but glass.

The new **Marinaside Crescent seawalk** is the latest extension to the seaside waterfront path, linking David Lam Park 220m east to Coopers' Park, near the Cambie Bridge. The new seawalk is lined with a number of innovative public art installations and numerous benches.

The development is widely hailed as a great success, and, judging by the cranes you'll find yourself surrounded by, things are moving full steam ahead. For a cool half a million dollars and

up, you too could call one of the magnificent glassed-in condos lining False Creek home! To find out more about the project, pop into the **Concord Place Presentation Centre** *(every day 10am to 5pm, 1550 Homer Mews, west of David Lam Park, ☎899-8800).*

Continue to Davie Street and turn left.

On your left, at the corner of Pacific Street, you'll see an interesting semi-circular structure. The beautifully restored **CPR Roundhouse ★** *(at the corner of Davie St. and Pacific Blvd.),* located opposite, is all that remains of the Canadian Pacific Railway (CPR) marshalling yard once located on this site. Erected in 1888, it was used for the servicing and repair of locomotives.

The roundhouse was built in this shape to allow grouping the inside tracks in a semi-circle. In front of the roundhouse, locomotives were driven onto a turntable that directed them

Engine 374

into a number of service bays.

Before you reach the entrance to the Roundhouse, you'll see the glassed-in **Engine 374 Pavilion ★** *(donations accepted; summer every day 11am to 3pm, rest of the year Thu-Sat 11am to 3pm; hours subject to change; Davie St. and Pacific Blvd., ☎684-6662)*, home to the locomotive that pulled the very first train to reach Vancouver, in 1887. Engine 374, built by the Canadian Pacific Railway in 1886, was restored by volunteers in time for Expo 86 after a period of neglect and deterioration in Kitsilano Park. Kids enjoy climbing aboard and tooting the whistle.

The actual roundhouse (entrance next door) has since been converted to the **Roundhouse Community Centre** *(181 Roundhouse Mews, ☎713-1800, www.roundhouse.ca)*, home to arts, community, cultural and sports activities, including rotating art exhibits and theatre. It too was restored for Expo 86, when it was a theme pavilion. Its redevelopment was financed by the Concord Pacific Development Corporation.

Head back down to the waterfront via Davie Street, if necessary, making a stop to refuel at **Urban Fare** *(see p 210).*

At the bottom of Davie Street is a marina served by the **Aquabus** *($2-$5; ☎689-5858)*, tiny little put-put ferries that look more like bath toys than seaworthy vessels. The Aquabus serves **Science World** *($3 one way; Sat and Sun only, departures 10:10am to 6:15pm every 30min, similar return schedule)* as well as **Granville Island** *($3 one way; every day departures every 30min on the hour and half hour 7am to 8:30pm, every 15min from 8:45am to 6:15pm, similar return schedule; ferry stops at Stamps Landing en route)*. If you choose to visit both sites, you can also take the Aquabus from one to the other on Saturdays and Sundays *($5 one way; departs Granville Island 10am to 6pm every 30 min, departs Science World 10:30am to 6:30pm)*. **False Creek Ferries**, *($5 one way; ☎684-7781)*, however, also runs the latter route and departs every day *(from Science World every 30min, at 15 and 45 past the hour; from Granville Island at 25 and 55 past the hour)*.

If the ferry schedule doesn't suit you, you can conceivably walk all the way to Science World. Continue your promenade to Cooper's Park, in the shadow of the Cambie Bridge, also a favourite for dogs and their walkers. The paving stones and lights of the walkway continue until the Plaza of

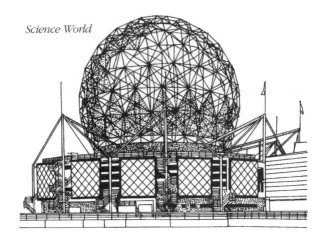

Science World

Nations, but beyond that you'll have to duck your way in and out of fenced-off areas until Science World, about a 12min walk from the Plaza.

On your way to Science World, you can spot the gray dome of GM Place and the white dome of BC Place Stadium, next to it. The 60,000 seats in **BC Place Stadium** *(777 Pacific Blvd. N., ☎669-2300, 661-7373 or 661-2122)* are highly coveted by fans of Canadian football, who come here to cheer on the B.C. Lions. Large trade fairs and rock concerts are also held in the stadium. Beside it is **GM Place** *(Pacific Blvd. at the corner of Abbott St., ☎899-7400)*, a 20,000-seat amphitheatre that was completed in 1995 and now hosts the home games of

the local hockey and basketball teams, the Vancouver Canucks and Grizzlies respectively.

In front of BC Place, you'll see the dozens of naked flagpoles lining the waterside **Plaza of Nations**, a convention and reception facility and legacy of Expo 86.

Science World ★ *($12.75 or $15.75 with movie; 1455 Québec St., ☎443-7440)* is the big silver ball at the end of False Creek. Architect Bruno Freschi designed this 14-storey building as a welcome centre for visitors to Expo 86. It was the only pavilion built to remain in place after the big event. The sphere representing the Earth has supplanted the tower as the quintessential symbol of these fairs since

Expo 67 in Montréal. Vancouver's sphere contains an **OMNIMAX** theatre that presents films on a giant, dome-shaped screen. The rest of the building is now occupied by a museum that explores the secrets of science from all different angles.

Included are both high- and low-tech puzzles and displays for kids, many of which have a strong environmental message, including a display demonstrating the enormous waste of water involved in the simple act of flushing a toilet, a film called *Burgerworks*, which explains the energy and resources that go into the making of a hamburger, and an explanation of how electricity runs household appliances. The majority of Science World's visitors are school-aged children under 14, for whom most of the exhibits are geared. Don't leave without spending a few moments watching the delightful Tower of Bauble, a giant kinetic sculpture located outside the main entrance.

When you leave Science World, you may want to stroll over to **Pacific Central Station** *(1150 Station St.)*, which features a long, impressive Beaux Arts facade. Determined not to be outdone, Canadian National (formerly the Canadian

Northern Pacific Railway Company) copied the Canadian Pacific Railway by building a second transcontinental railway. It ran parallel to the first and ended at this station, erected in 1919 on the embankment of False Creek. Today, it welcomes Canadian VIA trains and U.S. Amtrak trains as well as various private trains which use the tracks running through the Rockies for scenic tours.

If you're heading to the market at **Granville Island** ★ ★ *(every day 9am to 6pm, www.granville-island. net)* by ferry, take the ramp down to the False Creek Ferries dock. If you're driving (a bad idea, as traffic is heavy and parking is limited) or cycling (possible via the Seaside Bicycle Route), just take the Granville or Burrard Bridge and follow the signs from there. To reach the island without following the False Creek tour, take bus number 50 heading south from Howe Street downtown. You'll notice the vaguely Art Deco pillars of the Burrard Street Bridge (1930).

In 1977, this artificial island, created in 1914 and once used for industrial purposes, saw its warehouses and factories transformed into a major recreational and commercial centre. The area has since come to life thanks to a revitalization project. A public market, museums, many shops and all sorts of restaurants, plus theatres and artists' studios are all part of Granville Island.

The **Granville Island Market** ★★ is a must-see. Grab yourself a herbal chai at the Granville Island Tea Co. or an organic fair-trade coffee at Origins Coffee Company, and feast every sense: there are stalls of oriental orchids, fish-mongers with salmon in every shade of red (the Indian candy is a must), focaccia and fig-and-anise loaf at the wonderful Terra Breads, bowls of smoked-salmon chowder at Stock Market, and atmosphere to spare. Sit yourself down on a bench by False Creek and partake of the festive atmosphere. The view of the development's high- and low-rises on the north shore is not particularly inspiring, but with such creature comforts in hand, chances are you won't really mind.

Outside the market, spend some time shopping in the many handicraft shops that fill the tiny island's streets. They feature some truly unique products.
If you've got the little ones in tow, you might dare to venture into the **Kid's Market**, located beneath the

bridge. It's packed with two floors of pint-sized consumer frenzy, as well as some games and a restaurant counter.

You will also find a community centre and the **Emily Carr College of Art and Design**, which was enlarged considerably in 1996 and presents students exhibitions in the Concourse Gallery and international works in the Charles H. Scott Gallery.

The popular **Granville Island Brewing Company** *(every day 10am to 7pm; guided tours $8.75, every day noon, 2pm and 4pm; call ahead to verify hours and tour schedules; 1441 Cartwright St., ☎687-BREW)* offers tours of its facilities, which include a specialty beer and wine store, a tasting-room and a brewhouse.

Take Anderson Street south beneath the Granville Bridge, then turn left on Park Walk. The museum is at the junction, to your right.

Granville Island Museums ★ *(1502 Duranleau St., Granville Island, ☎683-1939)* is actually three separate museums in one location, a stone's throw from the market: the Sport Fishing Museum, the Model Trains Museum and the Model Ships Museum. While they are quite clearly special-interest museums, those of us uninitiated in the joys of fishing, model trains and model ships will still find some pleasure here.

The Sport Fishing Museum boasts an international collection of artifacts—some very old—related to sport fishing in British Columbia. Here, you enter a fascinating world full of rituals, where an understanding of ecology and entomology is a prerequisite to success. The exhibits dedicated to fly-fishing are impressive and very well laid-out. There are even some silk-screen prints of fish by renowned Haida artist Bill Reid, as well as some fish hooks and harpoon points used by First Nations people.

Once you have caught the "bug" after visiting this lovely museum, you will have the urge to equip yourselves and head for the great outdoors. The museum's information centre offers a complete list of outfitters, lodges, clubs and the best fishing spots in British Columbia.

In the Model Trains Museum, you'll find china and silverware from Canadian Pacific Railway (CPR) trains, in addition to countless model locomotives in display cases. Best of all, however, is a huge, working model train travelling

through a miniaturized depiction of B.C.'s Fraser and Kettle valleys, with over 6,000 handmade trees, all made of organic matter, and 300m of track. The Model Ships Museum includes West Coast working vessels, such as freighters, tug boats and fishing boats, but the real highlight is a 4m model of *HMS Hood*, which took its builder 20 years to complete.

Walk beneath the Granville Street Bridge, heading south along Anderson Street. Turn left at Park Walk. You will now enter the **False Creek Development** ★, a residential area begun in 1974 and built in stages by private developers on formerly polluted government land. Here, on the south shore of False Creek, was Vancouver's first planned community development, predating by two decades the twinkling, green-hued glass towers on the north shore.

It is pleasant to wander about on the pedestrian walkways and look at the carefully designed groups of houses.

If you'd like to continue your promenade, walk to **Charlson Park** *(corner W. Sixth Ave. and Laurel St.)*, a 6ha park where you'll find a duck pond, a waterfall, a field and a playground with

Vancouver

a panoramic view of Vancouver.

To return to downtown Vancouver, hop aboard the Aquabus at the Arts Club dock (which will take you back to Yaletown or to the foot of Hornby Street, further west), or False Creek Ferries (which will take you to the Aquatic Centre at the foot of Thurlow Street), on the next dock.

Tour H: The West Side

The culture of the Pacific as well as the history and traditions of the Aboriginal peoples are omnipresent throughout this tour, which follows the shore of the vast peninsula that is home to the majority of Vancouver's residents. Posh residential neighbourhoods, numerous museums, a university campus and several sand and quartz beaches from which Vancouver Island is visible on a clear day all make up this tour. This is a driving tour, as it extends over 15km. The first four attractions are accessible aboard bus no. 22 from downtown or by taking bus no. 4 directly to the University of British Columbia campus. You can also get to the starting point in Vanier Park via False Creek Ferries *(departure at Aquatic Centre, foot of Thurlow St.; ☎684-7781 for schedule).*

Exit the downtown area by the Burrard Street Bridge.

Keep right, and immediately after going down the roadway leading off the bridge, take a right on Chestnut Street to get to **Vanier Park** (directions well indicated), which is home to three museums.

The **Vancouver Museum** ★★ *($10; Tue-Sun 10am to 5pm, Thu until 9pm; 1100 Chestnut St., in Vanier Park, ☎736-4431)* forms its centrepiece. This delightful museum, whose dome resembles the

---

● ATTRACTIONS

1.	Vanier Park	6.	Museum of Anthropology
2.	Tatlow Court	7.	Asian Centre
3.	Pioneer Park	8.	First Nations House of Learning
4.	Jericho Beach Park	9.	UBC Botanical Garden and
5.	University of British Columbia		Centre for Plant Research

◯ ACCOMMODATIONS

1.	UBC Housing and Conference Centre	2.	Vancouver International Hostel

● RESTAURANTS

1.	True Confections

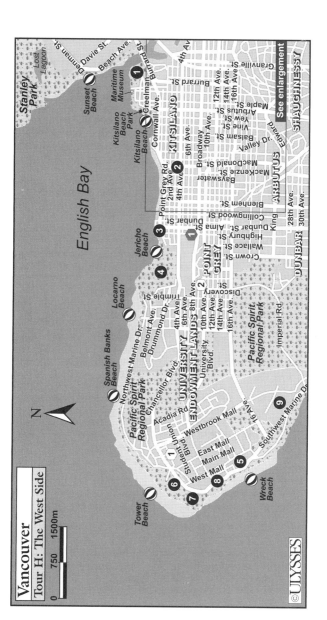

Vancouver
Tour H: The West Side

0 750 1500m

N

English Bay

Stanley Park
Lost Lagoon

Davie St.
Denman St.
Beach Ave.

Sunset Beach
Maritime Museum
Kitsilano Beach Park
Kitsilano Beach
Greelman
Cornwall Ave.
Burrard St.
4th Ave.

KITSILANO

Point Grey Rd.
2nd Ave.
4th Ave.
6th Ave.
Broadway
10th Ave.
Bayswater
MacKenzie St.
Blenheim St.
Collingwood St.
Dunbar St.
Alma St.
Highbury St.

Jericho Beach
Locarno Beach
Spanish Banks Beach
Northwest Marine Dr.
Belmont Ave.
Drummond Dr.
Trimble St.

Pacific Spirit Regional Park

Chancellor Blvd.
Acadia Rd.

UNIVERSITY
ENDOWMENT LANDS

4th Ave.
6th Ave.
8th Ave.
Discovery St.
University Blvd.
10th Ave.
12th Ave.
14th Ave.
16th Ave.

POINT GREY
Wallace St.
Crown St.

DUNBAR

Graniville St.
12th Ave.
14th Ave.
16th Ave.
Burrard St.
Arbutus St.
Yew St.
Vine St.
Maple St.
Valley Dr.
Edwards
28th Ave.
30th Ave.

ARBUTUS

SHAUGHNESSY

See enlargement

Student Union Blvd.
Westbrook Mall
East Mall
Main Mall
West Mall
16 Ave.
Southwest Marine Dr.

Pacific Spirit Regional Park
Imperial Rd.

Tower Beach
Wreck Beach

© ULYSSES

head-dress worn by the Coast Salish First Nation, presents exhibitions on the history of the different peoples who have inhabited the region.

In the Orientation Gallery, you'll find an eclectic collection, including items from all over the world that were once collected by Vancouverites. You'll also see a photograph of **Engine 374**, which pulled the first transcontinental train into Vancouver (see p 99), on May 23, 1887. Children will be delighted by this gallery, which features a collection of toys, thoughtfully displayed in child-height glass exhibit cases. You'll also be treated to some wonderful views of the West End and Stanley Park.

Much of the rest of the museum is divided into Vancouver Story Exhibits, each focused on a period in Vancouver's history and imaginatively arranged with enough realism to enthral both children and adults. You'll see replicas of the steerage quarters of an immigrant ship, circa 1860, complete with seasickness-inducing sound effects; an early-19th-century fur-trading post, complete with howling wolves; an actual "colonist car" locomotive; and the facade of a Victorian home (1890), recreated from demolished downtown and Eastside homes; and the interior of an Edwardian home. And if you enjoy it, you'll be pleased to know that the museum is planning to tell six new Vancouver stories in the coming years.

Also in the park is the **H.R. MacMillan Space Centre** *($12.75; Tue-Sun 10am to 5pm;* ☎ *738-7827, www.pacific-space-centre.bc.ca)*, which houses the H.R. MacMillan Planetarium and relates the creation of the universe. It has a telescope through which you can admire the stars. The **Maritime Museum** *($8; mid May to early Sep, every day 10am to 5pm; Nov to mis May Tue-Sat 10am to 5pm, Sun noon to 5pm; 1905 Ogden Ave.,* ☎ *257-8300, www.vmm.bc.ca)* completes the trio of institutions in Vanier Park. Being a major seaport, it is only natural that Vancouver should have its own maritime museum. The key attraction is the *Saint-Roch*, the first boat to circle North America by navigating the Panamá Canal and the Northwest Passage.

Get back on Chestnut Street and turn right on Cornwall Avenue, which becomes a scenic road named Point Grey Road.

You will now pass through **Kitsilano** *(between Burrard*

and Alma sts.), bordered to the north by a public beach on English Bay and to the south by 16th Avenue. This area, whose wooden Queen Anne and Western Bungalow Style houses are typical of the West Coast, was a middle-class neighbourhood in the early 20th century. By the 1960s, it was the centre of Vancouver's flower-power scene. Today, polar fleece has largely replaced paisley, but the area still has a strong counter-culture feeling to it. Around the corner of First Avenue and Yew Street, there are a number of restaurants, cafés and bars, conveniently located close to the beach.

If you want to leave no stone unturned during your tour of Kitsilano, take a look at Macdonald Street, between Fifth and Sixth streets. Around number 2100, a lovely row of shingled, gabled houses, each with a veranda in front, forms a cohesive whole. They date back to 1912.

Turn right on Sixth Avenue, then right again on Bayswater Street.

Tatlow Court *(1820 Bayswater St.)*, a group of neo-Tudor row houses built around a central court, is worth a quick look, particularly in spring, when the surrounding cherry trees are in bloom.

Turn left on Point Grey Road, then right on Alma Street, which leads to **Pioneer Park**, home of the **Hasting Mill Store** *(1575 Alma St.)*. Built in 1865, this former general store is the oldest building in Vancouver and has been converted to a small **museum** *(donations welcome; mid-Jun to mid-Sep Tue-Sun 11am to 4pm, rest of year Sat and Sun 1pm to 4pm; ☎734-1212)* displaying First Nations artifacts and pioneer memorabilia. Originally located east of Gastown, near the city's first sawmill, it was transported here by boat in 1930 and then restored by the Native Daughters of British Columbia, a charitable organization which, despite its name, has nothing to do with indigenous peoples.

Head south on Alma Street, then turn right on Fourth Avenue.

The area west of Alma Street as far as the University of British Columbia gates is known as **Point Grey ★★★**.

Fourth Avenue runs alongside lovely **Jericho Beach Park ★★**, a green space and beach rolled into one at the edge of English Bay. Turn right on Northwest Marine Drive, then left on

Vancouver

Belmont Avenue, driving up the hill, to see some of the loveliest houses on the West Side.

Return to Northwest Marine Drive and head west to **Spanish Banks Beach** ★★, where you'll get an unimpeded view of Vancouver and the north shore. It's a favourite place to watch the sunset. Just beyond Spanish Banks is **Pacific Spirit Regional Park** ★★ (☎224-5739), also known as the University Endowment Lands. This 763ha parcel of land encompasses the rocky beaches on the perimeter of UBC as well as an inland section that contains more than 40km of gentle hiking and biking trails. The beaches are unsupervised and clothing is optional. From here, you get a full panoramic view of the Strait of Georgia.

The tour continues onto the grounds of the **University of British Columbia** ★, or UBC. The university was created by the provincial government in 1908, but it was not until 1925 that the campus opened its doors on this lovely site on Point Grey. An architectural contest had been organized for the site layout, but the First World War halted construction work. It took a student demonstration denouncing government inaction on this matter to get the buildings

completed. Only the library and the science building were executed according to the original plans. To this day, the UBC campus is constantly expanding, so don't be surprised by its somewhat heterogeneous appearance. Quite frankly, the only redeeming feature of the campus is its view. If you're interested in a campus tour, nontheless, **Set Foot for UBC** (May to Aug, ☎822-TOUR) offers free tours organized by students.

There are, however, a few gems on the campus, including the **Museum of Anthropology** ★★★ ($7, free admission Tue 5pm to 9pm; mid-May to early Sep every day 10am to 5pm, Tue until 9pm, beg Sep to mid-May Tue 11am to 9pm, Wed-Sun 11am to 5pm; 6393 NW Marine Dr.; from downtown, take bus no. 4 UBC or bus no. 10 UBC; it's a 10 to 15min walk from the UBC bus terminal; ☎822-3825). It's not to be missed both for the quality of Aboriginal artwork displayed here, including totem poles, and for the architecture of Arthur Erickson. Erickson designed the Great Hall with big concrete posts and beams to imitate the shape of traditional Aboriginal houses. Inside are immense totem poles gathered from former Aboriginal villages along the coast and on the islands. Here you will learn that there are three types of

yellow cedar piece depicts the Raven, an infamous trick-ster in Haida his-tory, coaxing fearful human beings out of a clam shell after a great flood. This huge piece was lowered into the museum through the sky-light above it. In addition to wooden sculp-ture, you'll also find some fab-ulous carved silver and gold jewellery; the contemporary pieces you see in jewellery stores around the city have their roots in silver and gold coins, which the Haida hammered into bracelets and other objects and en-graved as early as the 1860s.

*Raven and the
First Men*

totem poles, classified ac-cording to function: sup-porting house poles, frontal beams, and memorial totem poles. Visitors are cautioned that "only those who know and have the right to the stories can tell the meaning of a totem pole." Some are contemporary, others over a century old.

A highlight of the museum is the *Raven and the First Men*, by renowned Haida artist Bill Reid and several assistants. This impressive

In addition to objects re-lated to the First Nations of B.C., including many pieces of intricate basketry, you'll also be astounded by the museum's rich collection of artifacts from other Cana-dian First Nations, as well as international items, such as Japanese dolls and masks, Chinese porcelain and representational art, and Polynesian, Australian, Southeast Asian and Indian art.

The museum's collection has exceedingly overgrown its display space; much of the collection, particularly the above-noted items, is crammed together in "visible storage," either in glass-topped drawers or squeezed into display cases. Each piece has a code, which can be looked up in a large book, something of a labourious process not usually found in contemporary museums. The process is soon to be computerized, and much more of the collection will be displayed in the coming years, thanks to upcoming renovations. It's a good idea to participate in a guided museum tour because the museum's interpretive signage is rather limited. There are political reasons for this: all cultural groups in British Columbia (there are seven major First Nations and a great number of language-based culture groups) must agree to any cultural interpretation—a long, contentious process.

On your way out (leave by the main entrance and turn right, turning again on the path), don't miss the outdoor exhibit, a 19th-century Haida house complex.

On the edge of the West Mall is the **Asian Centre** (*1871 West Mall*), capped with a big pyramidal metal roof. It houses the department of Asian studies and an exhibition centre. Behind the building is the magnificent **Nitobe Memorial Garden** ★ ★ (*$2.75 summer, free winter; $6 with Botanical Garden admission, see below; mid-Mar to mid-Oct, every day 10am to 6pm; winter, Mon to Fri 10am to 2:30pm;* ☎*822-9666*) which symbolically faces Japan on the other side of the Pacific.

Further along, the **First Nations House of Learning** ★ is a community centre for Aboriginal students that was completed in 1993. It was designed to be a modern version of a Coast Salish longhouse. The curved roof evokes the spirit of a bird. Totem poles surround the great hall, which can accommodate up to 400 people at a time.

The southwestern edge of the campus harbours a spot unlike any other—**Wreck Beach** ★ (*NW Marine Dr. at University St.*)—where students come to enjoy some of life's pleasures. Nudists have made this their refuge, as have sculptors, who exhibit their talents on large pieces of driftwood. Vendors hawk all sorts of items next to improvised fast-food stands. A long stairway, quite steep in places, leads down to the beach.

Just beyond Wreck Beach is the **UBC Botanical Garden and Centre for Plant Research** (*$4.75, $6 with Nitobe Memorial Garden admission; every day mid-Mar to mid-Oct 10am to 6pm; free admission mid-Oct to mid-Mar, open daylight hours; guided tours Apr to mid-Oct, Wed and Sun at 2pm from the main gatehouse; 6804 SW Marine Dr., ☎822-3928*), an attractive place for a stroll and a popular place to find many species that are extremely rare in Canada, many of which are for sale in its Shop in the Garden. Its annual Mother's Day perennial plant sale is a popular event.

Tour I: Shaughnessy and Surroundings

This short driving tour takes in a small neighbourhood in the West Side, Shaughnessy, as well as some nearby attractions. It begins, however, in the adjoining neighbourhoods of Mount Pleasant (city hall) and Fairview (Vancouver Genereal Hospital).

In the 1930s, the municipal government planned to make Mount Pleasant Vancouver's new downtown core in an effort to shift the city centre. This involved building a new city hall near Broadway. It is true that when you look at a map, you realize that Vancouver's business section is located at the northern edge of town, on a peninsula accessible mainly by bridges. Practical as it was, however, the project was a bitter failure, as illustrated by the solitary tower of City Hall, rising up amidst scores of cottage-style houses.

Shaughnessy Heights, the second area, is an affluent residential enclave laid out by the Canadian Pacific Railway (CPR) starting in 1907. It succeeded the West End as a refuge for well-heeled Vancouverites. The area was named after Thomas G. Shaughnessy, who was then president of the CPR. He lived in the house of the same name in Montréal, now part of the Canadian Centre for Architecture. A number of local streets, furthermore, were named after the eminent families of Montréal's Golden Square Mile, like the Hosmers, the Oslers and the Anguses.

The tour starts at the corner of Cambie Street and 12th Avenue. Take the Cambie Bridge from downtown.

On the northeast corner of Cambie and 12th Avenue, is **City Hall** (*453 West 12th Ave.*), a massive, austere-looking tower topped by public clocks and featuring both classical and Art Deco elements (1935).

Head west on 12th Avenue, a right turn, if you just crossed the bridge.

Next, you will pass **Vancouver General Hospital** *(855 West 12th Ave.)*, one of the largest hospitals in North America. Several of its buildings were erected in the Streamlined Art Deco style between 1944 and 1950. Unlike the geometric, vertical Art Deco style, the Streamline Deco or "steamship" style features rounded, horizontal lines which symbolize speed and modernism.

Turn left on Oak Street, then right on 16th Avenue. Sixteenth Avenue becomes Wolfe, which leads to Tecumseh Avenue, and finally to The Crescent, in Shaughnessy Heights. Here, the environment changes radically, with stately mansions suddenly appearing.

Park and walk around The Crescent to get a taste of the opulence of the houses in this area. The earliest Shaughnessy residences were large, built on spacious, handsomely landscaped lots of one-fifth to one-and-one-half acre and built in the Tudor and neoclassical styles of respectively, Renaissance England and the colonial United States. Many of these estates

have since been converted to multiple-family abodes.

One of the most elegant homes is definitely **Walter C. Nichol House** ★ *(1402 The Crescent, between Angus Dr. and McRae Ave; not open to the public)*, a masterpiece by Maclure and Fox that was built in 1912 for the former Lieutenant Governor of British Columbia. The Tudor-style half-timbering and mullioned windows of many of these homes are clear reminders of the British roots that characterize this province, despite its great distance from the mother country.

Furthermore, as the climate is similar to that of England, these houses boast front gardens as lovely as those found on the outskirts of London.

Between Hudson and Angus, you'll see **MacDonald House** *(1388 The Crescent)*, elegantly built in the neoclassical style in 1913, complete with all the typical classical details. Weddings were held here in the 1950s and the house was thereafter subdivided, but is again a single-family dwelling today.

Take Hudson Street to Matthews Avenue and turn right.

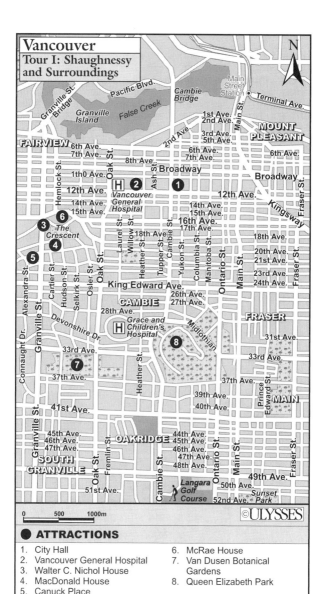

Vancouver
Tour I: Shaughnessy and Surroundings

N

Granville St. Bridge

Pacific Blvd.

Cambie Bridge

Main Street Station

Terminal Ave.

Granville Island

False Creek

1st Ave.
2nd Ave.
3rd Ave.
5th Ave.

MOUNT PLEASANT

FAIRVIEW

6th Ave.
7th Ave.
8th Ave.

6th Ave.
7th Ave.

6th Ave.

Broadway

Broadway

H ② ①

1th0 Ave.
12th Ave.
14th Ave.
15th Ave.

Vancouver General Hospital

12th Ave.

14th Ave.
15th Ave.
16th Ave.
17th Ave.
18th Ave.

Kingsway

③
The Crescent
⑥
④

⑤

King Edward Ave.

18th Ave.

20th Ave.
21st Ave.
23rd Ave.
24th Ave.

26th Ave.
27th Ave.

CAMBIE

28th Ave.

FRASER

H Grace and Children's Hospital

⑧

31st Ave.

33rd Ave.

⑦

33rd Ave.

37th Ave.

MAIN

37th Ave.

39th Ave.
40th Ave.

41st Ave.

45th Ave.
46th Ave.
47th Ave.

OAKRIDGE

44th Ave.
45th Ave.
46th Ave.
47th Ave.
48th Ave.

SOUTH GRANVILLE

49th Ave.

51st Ave.

Langara Golf Course

50th Ave.
52nd Ave.

Sunset Park

0   500   1000m

©ULYSSES

● ATTRACTIONS

1. City Hall
2. Vancouver General Hospital
3. Walter C. Nichol House
4. MacDonald House
5. Canuck Place
6. McRae House
7. Van Dusen Botanical Gardens
8. Queen Elizabeth Park

Just after Granville, on the left-hand side, is elegant **Canuck Place** *(1690 Matthews Ave.)*, formerly known as Tait House. It was built in 1911 by a homesick Scot who longed for the castles of his native land. After an ugly history as a base for celebrations by the Kanadian Knights of the Klu Klux Klan, who purchased it in 1925, the house has a more noble vocation today as a children's hospice.

Steal along McRae Avenue, where you'll find the largest home in Shaughnessy Heights, **McRae House** ★ *(1489 McRae Ave.)*, also known as Hycroft. Built in 1909 for General Alexander McRae, it was designed by Thomas Hooper. The long facade has a projecting portico in the Beaux Arts spirit.

The interior, decorated by Charles Marega, who sculpted the lions for Lions Gate Bridge, boldly combines Italian rococo with English neoclassicism. Like many other mansions across Canada, McRae House was abandoned by its owners and liveried servants after the stock market crash of 1929. Since 1962, it has been occupied by the University Women's Club. The interior can be viewed during the club's open house and Christmas craft fair.

Go back and complete the loop of The Crescent, then take Osler Avenue southward out of Shaughnessy Heights.

Turn left on 33rd Avenue, then right on Oak Street and right again on 37th Avenue, where you'll find

Canuck Place

the entrance to the **Van Dusen Botanical Gardens** ★★ *(summer $7, winter $5; Apr to Oct every day 10am to night-fall, Oct to Apr 10am to 4pm; free guided tours every day Apr to Oct 2pm; group tours can also be arranged; 5251 Oak St., ☎878-9274).* Since Vancouver is so blessed by Mother Nature, a number of lovely gardens have been planted in the area, including this one, which boasts plant species from all over the world. The Great Lawn is the last remnant of the golf course that occupied this property from 1912 to 1964.

When the rhododendrons are in bloom *(late Mar to late May)*, the garden deserves a third star. In bloom simultaneously, the Laburnum Walk is also a delight. At any time of year, don't miss the maze, and leave yourself enough time to find your way out! At 22ha, the garden is a much smaller, wilder alternative to Victoria's Butchart Gardens.

At the far end is a housing co-op that blends in so perfectly with the greenery that it looks like a gigantic ornamental sculpture (McCarter, Nairne and Associates, 1976).

Back on Oak Street, turn right on 33rd Avenue.

Further east on 33rd Avenue is another magnificent green space, **Queen Elizabeth Park** ★★ *(corner of 33rd Ave. and Cambie St.),* laid out around the **Bloedel Floral Conservatory** ★ *($3.90; Apr to Sep, Mon to Fri 9am to 8pm, Sat and Sun 10am to 9pm; Oct, Feb and Mar every day 10am to 5:30pm, Nov, Dec and Jan every day 10am to 5pm; top of Queen Elizabeth Park, ☎257-8570).* The latter, shaped like an overturned glass saucer, houses exotic plants and birds, the latter flying freely through this delightfully tropical environment. It's a tiny space that gets quite crowded with visitors in the summer. Visit in the morning, when the birds are awake but the crowds of visitors aren't. The Bloedel company, which sponsored the conservatory, is the principal lumber company in British Columbia. This park's rhododendron bushes also merit a visit in springtime. Finally, the outdoor gardens offer a spectacular view of the city, English Bay and the surrounding mountains. **Seasons in the Park** (see p 219) restaurant has a wonderful scenic location—where else?—in the park, which makes it a favourite spot for many visitors.

Vancouver

Tour J: Richmond and Steveston

South of Vancouver, visitors with cars can visit the second-largest **Buddhist temple** in North America *(every day 9:30am to 5:30pm; 9160 Steveston Hwy., Richmond, ☎274-2822)*. To get there, take Oak Street southward toward Highway 99, which leads to the ferry for Victoria, and get off at the Steveston Highway West exit. Visitors are gracefully received and can have the various elements of Buddhism explained to them.

Get back on the Steveston Highway heading west, turn left on Fourth Avenue, and continue to the end. The **Gulf of Georgia Cannery National Historic Site ★** *($6.50; early Jun to early Sep every day 10am to 5pm, early Apr to end May and beg Sep end Oct Thu-Mon 10am to 5pm; guided tours every hour; 12138 Fourth Ave., Richmond, ☎664-9009)*, restored by Parks Canada, retraces the history of the fishing industry in Steveston. This historic spot explains the steps involved in conserving fish, especially salmon, and also shows how herring is transformed into pet food and oil. Very interesting. Leav-

ing this establishment, stay along the seashore by way of the wooden walkway near the fishing boats. Fishing remains an important economic activity in this region. A commercial area with restaurants and shops invites you to relax. The day's catch is served in the restaurants.

Turn back along the Steveston Highway, this time heading east, and take Route 99 toward the ferry pier for Victoria; take the Ladner exit after the tunnel. Go along this road and follow the signs to the **George C. Reifel Bird Sanctuary ★★** *($4; every day 9am to 4pm, 5191 Robertson Rd., Delta, ☎946-6980)*. Each year more than 350 species of birds visit this magical spot in the marshlands at the mouth of the Fraser River.

Excursions from Vancouver: The Southern Gulf Islands

Among the many reasons to appreciate Vancouver, one in particular stands out. Unlike certain cities, where nearby suburbs are often the only place to get away for the weekend, Vancouver offers a wide choice of nearby destinations: **Victoria**

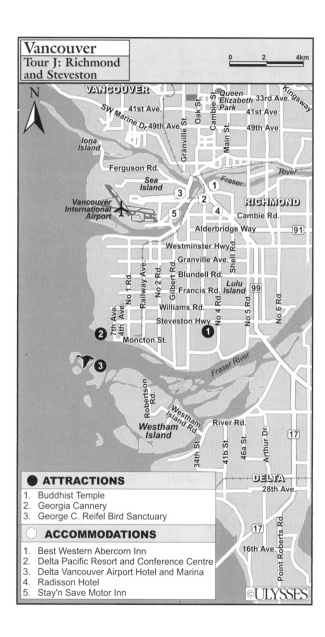

Vancouver
Tour J: Richmond and Steveston

N

0   2   4km

VANCOUVER

41st Ave.

SW Marine Dr. 49th Ave.

Queen Elizabeth Park 33rd Ave.

Kingsway

41st Ave.

49th Ave.

Granville St.

Oak St.

Cambie St.

Main St.

Iona Island

Ferguson Rd.

Sea Island

Fraser River

Vancouver International Airport

RICHMOND

Cambie Rd.

Alderbridge Way

91

Westminster Hwy.

Granville Ave.

Shell Rd.

Blundell Rd.

Francis Rd.

Lulu Island

99

No 1 Rd.

Railway Ave.

No 2 Rd.

Gilbert Rd.

Williams Rd.

No 4 Rd.

No 5 Rd.

No 6 Rd.

Steveston Hwy

7th Ave.

4th Ave.

Moncton St.

Fraser River

Robertson Rd.

Westham Island Rd.

River Rd.

Westham Island

34th St.

41b St.

46a St.

Arthur Dr.

17

DELTA

28th Ave.

17

16th Ave.

Point Roberts Rd.

© ULYSSES

● ATTRACTIONS
1. Buddhist Temple
2. Georgia Cannery
3. George C. Reifel Bird Sanctuary

⬡ ACCOMMODATIONS
1. Best Western Abercorn Inn
2. Delta Pacific Resort and Conference Centre
3. Delta Vancouver Airport Hotel and Marina
4. Radisson Hotel
5. Stay'n Save Motor Inn

(see p 253), **Whistler** (see p 305), and the **Gulf Islands** are the most famous.

These islands have retained their wild essence and charm by not being overly commercially developed; with no concrete and few cars to mar their beauty, these islands constitute havens of peace for stressed-out Vancouverites.

Getting There

Ferry transportation between islands is very inexpensive. Contact **BC Ferries** (☎888-223-3779 in B.C., out of province: 250-386-3431, www.bcferries.bc.ca) for information. The Southern Gulf Islands, described below, can all be reached by ferry via Tsawwassen, south of Vancouver.

Salt Spring Island

With many art galleries, restaurants and boutiques, Salt Spring is the most developed of the Gulf Islands. During the summer, artists and artisans flood the streets, exhibiting their work. Throughout the island, "Studio" signs line the streets, indicating that is it possible to visit artists in their studios.

Salt Spring Island boasts a great many bed and breakfasts, hotels and log cabins by the water as well as a youth hostel (☎537-4149). Accommodations fill up quickly in the summer. Try the lovely **Quarrystone House B&B** (*$$$$*; ☎250-537-5980 or 800-537-5980) located atop a cliff and surrounded by orchards and pasturage. For further details, contact the **Salt Spring Island Visitor Information Centre** (☎250-537-5252).

Mayne Island

Unlike Salt Spring, Mayne does nothing to court tourists. Roadsigns are virtually non-existent. It is therefore recommended that you study the only public road map set up near the harbour. Only a few remaining historic buildings testify to the island's past role as a prison; then it was nicknamed "Little Hell". Relics confirm the island was once a colonial outpost with old trading posts and shops; the old **Mayne Inn Hotel** (☎250-539-3122), with its period architecture, remains intact. For provisions and camping or hiking gear, **Miners Trading Post** (☎250-539-2214), in the village of **Fernhill**, is a good bet. The **Arbutus Bay Deer Farms** (☎250-539-2301) sells venison and beef for barbecues. **Bennett Bay Beach** is a lovely place for a stroll. Both **Pacific Spirit Air** (☎800-665-2359) and **Harbour Air** (☎800-665-0212) offer direct flights between Vancouver and Mayne Island.

Pender Islands

Linked by a wooden bridge, the two Pender Islands, much like Mayne, are very quiet. Visitors come here especially to go bike riding and stroll along the long stretch of **beaches**. Mount Normand has a good reputation among hikers. The summit offers a unique view of the San Juan Islands. The "hippie-cool" ambiance of these islands is obvious; natural food stores and organic produce farms prevail here. Try the **Southridge Farms Country Store** (☎250-629-2051) for organic fruits and vegetables. Sample excellent cuisine at the **Islanders Restaurant** (*$$$-$$$$; 1325 Mackinnon Rd.;* ☎250-629-3929) Bed and breakfasts ensure accommodation. Try **Hummingbird Hollow B&B** (*$$;* ☎250-629-6392), in the forest by a lake, or **Alice's Shangri-La Oceanfront B&B** (*$$$$;* ☎250-629-3433 or 877-629-6555), which offers a breathtaking 360° view.

Galiano Island

The first thing you will notice upon arriving in Galiano is the scarcity of infrastructure and commercial development. The inhabitants' passionate protests to protect the ecological balance have attracted worldwide attention. Their efforts have enabled Galiano to preserve its vast stretches of great natural area. The island also has many meditation centres and retreats for New Age enthusiasts, such as **Serenity By-the-Sea** (☎800-944-2655, *www.serenitybythesea.com*). **The Bellhouse Inn** (*$$$;* ☎250-539-5667 or 800-970-7464), a historic house on a 2.4ha farm, offers a warm welcome and four confortable rooms.

Galiano also features many bed and breakfasts and rustic cabins for rent as well as **campsites** in **Montague Harbour** (☎250-539-2115). There is also a good selection of restaurants here. **La Berengerie** (☎250-539-5392) is renowned for its Algerian food and lamb chops; it is also a bed and breakfast.

Call **Galiano TravelInfoCentre** (*☎250-539-2233 for B&B reservations*). They also offer adventure packages. For more information, call the **Galiano Island Chamber of Commerce** (☎250-539-2233, *www.galianoisland.com*).

Saturna Island

Saturna is perhaps the most isolated and least accessible of the Southern Gulf Islands, and its inhabitants

Vancouver

are determined to keep it that way. It has very limited facilities. Nevertheless, there are many good reasons to visit the island. Nature lovers will be fascinated by its unusual fauna and flora, like the **giant mushrooms** at the base of **Mount Warburton**. On Canada Day (July 1st), a great annual lamb barbecue is organized. It is the largest gathering of the year on the island. **Saturna Lodge** (☎250-539-2254) is one of the few inns here. Camping is forbidden on Saturna. For more information on accommodations, call ☎250-539-2930. Ferry reservations are essential during the summer.

Outdoor Activities

Located where the mountains meet the sea, a short distance from the wilds of British Columbia, Vancouver offers an extremely wide range of outdoor activities. Downhill skiing, hiking in the woods, hanggliding, salt-water swimming in the Strait of Georgia, sun-bathing on sandy beaches, sailboarding and surfing can all be enjoyed just 30min or less from downtown.

The ski resorts of the Coast Mountains, north of Vancouver, are easily accessible by car via the Lions Gate Bridge. They boast substantial vertical drops of more than 1,000m and offer a year-round cable car service to scenic lookouts on various mountaintops, from which visitors can take in outstanding views of the city. To the south, the beaches flanking the central neighbourhoods mean that Vancouverites can go swimming in the ocean without leaving town—and the water isn't as polluted as you might think! Among the other popular activities, cycling, jogging and in time skating in Stanley Park have become something of a ritual for many of the city's residents.

The local sports mania doesn't end there, however. Within the past few years, the city has built some impressive facilities for professional sports like football, hockey and most recently, basketball. This last sport, much more popular in the United States than in Canada, is indicative of the growing influence of American culture here in Vancouver.

For general information on all outdoor activities in the Greater Vancouver area, contact **Sport B.C.** (409-1367 Broadway, Vancouver, V6H 4A9, ☎737-3000, www.sportbc.ca) or the **Out-**

door Recreation Council of B.C. *(334-1367 W. Broadway, Vancouver, V6H 4A9,* ☎*737-3058, www.orcbc.ca).* Both organizations offer many suggestions and information.

Vancouver Parks & Recreation
☎*257-8400*
www.city.vancouver.bc.ca/parks
Vancouver Parks & Recreation provides information on sports and recreation activities.

Beaches

The Vancouver shoreline is made up in large part of easily accessible sandy beaches. All these beaches lie along English Bay, where it is possible to walk, cycle, play volleyball and, of course, take a dip in the sea to fully enjoy the setting. Stanley Park is fringed by **Third Beach** and **Second Beach**, and then, further east, along Beach Avenue, by **First Beach**, where hundreds of bathers brave the icy water to celebrate the New Year on January 1. A little farther east, **Sunset Beach** celebrates the day's end with gorgeous sunsets. At the southern edge of English Bay are **Kitsilano Beach**, **Jericho Beach**, **Locarno Beach**, **Spanish Banks Beach**, **Tower Beach** and, finally,

Wreck Beach at the western edge of the University of British Columbia campus.

Kitsilano Beach is enlivened by beach volleyball tournaments and by an assortment of sports facilities, including a basketball court. Locarno, Jericho and Spanish Banks beaches are quieter spots for family relaxation, where walking and reading are key activities.

Hiking

Stanley Park is definitely the best place go hiking in Vancouver with over 50km of trails through forest and greenery along the seashore, lakeshores, including the **Seawall**, an outstanding 9km trail flanked by giant trees.

There are lots of places to go walking in the Point Grey area. Myriad trails crisscross the **University of British Columbia (UBC) Endowment Lands**, now known as **Pacific Spirit Regional Park** *(access via Northwest Marine Dr. And Southwest Marine Dr., east of the UBC campus, as well as 16th Ave., where there is parking, and the Park Centre;* ☎*224-5739).* Pick up a trail map from the centre or download one from *www.gvrd.bc.ca.* There is a

Vancouver

40km network of trails through the forest, and since UBC is located on a peninsula, all trails ultimately lead to the beach.

On the other side of Lions Gate Bridge, in North Vancouver, Capilano Road leads to **Capilano River Regional Park** (☎224-5739), where you'll find a trail offering sweeping views of the Capilano River. During summer, you can see the salmon swimming upriver. Maps are available on the following Web site: *www.gvrd.bc.ca.*

Mountain hiking is also accessible near the city centre. **Cypress Provincial Park** (☎924-2200), north of the municipality of West Vancouver, has several hiking trails, among them the Howe Sound Crest Trail, which leads to different mountains, including The Lions and Mount Brunswick. The views over the west shore of Howe Sound are really quite spectacular. You must wear good shoes and bring food and water for these hikes. To get to Cypress Park by the Lions Gate Bridge, follow the signs west along the Trans-Canada Highway and take the Cypress Bowl Road exit. Take the time to stop at the lookout to contemplate Vancouver, the Strait of Georgia and, on a clear

day, Mount Baker in the United States.

The hike up **Grouse Mountain** ★★★ (☎984-0661), known as the Grouse Grind, is not particularly difficult, but the incline is as steep as 25° in places, so you have to be in good shape. It takes about 2hrs to cover the 3km trail, which starts at the parking lot for the cable car. The view of the city from the top of the mountain is fantastic. If you are too tired to hike back down, take the cable car for the modest sum of $5. Note that the trail is subject to closures due to inclement weather or other dangerous conditions.

Mount Seymour Provincial Park ★★ (☎986-2261) is another good hiking locale, offering two different views of the region. To the east is Indian Arm, a large arm of the sea extending into the valley.

A little further east in this marvellous mountain range on the north shore, magnificent **Lynn Canyon Park** ★★★ (☎981-3103) is scored with forest trails. It is best known for its footbridge, which stretches across an 80m deep gorge. Definitely not for the faint of heart! There is also an ecology centre on-site. To get there, take Highway 1 from North Vancouver to the Lynn Valley Road exit and follow the signs, then turn right on Peters Road.

Lighthouse Park, in West Vancouver, is well suited to hiking on flatter terrain. From this site, you will be facing the University of British Columbia, the entrance to English Bay, and the Strait of Georgia. Take the Lions Gate Bridge and follow Marine Drive West, crossing the city of West Vancouver and hugging the seashore until you reach the western edge of English Bay. Turn left at Beacon Lane toward Lighthouse Park.

If you get off Highway 99 just after West Vancouver and head west to Horseshoe Bay, you'll come to lovely little **Whytecliff Park**, located on the seashore. Most people come here to go picnicking or scuba diving. For an interesting little excursion, follow the rocky trail out to **Whyte Island** at low tide. Before heading out to this big rock, make sure to check what time the tides are due to come in, or you'll end up with wet feet.

A 15min **ferry** *(BC Ferries, ☎888-223-3779)* ride from Horseshoe Bay transports you to **Bowen Island** ★★★ *(☎947-2216)*, where hiking trails lead through a lush forest. Although you'll feel as if you're at the other end of the world, downtown Vancouver is only 5km away as the crow flies.

Cycling

The region has a multitude mountain-biking trails. Just head to one of the mountains north of the city.

A pleasant 9km ride runs along the Seawall in Stanley Park, part of Vancouver's oldest, and no doubt best, bike path, the **Seaside Bicycle Route**. It extends from Coal Harbour, just west of the Pan Pacific Hotel, west to the Stanley Park Seawall, and from there along English Bay and False Creek to Spanish Bank West. If you include the Stanley Park Seawall, the entire route measures about 30km and is an excellent way for visitors to explore the beauty of the city. Shortcuts can be taken along the Cambie and Burrard bridges, the latter being a good choice if you want to head directly to Granville Island. A handy map of bike paths in Vancouver can be obtained by contacting the **Bicycle Hotline** at ☎871-6070.

Bicycle rentals are available at **Spokes Bicycle Rental** *(1798*

Vancouver

West Georgia St., corner of Denman, ☎688-5141).

Outside Vancouver, you can go cycling in the Fraser Valley, near farms or along secondary roads.

More courageous visitors can follow the **Spanish Banks** beach all the way to UBC. You have to ride along roads during certain parts of the trip. To avoid getting lost, follow the green-and-white signs specifically posted for cyclists.

The 15min ferry ride from Horseshoe Bay out to little **Bowen Island ★★★** (☎947-2216) is a worthwhile excursion. This perfectly lovely residential island has a network of quiet little country roads. You are likely to come across a deer or two, and make sure to keep an eye out for eagles soaring overhead. After a day of pedalling, you can enjoy a relaxing drink

Bald eagle

by the harbour at Snug Cove.

Bird-watching

Birders should make a trip to the **George C. Reifel Bird Sanctuary ★★** (*5191 Robertson Road, Delta,* ☎946-6980) on Westham and Reifel islands. Dozens of species of migratory and non-migratory birds draw orthinology enthusiasts year-round to see aquatic birds, birds of prey, and many other varieties. Further south, several species can also be observed at Boundary Bay and Mud Bay as well as on Iona Island closer to Vancouver, next to the airport.

Whytecliff Park (*near Horseshoe Bay, West Vancouver*) is a lovely park, located on the seashore. Keep your ears tuned and your eyes peeled and you will probably spot some bald eagles in the tops of the tallest trees.

The largest bald eagle population in the world is found just 70km from Vancouver, at the **Brackendale Eagles Provincial Park** (☎898-3678), which lies alongside Highway 99, west side of Squamish

River, on the way to Whistler. Eagle viewing is at its best from mid-December to mid-January. Eagles can be viewed from the "Eagle Run" on Goverment Road *(Exit Hwy. 99 at Mamquam Rd. and head north on Government Rd.).*

Eagle buffs mingle at the **Brackendale Art Gallery** *(Sat and Sun and statutory holidays, noon to 10pm;* ☎898-3333).*

Windsurfing

The pleasures afforded by the sea in Vancouver are definitely not to be taken lightly. **Howe Sound**, located alongside Highway 99 North on the way to Squamish, was slated to become a major harbour for giant freighters, but, to the great relief of local windsurfers, never did. The wind rushes into the hollow formed by the mountains on either side of the fjord, making this part of British Columbia a paradise for high-speed sailboarding. You can obtain all the necessary information about where to go at the **Squamish tourist office** *(37950 Cleveland Avenue,* ☎892-9244). To find out about wind conditions, call the **Windtalker Windline** *(*☎926-9463). More informa-tion is available from the **Squamish Windsurfing Society** *(*☎734-0114, kutz@telus.net).* A $10 fee covers insurance and potential rescue costs.

Paddling

Like the mountains, the water is a key part of life in Vancouver, and there is an almost unlimited number of ways to get out and enjoy the sea. One option is to tour the city by sea kayak. **False Creek** stretches all the way to Main Street and Science World, and you'll pass Granville Island along the way; by paddling around **Stanley Park**, you can reach Canada Place and the skyscrapers downtown. More courageous visitors can set out along **Indian Arm** ★★★ from Deep Cove, an expedition likely to include a few encounters with seals and eagles.

A completely no-hassle way to get there is to take part in an organized expedition, such as the ones available from:

Lotus Land Tours Inc.
2005-1251 Cardero St.
Vancouver V6G 2H9
☎**684-4922**
Knowledgeable guide Peter Loppe and his staff will pick you up from your

Vancouver

hotel and take you kayaking in scenic Indian Arm. A barbecued-salmon lunch is provided ($145). No experience required.

Ecomarine Ocean Kayak Centre
1668 Duranleau St.
Granville Island
☎689-7520
This Granville Island outfit offers kayak rentals as well as 2.5hr and 4hr tours *($49 and $89 respectively)* of False Creek and English Bay. This company also offers instruction.

Further information:
Whitewater Kayaking Association of B.C. *(PO Box 91549 West Vancouver Postal Outlet V7V 3P2, ☎515-6376, www.whitewater.org).*

Rafting

Thrill-seekers will certainly appreciate the water-ways around Vancouver. A white-water

rafting paradise awaits visitors in the heart of Cascade Mountains, a semi-arid region less than 2hrs away from the city by car, on the **Fraser River**, the greatest waterway in British Columbia in terms of flow. Certain parts of the river are sure to make your hair stand on end.

The **Thompson River** (a tributary of Fraser River) is the best-known for white-water rafting. This beautiful emerald-green river runs through a magnificent rocky, arid landscape. Experts will tell you the Thompson River descent is a real roller-coaster ride. Good luck!

The **Coquihalla River** is another interesting and worthwhile destination. This powerful little river runs at the bottom of a deep canyon, offering spectacular scenery. Another tumultuous little river, the **Nahatlatch**, is less frequented than its renowned counterparts, but worth considering nonetheless. The river closest to Vancouver on which to go rafting is the **Chilliwack**. Despite its proximity to large urban centres, this river runs through a wild landscape. Over the course of the years, it has acquired a solid reputation among kayakers and canoeists.

Fraser River Raft Expeditions
☎863-2336 or 800-363-7238
Fraser River Raft Expeditions is located in the heart of the Fraser River canyon, 2 to 3hrs from Vancouver and specializes in expeditions on the Fraser, Thompson, Coquihalla and Nahatlatch rivers.

Hyak Wilderness Adventures
☎734-8622 or 800-663-7238
This is a major rafting enterprise with an excellent reputation. It has the practical advantage of having its offices in Vancouver and offers expeditions on the Chilliwack, Fraser and Thompson rivers.

REO Rafting Adventures
☎461-7238 or 800-736-7238
REO Rafting Adventures is a big agency that organizes white-water rafting on the Chilliwack, Nahatlatch and Thompson rivers. Group rates.

Sailing

Sailing is the best way to visit some of the lovely spots in **Vancouver Harbour**. Jericho Beach, in the Kitsilano area, is an excellent starting point. You can rent your own sailing dinghy or Hobie Cat at the **Jericho Sailing Centre Association** *(1300 Discovery St., ☎224-4177)*, or climb aboard a larger sailboat for a cruise of several hours or several days. The **Cooper Boating Centre** *(1620 Duranleau St., Granville Island, ☎687-4110)* is a good place to keep in mind.

Pleasure Boating

Renting an outboard **motor boat** is as easy as renting a car. No special permit is required for you to putter around at your leisure or speed across the water, as long as you stay near the shore. You'll find everything you need at **Granville Island Boat Rentals** *(16296 Duranleau Street, Granville Island, ☎682-6287)*.

Fishing

Salt-water Fishing

Vancouver is the starting point for unforgettable fishing. When it comes to sea fishing, salmon reigns supreme. Before casting your line, you must obtain a permit from a specialized outfitter from whom you can also rent out the necessary equipment. They have boats, know the best locations, and supply equipment and often meals, too. Make sure you are dressed appropriately. Even when the sun is out, it can get very cold on the open sea. It is also essential that you not forget your fishing license. You will find a mine of information from:

Sport Fishing Institute of British Columbia
Sport Fishing Museum
200-1676 Duranleau St.,
Granville Island, V6H 3S4
☎*689-6438*
www.sportfishing.bc.ca

The following charter company can make all the arrangements for you:

Bites-On Salmon Charters
1128 Hornby St.
Granville Island
☎*877-688-2483*
A 5hr trip will run you about $425.

Westin Bayshore Yacht Charters
1601 West Georgia St.
☎*691-6936*
Westin Bayshore Yacht Charters has an impressive fleet of fishing yachts.

Fresh-water Fishing

With an infinite number of lakes and rivers, trout fishing in British Columbia is always excellent. Licenses are sold in all camping equipment stores as well as at **Ruddik's Fly Shop** *(1077 Marine Dr., N. Vancouver,* ☎*985-5650)*, a good shop for this sport. Thousands of flies for catching every kind of fish in the area can be purchased here. The owner will gladly offer advice. Vancouver is the starting point to equip yourself and make inquiries, though you will have to leave the city to fish on a river or lake. The interior region and Cariboo Country are prime destinations for anglers from Vancouver. You can also purchase an issue of ***BC Outdoors Sports Fishing*** magazine at almost any newsagent's or call on fishing clubs or outfitters.

For more information on fresh-water fishing, contact the **Sport Fishing Institute of British Columbia** (see above).

Whale-watching

Visitors can admire great marine mammals on the outskirts of Vancouver, including **grey whales**, **killer whales** and other **finbacks**. There are a great many whale-watching tour operators on Vancouver Island.

Orca

considered the second-largest monolith in the world, after El Capitan in California. Squamish Chief boasts rock climbing routes: you have only to hook your karabiners. To get there from Vancouver, take Highway 1 to Highway 99, which will take you the 40km to Squamish.

Mountaineering

A trip to Vancouver without tackling the snow-covered peaks that surround the city would be a real shame. The **Federation of Mountain Clubs of B.C.** *(47 W. Broadway, Vancouver, V5Y 1P1, ☎737-3053, www.mountainclubs. bc.ca)* is a very reliable club with experienced instructors. Excursions are organized on a regular basis.

Rock-climbing

Vancouver is surrounded by mountains, and rock-climbing sites are hardly lacking. One of the best known in western North America, **Squamish Chief**, lies 60km from Vancouver. With a rock face of 600m, it is

Helicopter Sightseeing

If Vancouver's scenery has already won you over, here is something that will truly take your breath away! A glacier-skimming helicopter ride over snow-covered peaks and turquoise lakes is a must. Some agencies even offer landings on the glaciers. Though somewhat pricey, you will have unforgettable memories and extraordinary photographs too.

Vancouver Helicopters
5455D Airport Rd. S.
Richmond
☎270-1484 or 800-987-4354
Vancouver Helicopters is located right near Vancouver International Airport. This enterprise has a fine

Vancouver

reputation and will take you anywhere you want to go.

Kite Flying

With its 26km of beaches, Vancouver is the perfect place to go fly a kite. The most renowned spot for this activity is **Vanier Park**, which borders the beaches on English Bay, behind the Vancouver Museum. To get there, take the Burrard Bridge out of the downtown area and follow Chestnut Street through the pretty neighbourhood of Kitsilano.

Horseback Riding

Horseback riding opportunities are virtually limitless around Vancouver, with many bridle paths along forest roads. Contact **Back Country Horsemen Society of B.C.** *(25237-130th Ave., Maple Ridge, V4R 1C9 ☎574-7631)*, which has representatives throughout British Columbia. Keep in mind that this is a private club.

In-line Skating

In-line skating is a popular activity in Vancouver. Although you'll see skaters all over, the most popular place to go is around Stanley Park on the **Seawall**, a scenic, 9km trail flanked by a century-old forest. Skaters must travel counter clockwise (from Coal Harbour to English Bay), keep to the bicycle lane and not travel faster than 15km/hr. Skate rentals are available at many places along the beach, as well as near the entrance to the park at **Bayshore Bike Rentals** *($13.50/4hrs; 745 Denman St., ☎688-2453)*.

Golf

Vancouver is unquestionably the golf capital of Western Canada, with golf for all tastes and budgets. Golf courses in Vancouver and its surrounding areas are virtually all hilly and offer spectacular views of the ocean and especially the mountains that loom over all parts of the region. It should be noted that all golf clubs require appropriate attire. There are very few courses in Vancouver itself, but the suburbs boast one at practically every turn.

University Golf Club
5185 University Blvd.
☎**224-1818**
The University Golf Club is one of the best-known in town and among the priciest. It is situated a stone's throw from the University of British Columbia (UBC). Sean Connery has played here.

Peace Portal Golf Course
16900 Fourth Avenue, Surrey
☎**538-4818 or 800-354-7544**
The oldest public golf course, the Peace Portal Golf Course was founded in 1928 and is open year-round. It lies along Highway 99, near the U.S. border, in the suburb of Surrey.

Mayfair Lakes Golf and Country Club
5460 No. 7 Road, Richmond
☎**276-0585**
In Richmond, another of the city's southern suburbs, the Mayfair Lakes Golf and Country Club has a top-notch green surrounded by water.

Furry Creek
Britannia Beach
☎**922-9576 or 922-9461**
No golf course boasts a more spectacular setting than Furry Creek, located

just past the village of Lions Bay, on **Howe Sound**, (Highway 99 N). Nestled away in a splendid landscape, this course is more than just pleasant; imagine the sea stretched out beside towering, snow-capped peaks. Amazing.

Fraserview Golf Course
7800 Vivian Dr.
☎**280-1616**
The Fraserview Golf Course is an affordable golf course, managed by the City and located at the southern tip of Vancouver.

Langara Golf Course
6706 Alberta St.
☎**280-1818**
The Langara Golf Course is also a municipal golf course, situated southeast of town.

Gleneagles
6190 Marine Dr., West Vancouver
☎**921-7353**
Right near the lovely village of Horseshoe Bay and 15min from Vancouver, this very inexpensive golf course is sometimes jam-packed on weekends, but the scenery makes playing here worth the wait.

Seymour Golf and Country Club
3723 Mt. Seymour Pkwy
North Vancouver
☎**929-2611**
Seymour Golf and Country Club is located in a very mountainous region in North Vancouver. This

Vancouver

semi-private club is only open to the public Mondays through Fridays.

Burnaby Mountain Golf Club
7600 Halifax St., Burnaby
☎280-7355
The Burnaby Mountain Golf Club is located in a lovely setting, close to Simon Fraser University (SFU), 15min east of Vancouver.

Riverway Golf Course
9001 Riverway Pl., Burnaby
☎280-4653
The Riverway Golf Course is another beautiful golf course in Burnaby.

Westwood Plateau
Golf & Country Club
3251 Plateau Blvd., Coquitlam
☎552-0777 or 800-580-0785
The Westwood Plateau Golf & Country Club, a golf course with spectacular scenery and grounds is located in Coquitlam, a suburb northeast of Vancouver. Be advised, however, that the golf marshal is not overly fond of slow players and, considering the $99-$145 greens fee, you had best be a fine player!

Driving Ranges in Vancouver and Surrounding Areas

University Golf Club
5185 University Boulevard
☎224-1818

Musqueam Golf Club
3904 West 51st Avenue
☎266-2334.
An executive 18-hole par 60 course.

Seymour Golf and Country Club
3723 Mt. Seymour Parkway
North Vancouver
☎929-2611

Riverway Golf Course
9001 Riverway Place, Burnaby
☎280-4653

Westwood Plateau
Golf & Country Club
3251 Plateau Boulevard, Coquitlam
☎552-0777

Mayfair Lakes Golf Course
5460 No. 7 Road, Richmond
☎276-0505

Pitch & Putt

Pitch & Putt is a simplified version of golf. Although the rules are quite similar, you don't necessarily have to be a practiced golfer to play.

For about $12 per person (equipment included), you can spend a pleasant day with your friends or family outside amidst flowers and impeccable greenery. Vancouver has three Pitch & Putt courses, the best-known being the one in **Stanley Park** *(Parks Office,*

2099 Beach Ave., ☎*257-8400).* The other two are in **Queen Elizabeth Park** *(*☎*874-8336),* which stretches south of town, and **Rupert Park** *(3402 Charles St.,* ☎*257-8364),* to the east.

Health Clubs

If you are a member of a gym in your own country or home town, **your card could be accepted in Vancouver**. Many clubs, in fact, are part of international organizations. Check whether your card is valid by contacting your club or those in Vancouver. Those listed below are all located in the Vancouver area.

Bentall Centre Athletic Club
4 Bentall Centre, 1055 Dunsmuir St.
☎**689-4424**
The Bentall Centre Athletic Club is a typical business club, located in the business district.

Denman Fitness Company
1731 Comox St.
☎**688-2484**
Denman Fitness Company is a small, very pleasant neighbourhood sports club with many gay members.

Fitness Quest Gym
444 West Sixth Ave.
☎**879-7855**
The Fitness Quest Gym is a well-equipped independent club.

Fitness World
1214 Howe St.
☎**681-3232**
Fitness World is part of the biggest chain of health clubs in Vancouver.

Fitness World
1989 Marine Dr., North Vancouver
☎**986-3487**
This centre is the largest and poshest link in the Fitness World chain. An absolute must. Easy parking.

Fitness World
555 West 12th Ave.
☎**876-1009**
This Fitness World is ultra-high-tech and sometimes jam-packed at the end of the day.

Olympic Athletic Club
212 First Ave. W.
☎**708-9441**
Located far to the west of the city, this club has an excellent reputation.

RZ Sports Club
200-1807 West First Ave.
☎**737-4355**
This gym has both a mixed and a women-only section.

Vancouver

Cross-country Skiing

Less than a 30min drive from Vancouver, three ski resorts welcome snow-lovers from morning to evening. In **Cypress Provincial Park**, on Cypress Mountain (*$15; ☎926-5612*) there are nearly 25km of mechanically maintained trails suitable for all categories of skiers. These trails are frequented day and evening by cross-country skiers. There are also trails at Grouse Mountain (*☎984-0661*) and Mount Seymour Provincial Park (*☎986-2261*).

Downhill Skiing and Snowboarding

What makes Vancouver a truly magical place is the combination of sea and mountains. The cold season is no exception, as residents desert the beaches and seaside paths to crowd the ski hills, which are literally suspended over the city. There are four ski resorts close to the city: **Mount Seymour** (*$29; 1700 Mount Seymour Rd., North Vancouver; Upper Level Hwy. heading east, Deep Cove Exit, ☎986-2261*), a family resort with beginner trails, situated east of North Vancouver, above Deep Cove; **Grouse Mountain** (*$35; 6400 Nancy Greene Way, North Vancouver; ☎984-0661*), a small resort accessible by cable car, which offers an unobstructed view of Vancouver that is as magnificent by day as it is by night; **Cypress Mountain** (*$42; from North Vancouver, take Trans-Canada Highway 1, heading west for 16km, then follow road signs; ☎926-5612*), a resort for the most avid skiers, also offers magnificent views of Howe Sound and of the city. For more affordable skiing, try the village-style **Hemlock Valley Resort** (*$34.50; Hwy. 1 heading*

east, Agassizou Harrisson Hot Springs Exit; ☎ *515-6300 or 866-515-6300).* Situated at the eastern tip of Vancouver's urban area, in the heart of the Cascade Mountains, this resort boasts an abundance of snow and a spectacular view of Mount Baker in the United States. As soon as enough snow blankets the slopes, in late November or early December, these four ski resorts are open every day until late at night, thanks to powerful neon lighting. It should be noted, however, that the first three resorts do not provide accommodation (consult Burrard Inlet in the "Accommodations" section, p 184 for the nearest hotels).

Those who prefer skiing outside the metropolitan area can head to Whistler (see p 305).

Accommodations

There are more than 10,000 hotel rooms in the downtown core and another 8,000 in the surrounding area. They include hotels, motels, bed and breakfasts, inns and hostels. According to Tourism Vancouver, the average rate is just over $100, with the lowest at around $60. In our experi-

ence, however, during peak summer season, you'll pay well over $150 for a decent room and over $200 for really top-notch digs. We've included reviews in all price ranges for those looking for the best value for their money, as well as for those looking for the best the city has to offer.

Accommodations can be booked for you by Super, Natural British Columbia Reservation and Information Service:

☎ ***800-HELLO-BC (North America)***
☎ ***(250) 387-1642 (overseas)***
☎ ***(604) 663-6000 (Greater Vancouver)***

Ulysses's Picks

Vancouver

Chinatown and East Vancouver

See map p 89.

Simon Fraser University
$
sb, ℝ
Room 212, McTaggart-Cowan Hall,
Burnaby
☎*291-4503*
⇥*291-5598*
This hill-top student residence is available from May to August. A room for two with linens costs $45 a night, while a single room with linens is $26, $20 without. SFU is 20 km east of downtown Vancouver.

Apricot Cat & Black Dog Bed and Breakfast
$$ bkfst incl.
pb/sb, 🐾
628 Union St.
☎*215-9898*
⇥*255-9271*
www.apricotcat.com
The Apricot Cat Guest House is an old restored house that is located east of downtown in the historic neighbourhood of Strathcona, near Chinatown. Despite the establishment's name, there is no cat—Apricot or otherwise—in the house, just a friendly dog. Breakfast is extended continental, with home-made goodies. Guests have access to a refrigerator, microwave, and self-serve coffee and tea. The atmo-

sphere is cozy, the five rooms are bright and airy, and you can have your breakfast on the deck with a view of the garden. An excellent choice for those on a budget who don't mind being somewhat removed from the downtown core. Telephone and fax available to guests.

Downtown

Vancouver Downtown YHA
$
sb
1114 Burnaby St.
☎*684-4565*
⇄*684-4540*
Vancouver Downtown YHA is a big hostel (223 beds) right downtown at the corner of Thurlow. Common kitchen and TV room; coin-laundry. Private rooms available.

Global Village Backpackers
$
1018 Granville St.
☎*682-8226*
⇄*682-8240*
A mostly young crowd has been lugging their backpacks along Granville Street's busy Entertainment District and up the stairs to Global Village since 1999. The place offers 220 four- and two-bed rooms, as well as a few private rooms. A frenetic, no-frills, colourful atmosphere reigns. Book a

few weeks in advance from May to October.

YMCA
$
sb, ≈, ℜ
955 Burrard St.
☎*681-0221*
⇄*681-1630*
This establishment on the corner of Nelson Street is not actually restricted to men; families are also welcome. The building is fairly new and offers rooms accommodating from one to four people, as well as laundry service.

YWCA
$$-$$$
pb/sb, ℝ, ≡
733 Beatty St.
☎*895-5830 or 800-663-1424*
⇄*681-2550*
www.ywcahotel.com
Forget whatever images you had of lodgings beginning with a *Y*. Far from dreary, this purpose-built (1995) high-rise offers 155 private rooms on 11 floors, each simply but brightly decorated and equipped with all the essentials. Open to men, women and families, it's safe and centrally located across from BC Place Stadium. In addition, it's a non-profit establishment, with proceeds invested in YWCA community programs. Guests have access to three common kitchens and can choose from a variety of room types. Discounts for seniors

Vancouver

and students. The only competition in the vicinity is the Kingston and the Victorian (see below), and a number of dreary motels and motor inns. Inexpensive private parking.

Kingston Hotel
Bed and Breakfast
$$-$$$ bkfst incl.
sb/pb, ○
757 Richards St.
☎*684-9024 or 888-713-3304*
⇌*684-9917*
www.kingstonhotelvancouver.com
This family-owned hotel, built in 1910, is a favourite with budget-conscious travellers—and with good reason. It offers 55 clean rooms, which range in size from a very small room with a sink and a shared bathroom (down the hall) to a large double-bedded room with desk, TV, armchairs, hair dryer and bathtub. All rooms have telephones and windows that open, and guests have ac-

cess to a coin-operated laundry, storage and sauna. Strictly no frills, however, this four-storey hotel has no elevator. A courtyard patio with a pub is in the works. Excellent downtown location. Continental breakfast.

🐚 **Victorian Hotel**
$$-$$$ bkfst incl.
pb/sb, K
514 Homer St.
☎*681-6369 or 877-681-6369*
⇌*681-8776*
www.victorian-hotel.com
More charming than the Kingston and the YWCA but still in the budget category, the Victorian Hotel is without a doubt the best deal in downtown Vancouver. Spotless and attractive, all rooms feature feather duvets, hardwood floors, high ceilings and sinks; some have antique furniture, bay windows and bathtubs. All rooms have telephones and TVs and there are laundry facilities

---

○ **ACCOMMODATIONS**

1. Best Western Downtown Vancouver	12. Sheraton Vancouver Wall Centre
2. Bosman's Hotel	13. Sutton Place Hotel
3. Fairmont Hotel Vancouver (R)	14. Terminal City Club
4. Fairmont Waterfront Hotel	15. Travelodge Vancouver Centre
5. Global Village Backpackers	16. Vancouver Downtown YHA
6. Hampton Inn & Suites	17. Victorian Hotel
7. Kingston Hotel	18. Wedgewood Hotel (R)
8. Le Soleil Hotel	19. Westin Grand
9. Metropolitan Hotel	20. YWCA
10. Pan Pacific Hotel Vancouver	
11. Sandman Hotel	(R) establishment with restaurant (see description)

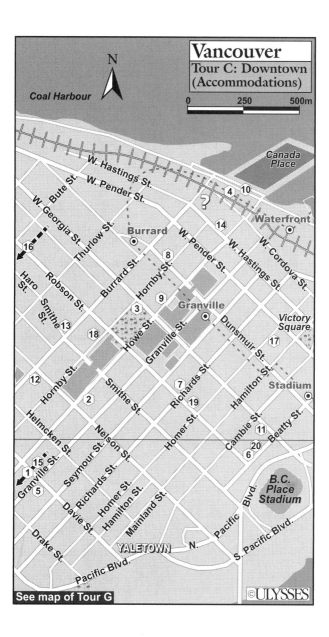

Vancouver

Tour C: Downtown (Accommodations)

Coal Harbour

N

0   250   500m

Canada Place

W. Hastings St.

W. Pender St.

4 10

?

14

Waterfront

Burrard

W. Pender St.

W. Hastings St.

W. Cordova St.

8

Bute St.

W. Georgia St.

Thurlow St.

16

Haro St.

Robson St.

Smithe St.

Burrard St.

Hornby St.

9

Granville

Dunsmuir St.

Victory Square

3

Granville St.

Howe St.

17

13

18

Hamilton St.

12

Hornby St.

2

Smithe St.

7

Richards St.

19

Homer St.

Stadium

Cambie St.

Beatty St.

11

Helmcken St.

Nelson St.

20

6

15

Granville St.

1

5

Seymour St.

Richards St.

Homer St.

Hamilton St.

B.C. Place Stadium

Davie St.

Mainland St.

Pacific Blvd.

Drake St.

YALETOWN

N.

Pacific

S. Pacific Blvd.

Pacific Blvd.

See map of Tour G

©ULYSSES

on-site and reasonably priced, secure parking ($10). Bike rentals are also offered. A continental breakfast is included. Your hosts Miriam and Andrew speak German, French, Dutch, Czech and Slovak, to the delight of their many European guests. A real find.

Travelodge Vancouver Centre
$$$
ℜ, ≡, ≈
1304 Howe St.
☎*682-2767*
⇄*682-6225*

The Travelodge Vancouver Centre offers a discount to seniors and groups. Relax in the heated outdoor pool before dining at its restaurant.

Bosman's Hotel
$$$
≡, ≈, ℜ, 🐾
1060 Howe St.
☎*682-3171 or 888-BOSMANS*
⇄*684-4010*
www.bosmanhotel.com

Bosman's Hotel is in the heart of the city, close to the Vancouver Art Gallery. The rooms are spacious and modern.

Sandman Hotel
$$$$
ℜ, ℝ, ≡, 🐾, ⊛
180 West Georgia St.
☎*681-2211*
⇄*681-8009*

Situated near theatres and downtown, the Sandman Hotel has some 300 com-

fortable rooms. The Shark Club (see p 225) is the hotel restaurant.

Hampton Inn & Suites
$$$$ bkfst incl
☺, ≡, ℝ, ≡
111 Robson St.
☎*602-1008*
⇄*602-1007*

The rooms at the Hampton Inn & Suites are spacious and cozy. Only a stone's throw away from the major theatres and the Library Square.

🌴 Westin Grand
$$$$-$$$$$
K, ≡, =, ☺, ℜ, △
433 Robson St.
☎*602-1999 or 888-680-9393*
⇄*647-2502*
www.westingrandvancouver.com

A new kid on the block (1999), the all-suite Westin Grand has become a highlight among downtown hotels in no time at all. Its suites offer floor-to-ceiling windows for some incredible city views. Decorated in warm sand tones with beech and walnut furnishings and original artwork, they are tasteful and understated, and the beds, linens, showers and soaker tubs are designed with the utmost comfort in mind. Furthermore, the service is friendly and professional throughout. An excellent spot for business travellers, 23 of its 207 suites are fully equipped "guest offices." Conveniently located within easy walking distance of Yaletown, the heart of the downtown core, Gastown and Chinatown. Highly recommended.

Best Western Downtown Vancouver
$$$$$

⌂, ☺, ≡, K, 🐾

718 Drake St., corner Granville St.

☎*669-9888*

≈669-3440

Facing Granville Street, this brand-new, comfortable hotel is situated near interesting attractions. If you don't have a car, there's a bus stop just before the entrance to the Granville Bridge.

Terminal City Club
$$$$$

ℜ, ☺, ≈, ≡, ⌂, K, ⊛

837 West Hastings St.

☎*681-4121*

≈681-9634

www.tcclub.com

The favourite place for business travellers, this luxurious establishment has an elegant style. It has 60 cozy rooms with a cheerful decor. Its poolroom, golf simulator, ocean view and attentive service will make your stay memorable.

Fairmont Waterfront Hotel
$$$$$$

≈, ☺, 🐾, ≡, ⌂, ℜ

900 Canada Place Way

☎*691-1991 or 800-441-1414*

≈691-1999

The Fairmont Waterfront Hotel is a luxury hotel lo-

cated just a few steps from Gastown. It has 489 rooms.

Le Soleil Hotel
$$$$$$

ℜ, ≡, 🐕

567 Hornby St.

☎*632-3000 or 877-632-3030*

www.lesoleilhotel.com

The Sun King would have been so proud. This swish and stylish boutique hotel, housing 119 suites, was purpose built in Vancouver's financial district in 1999, on the vanguard of Vancouver's burgeoning boutique hotel scene. From its opulent, gilded lobby to the 18ft vaulted ceilings and black whirlpool bath in its magnificent penthouse suite, each suite is magnificently done up in shades of gold or crimson, with blond-wood furniture and brocade duvets on beds with padded headboards. Each has an in-room safe, two TVs so you never have to miss your favourite programs, bedside cordless phone, deep soaker tub, high-speed Internet hook-ups, as well as the usual accoutrements (coffee makers, ironing boards, etc.). True to European style, the rooms are a tad on the cozy (i.e. small) side, but their style and comfort is undeniable. The daily newspaper is delivered to your door, along with fruit and bottled water. While the price tag is clearly beyond the reach of many, inquire about the off-peak rates, which may actually be a relatively good deal.

Wedgewood Hotel

$$$$$$

☉, △, ≡, ℜ, ℝ

845 Hornby St.

☎ *689-7777 or 800-663-0666*

⇄ *668-3074*

www.wedgewoodhotel.com

The Wedgewood Hotel is small enough to have retained some character and style. In particular, It features a lovely lobby complete with shiny brass accents, cozy fireplace and distinguished art, and is large enough to offer a certain measure of privacy and professionalism. This is a popular option for business trips, with an on-site business centre, and romantic weekend getaways.

Fairmont Hotel Vancouver

$$$$$$

≈, ☉, △, ℜ, ✻, ۞, ≡

900 West Georgia St.

☎ *684-3131 or 800-441-1414*

⇄ *662-1929*

www.fairmont.com

The storied Hotel Vancouver, formerly a Canadian Pacific Hotel, is actually the third incarnation of the hotel by this name. Completed in 1939 in the château-style characteristic of Canadian railway hotels, it replaced two earlier Hotel Vancouvers, the first located at Georgia and Granville (1887), the second nearby

on the site of Pacific Centre Mall (1916). Soon after opening, it hosted George VI and Queen Elizabeth, the first British monarchs to visit Canada. You will find tranquillity and luxury in the heart of downtown near Robson Street and Burrard Street. The hotel has some 550 rooms and a popular on-site bar.

Metropolitan Hotel

$$$$$$

☉, ⊛, ≡, ✻, ℜ, △, ≈

645 Howe St.

☎ *687-1122 or 800-667-2300*

⇄ *689-7044*

The Metropolitan Hotel is located right downtown, just steps from the business district. These luxury accommodations also have a luxurious price tag. Diva, the hotel's restaurant, has a pleasant staff and a cozy ambiance, and is worth trying.

Pan Pacific Hotel Vancouver

$$$$$$

≡, ⊛, ☉, ≈, △, ℜ, ✻, ℝ

300-999 Canada Place

☎ *662-8111*

☎ *800-663-1515 in Canada*

☎ *800-937-1515 in the US*

⇄ *685-8690*

www.panpacific.com

The luxurious Pan Pacific Hotel Vancouver is located in Canada Place, on the shore of Burrard Inlet facing North Vancouver. Everyone from Elizabeth Taylor to Sly Stallone has called the landmark Pan Pacific home. Connected to Canada Place and the Vancouver Convention and Exhibition Centre, its fabulous atrium lobby with fountain and armchairs looks out over the harbour, where sea planes land and cruise ships dock, and the Coastal Mountains to the north—apparently, Liz couldn't tear herself away from the window of her deluxe suite. All of the 504 rooms were recently redecorated and feature tasteful neutral tones, with bird's-eye maple furnishings and feather duvets. High-speed Internet access in all rooms.

Sheraton Wall Centre Hotel
$$$$$$
ℜ, ☺, 🐾, △, ≡, ℝ, *K*, ✪, ≈
1088 Burrard St.
☎*331-1000 or 800-663-9255*
⇄*331-1001*
www.sheratonwallcentre.com
With the recent addition of a second tower (2001), this mega-hotel now offers over 700 guest rooms and takes up an entire city block. The best feature of the guest rooms is their floor-to-ceiling windows, offering an unequalled city view and as much natural light as you can get in this frequently overcast city. The contemporary decor is understated, warm and tasteful, with

beige tones, gorgeous linens and duvets, and original photographs taken on site. The decor in the original south tower, which dates from 1996, is still fresh and attractive. All rooms have safes, bathrobes, irons, hair dryers and coffee makers, as well as high-speed, ethernet Internet access via a TV screen and wireless keyboard. A plethora of meeting rooms and up-graded "club" rooms make this a choice lodging for business travellers with a hefty expense account.

The West End

Buchan Hotel
$$
sb/pb, ℜ
1906 Haro St.
☎*685-5354 or 800-668-6654*
⇄*685-5367*
Buchan Hotel is located in the West End residential area, near Stanley Park, beneath the trees. At the end of Haro Street, on Lagoon Drive, three municipal tennis courts are accessible to guests. Other tennis courts, a golf course and hiking trails can be found near this 61-room, three-storey hotel. Smoking on the premises is prohibited. Children under 12 free.

Vancouver

Barclay Hotel
$$$
≡, ℜ, ℝ
1348 Robson St.
☎*688-8850*
⇌*688-2534*
www.barclayhotel.com
Of the handful of budget
accommodations concen-
trated at the intersection of
Robson and Broughton
streets, the Barclay, along
with the Robsonstrasse (see
below) are probably the
least objectionable choices.
That being said, its 90
rooms are rather
shabby—the tiny windows
and the flickering fluores-
cent lights make for a dark,
uninviting ambiance, ade-
quate only for those who
plan on spending more
time in nearby Stanley Park
than in their room.

 Sylvia Hotel
$$$
K, ℜ, ✘
1154 Gilford St.
☎*681-9321*
⇌*682-3551*
www.sylviahotel.com
Located just a few steps
from English Bay, this
charming old hotel, built in
the early 1900s, offers unspoiled views and has 118
simple rooms. People come
for the atmosphere, but also
for food and drink at the
end of the day. For those
on lower budgets, rooms
without views are offered at
lower rates. The manager of
this ivy-covered hotel is a
Frenchman who is fully and
justifiably dedicated to his
establishment. Request a
southwest-facing room (one
facing English Bay) in order
to benefit from magical
sunsets over the bay.

⬡ ACCOMMODATIONS

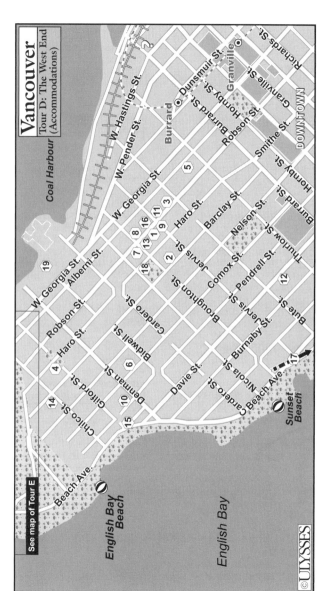

Vancouver
Tour D: The West End (Accommodations)

See map of Tour E

Coal Harbour

English Bay Beach

Sunset Beach

English Bay

DOWNTOWN

© ULYSSES

Tropicana Motor Inn
$$$
K, ℜ, ⌂, ≈
1361 Robson St.
☎687-6631
⇌687-5724

The relatively affordable Tropicana Motor Inn is another dreary option on this hotel-heavy corner. Its shabby rooms are all equipped with kitchenettes, its beds are uncomfortable, the hallway is redolent with the odours of other peoples' cooking and the elevator is mind-numbingly slow—and it isn't even particularly cheap! Nevertheless, like its equally shabby neighbours, it is well located and might be acceptable to people who are watching their pennies.

Robsonstrasse Hotel
$$$
K, ≡, ☉
1394 Robson St.
☎687-1674 or 888-667-8877
⇌685-7808
www.robsonstrassehotel.com

The Robsonstrasse Hotel is another relatively affordable Robson Street option, and is similar to that of the Tropicana (see above).

Oceanside Hotel
$$$
K, ≡, 🐕
1847 Pendrell St.
☎682-5641

The Oceanside Hotel is a small hotel offering complete apartments, with separate bedrooms. Well located in the West End a walk away from the major attractions.

Greenbrier Hotel
$$$-$$$$
K
1393 Robson St.
☎683-4558
⇌669-3109

The Greenbrier Hotel is popular with globetrotters. You'll meet world travellers who have decided to take a break in Vancouver, that is, if the cold, indifferent reception doesn't turn you off first. Weekly and monthly rates.

Rosellen Suites
$$$$
K, ℨ
2030 Barclay St.
☎689-4807
⇌684-3327
www.rosellensuites.com

Located in the heart of the West End near Stanley Park and downtown, these completely furnished suites have one or two bedrooms, kitchenettes and all the modern conveniences. They can be rented on a short- or long-term basis. Cost varies slightly depending upon the length of stay. Minimum three-night stay. Laundry facilities.

Blue Horizon Hotel
$$$$
ℜ, △, ≈, ≡, ⊛, ⊘, ℝ
1225 Robson St.
☎ *688-1411 or 800-663-1333*
⇌ *688-4461*
Each of the Blue Horizon's 214 rooms affords an exceptional view of the city. Reasonably priced meals are served in the interior "granite" decor or out on the terrace facing Robson Street. Banquet rooms and special features for those with hearing impairments.

West End Guest House Bed & Breakfast
$$$$ bkfst incl.
⊛
1362 Haro St.
☎ *681-2889 or 888-546-3327*
⇌ *688-8812*
www.westendguesthouse.com
This Victorian-style B&B houses eight cozy guest rooms, all decorated with the requisite flowered wallpaper and antiques, as well as ceiling fans and luxurious linens. Some of the rooms are a bit small, however, and most have showers rather than baths. Attentive host Evan Penner likes his guests to socialize, so he offers an informal afternoon sherry service by the cozy gas fire in the living room. An elaborate full breakfast is served and cookies await at bedtime. A popular, gay-friendly spot. Children over 12 are welcome.

Parkhill Hotel
$$$$
⊘, ℜ, △, ≈, ≡, ℝ
1160 Davie St.
☎ *685-1311 or 800-663-1525*
⇌ *681-0208*
www.parkhillhotel.com
The Parkhill Hotel is right in the middle of Vancouver's gay village. Despite their purely utilitarian furnishings, the rooms are comfortable and offer a truly phenomenal view of English Bay from the 18th floor upwards ($20 surcharge). Originally built as apartments, each guest room is actually a very spacious studio suite with a king-size or two queen-size beds, ordinary furnishings and a balcony with sliding glass doors for you to really appreciate the view. Inexpensive parking available. A very good, mid-range option. Don't bother with the overpriced buffet breakfast, though—there are plenty of much better options right nearby.

Barclay House in the West End
$$$$ bkfst incl.
ˢ̃
1351 Barclay St.
☎ *605-1351 or 800-971-1351*
⇌ *605-1382*
www.barclayhouse.com
This five-room Victorian bed and breakfast provides personalized service and a conservative, neutral-toned decor. From the West room, a small room with king-size sleigh bed and its own bal-

cony, to the garden suite, a cozy hideaway with its own entrance and gas fire place, all rooms are furnished with antiques, luscious down duvets, bathrobes, telephones, VCRs and CD players. A three-course breakfast is served, and sherry and cookies await in the sitting room, by the grand piano. Off-season rates are a super value.

Empire Landmark Hotel
$$$$$
®, ☉, ℜ, ◠, ≈, ≡, ℝ
1400 Robson St.
☎*687-0511 or 800-830-6144*
⇄*687-2801*
www.asiastandard.com/hotel/van couver

The recently renovated Empire Landmark Hotel truly is a landmark, with 40 floors and a revolving restaurant and bar at the top. The view is wonderful and quite an experience!

Vancouver's Suites By the Sea
$$$$$
K, ☉, ⅏, 🐾
The Meridien at 910 Beach
☎*609-5100*
⇄*609-5111*

Suites by the Sea offers one- to three-bedroom suites or small apartments with a magnificent view of the sea. Fully equipped kitchen and washer and dryer. Rates vary according to the length of stay. Many interesting attractions nearby.

Coast Plaza Hotel and Suites
$$$$$
≈, ◠, ☉, ℜ, K, 🐾, ≡
1763 Comox St.
☎*688-7711 or 800-663-1144*
⇄*688-5934*

If you are looking for a big, modern, American-style hotel close to the beach, this 267-room establishment is a good choice. The restaurant serves everything, and the food is decent.

Carmana Plaza
$$$$$$
K, ☉, ≡
1128 Alberni St.
☎*683-1399*
⇄*683-1391*

The Carmana Plaza is a luxurious, all-suite facility. Each suite has a view of the sea or city. Enjoy its numerous amenities, including a kitchen, office and conference rooms for business travellers, fitness centre, cleaning service, security guard and parking.

Listel Vancouver
$$$$$$
≡, ℜ, ☉
1300 Robson St.
☎*684-8461 or 800-663-5491*
⇄*684-7092*
www.listel-vancouver.com

This six-storey, 129-room hotel has recently decked out most of its rooms with works of art from local galleries (fourth and fifth floors) and the Museum of Anthropology (sixth floor). The latter, our favourite, achieve a contemporary, minimalist look by means of pale, neutral colours, cedar and hemlock furnishings (most B.C.-made), natural fabrics and Northwest Coast artwork (for sale). Gallery rooms have a more traditional hotel decor, albeit spruced up by mahogany furnishings, comfortable armchairs, window seats and original artwork. Strangely enough, however, the museum floors are the less expensive of the two. There are also two floors of standard rooms awaiting renovations. On site, O'Doul's Restaurant and Bar stages jazz acts Thursdays to Saturdays.

Pacific Palisades Hotel
$$$$$$
≈, ℜ, ℝ, K, ⊙, ≡, ⊛, 🐕
1277 Robson St.
☎*688-0461 or 800-663-1815*
⇄*688-4374*
www.pacificpalisadeshotel.com
The Pacific Palisades Hotel is part of the Kimpton Group Hotels chain. Its two towers, totalling 233 rooms, offer peekaboo views of the sea and the mountains. Recently completely revamped, the new decor is clearly meant to endear the establishment with a young (or young at heart), well-heeled clientele. Described as "South Beach meets Stanley Park," its look is fun, modern and retro, with a little whimsy thrown in for good measure. The guest rooms, all suites, are

decked out in lime-green and yellow, with furnishings straight out of the Ikea catalogue. It is entirely too big to be a boutique hotel, as the PR would have you believe, but this truly is a fun place, unique in the city. A big pool and a well-equipped gymnasium are available to guests. The staff is friendly and professional.

Westin Bayshore Resort
$$$$$$
ℜ, △, ≈, ≡, 🐕, ⊙, ✿
1601 Bayshore Dr.
☎*682-3377*
⇄*687-3102*
www.westinbayshore.com
The Westin Bayshore Resort is a very classy place. Its setting is typically "Vancouver" with the surrounding mountains, the proximity of the sea and the city. The 510 rooms each have their own charm, not to mention the stunning views. Staying here is like staying at a tropical resort.

Sutton Place Hotel
$$$$$$
⊛, ⊙, ≈, △, ℝ, ℜ, ≡, 🐕
845 Burrard St.
☎*682-5511 or 800-961-7555*
⇄*682-5513*
www.suttonplace.com
The Sutton Place Hotel has 397 rooms and the full range of five-star services normally provided by the top hotel chains. The decor, all peachy pinks, coffered ceilings, elaborate mouldings, golden chandeliers

and marble, drips with traditional European elegance. Next to the main hotel is La Grande Résidence, a travel apartment for stays of a week or more. It's a favourite with film crews. If you are a chocolate lover, don't miss the chocolate buffet *(Thu-Sat 6pm and 8:30pm)*. And not only can you bring Whiskers, you can even regale her with Alberta T-bone or fresh tuna steak and caviar!

Executive Accommodations
$800/week
K, 🦜, 🐾, ⊘
☎*800-557-8483*
"Like home" is the motto of the Executive Accommodations chain, which offers apartments and completely furnished homes, including daily cleaning service.

🌴 Chez Phillipe
$1,750/month
K
☎*649-2817*
Chez Phillipe is located in the heart of Vancouver in the West End neighbourhood, two steps away from False Creek in a very resort-like setting. It's a luxurious apartment on the 17th floor of a modern highrise built at the entrance to the Seawall. Guests

can cook for themselves and have access to a dishwasher, a washing machine and a dryer as well as a full bathroom with a separate shower and a terrace.

Burrard Inlet

See map p 123.

Horseshoe Bay Motel
$$
6588 Royal Ave., West Vancouver
☎*921-7454*
⇄*921-7464*
The Horseshoe Bay Motel, in the chic neighbourhood of West Vancouver, is advantageously located near the charming little town of Horseshoe Bay and the dock for the ferry to Nanaimo on Vancouver Island.

Canyon Court Inn and Suites
$$$
≡, ≈, *K*
1748 Capilano Rd., North Vancouver
☎*988-3181 or 888-988-3181*
⇄*904-2755*
www.canyoncourt.com
Canyon Court Inn and Suites is located right next to the Capilano Suspension Bridge, the Lions Gate Bridge and the Trans-Canada Highway. It is very comfortable and reasonably priced.

Grouse Inn
$$$ bkfst incl.
≡, ≈, *K*, ℜ
1633 Capilano Rd., North Vancouver
☎*988-7101 or 800-779-7888*
⇜*988-7102*

The Grouse Inn, located close to the Grouse Mountain cable car, is great for those who like to be near the mountains.

Capilano Bed & Breakfast
$$$ bkfst incl.
K, ℜ
1374 Plateau Dr.
☎*990-8889 or 877-990-8889*
⇜*990-5177*
www.capilanobb.com

The Capilano Bed & Breakfast is located close to Lions Gate Bridge. Skiers can easily get to Cypress Mountain (15min) and Grouse Mountain (8min). Except during rush hour, the hotel is 5min from Stanley Park, 10min from downtown and Chinatown, and about 25min from the airport. The rooms are attractive, and some have nice views. The complete breakfasts are delicious. Prices for weekly stays can be negotiated.

Lonsdale Quay Hotel
$$$
≡, ⊘, ℜ, ℝ
123 Carrie Cates Court
North Vancouver
☎*986-6111 or 800-836-6111*
⇜*986-8782*
www.lonsdalequayhotel.com

The Lonsdale Quay Hotel is a lovely hotel set magnificently near the shores of Burrard Inlet, above the huge covered Quay Market. The rooms enjoy extraordinary views of downtown Vancouver.

Palms Guest House
$$$$ bkfst incl.
≡, ℝ, ℑ, ⊛
3042 Marine Dr.,
West Vancouver
☎*926-1159 or 800-691-4455*
⇜*926-1451*
www.palmsguesthouse.com

Palms Guest House offers luxurious, if somewhat over-decorated, rooms with private balconies and a view of the ocean. Inquire about off-season prices. Conveniently located for attractions in North and West Vancouver.

False Creek

See map p 131.

Granville Island Hotel
$$$$$
ℜ, ≡, 🐾, △
1253 Johnston St.
☎*683-7373 or 800-663-1840*
⇜*683-3061*
www.granvilleislandhotel.com

If you want to be really close to the market, you might enjoy staying at the Granville Island Hotel. Recently expanded, its 84 guest rooms offer a very acceptable, if rather generic, colonial-style decor. Try to get a room with a view of the water, offered for no extra charge. Rooms offer

Vancouver

all the standard accoutrements (hair dryers, coffee
makers, iron and board).
Excellent brew pub and
restaurant on site (see
p 212). The rates, however,
are comparable to those of
the city's finest downtown
hotels, and considering the
volume of traffic on the
island, many will probably
prefer to stay in the downtown area.

Opus Hotel
$$$$$$
ℜ, ≡, ℑ, ⊘, 🐾
322 Davie St.
☎*642-6787 or 866-642-6787*
⇄*642-6780*
www.opushotel.com
Vancouver's newest bou-
tique hotel opened during
the summer of 2002.
Purpose-built to blend in
with the neighbouring in-
dustrial brick buildings of
Yaletown, its 97
innovatively designed
rooms and suites sport one
of five different decor
schemes to appeal to differ-
ent lifestyle types, all of
them packing thick wallets.
Each provides contempo-
rary furnishings, European
bedding, robes and slip-
pers, 24-hour room service,
cordless telephones with
private voice mail, high-
speed Internet connections,
27" televisions and CD play-
ers. On-site bar and
brasserie-style restaurant to
see and be seen in. For the
spoilt starlet in you.

The West Side

See maps p 139 and p 215.

**Vancouver International Hostel
Jericho Beach**
$
pb/sb
1515 Discovery St.
☎*224-3208 or 888-203-4303*
⇄*224-4852*
www.hihostels.ca
Located in Jericho Park, this
youth hostel is open day
and night; take bus no. 4
from downtown to reach it.
With Locarno and Jericho
beaches nearby, this is a
great spot for budget travel-
lers. There are co-ed, men-
only and women-only
dormitories as well as pri-
vate rooms. The cafeteria is
open from April to October.
Members $18, non-members
$22.

**UBC Housing and
Conference Centre**
$-$$$
sb/pb, K, ℝ
5961 Student Union Blvd.
☎*822-1001*
⇄*822-1010*
www.conferences.ubc.ca
In addition to a year-round
48-suite hotel, the UBC
campus offers rental apartments from May to August.
Inexpensive and well lo-
cated near museums,
beaches and hiking trails,
this spot also provides
tranquility.

Johnson Heritage House Bed & Breakfast
$$$ bkfst incl.
ℑ, ⊛
May to Nov
2278 West 34th Ave., Kerrisdale
☎/⇄ *266-4175*
www.johnsons-inn-vancouver.com

The Johnson Heritage House Bed & Breakfast occupies a magnificent, fully renovated house from the 1920s with an extra floor added. The owners, Sandy and Ron Johnson, carried out the work and furnished the place with antiques.

Accommodations by Pillow Suites
$$$
ℝ, K, ℑ,
2859 Manitoba St.
☎ *879-8977*
⇄ *897-8966*
www.pillow.net

Accommodations by Pillow Suites is three adjacent heritage houses dating back to the early 1900s, and the decor and ambiance attest to it. Individually decorated with taste and originality, they are complete apartments with kitchens and living rooms. Not only lovely, they are also good value, especially for families or a small group of friends. Monthly rates available.

Penny Farthing Inn Bed & Breakfast
$$$ bkfst incl.
sb/pb, ℝ, ℑ
2855 W. Sixth Ave., V6K 1X2
☎ *739-9002 or 866-739-9002*
⇄ *739-9004*
www.pennyfarthinginn.com

A warm welcome awaits at Penny Farthing Inn, situated in lovely Kitsilano, a short distance from downtown. Easy-going host Lyn Hainstock has four guest rooms in her 1912 home, all brightly and cheerfully decorated. An experienced cook, Lyn prepares full breakfasts, which can be enjoyed in the dining room or the English garden. Three cats in residence. British-style country ambiance guaranteed.

Ramada Vancouver Centre
$$$$
ℜ, ≡, ℝ, 🐕
898 W. Broadway Ave.
☎ *872-8661*
⇄ *872-2270*
www.ramada.ca/vancinn.html

Located in Vancouver's West Side, this hotel belongs to the Ramada hotel chain, which specializes in accommodations for large groups and families. Comfortable rooms and impeccable, personalized service.

Vancouver

Plaza 500 Hotel
$$$$
ℜ, ℝ, ≡
500 W. 12th Ave.
☎*873-1811 or 800-473-1811*
⇄*873-5103*
www.plaza500.com
Located 15min by car from
downtown just after the
Cambie bridge, this recently
renovated hotel has attractive rooms, many with balconies, and a view of the
city. Broadway Street, only
2min away, has a variety of
shops, restaurants and bars.
The perfect place for large
groups or conferences.

Richmond

See map p 151.

If you need to stay near the
airport, here are a few
options in the Richmond
area.

Accent Inns
$$$
K, ℜ, ☺, ⊛, 🐾, ≡
10551 St. Edwards Dr.
☎*273-3311*
⇄*273-9522*
www.accentinns.com
This decent facility, located
near the airport, has com-
fortable rooms and a family-
style restaurant.

**Best Western Abercorn
Inn**
$$$
≡, ℜ, ⊛
9260 Bridgeport Rd.
☎*270-7576 or 800-663-0085*
⇄*270-0001*
The Best Western Abercorn
Inn is relatively affordable
for its category. It is located
close to the airport and
many shopping malls. A
good choice for travellers
looking for something halfway between the airport
and downtown.

**Radisson President Hotel and
Suites Vancouver Airport**
$$$$$
≈, ℝ, ℜ, ☺, ≡, K
8181 Cambie Rd.
☎*276-8181 or 800-333-3333*
⇄*279-8381*
www.radissonvancouver.com
Located near the airport, the
Radisson Hotel offers a high
level of comfort. Rooms
have coffee-makers and
refrigerators, as well as
work desks. Decor in the
guest rooms, meeting
rooms and restaurants is
modern and classic, providing a relaxing atmosphere.
Next to the hotel is a very
impressive Chinese super-
market with a Buddhist
temple above it; the hotel is
located in Richmond, a
suburb with a large Chinese
population.

Delta Vancouver Airport
$$$$$$
≈, ≡, ⊘, 🐕, ℜ
3500 Cessna Dr.
☎*278-1241 or 800-268-1133*
⇄*276-1975*
www.deltahotels.com
The exciting spectacle of planes and seaplanes landing is part of staying at the Delta Vancouver Airport. This hotel offers all the amenities you would expect in a Delta hotel. It is located on the edge of the airport, close to the Fraser River.

Restaurants

Food critics from far and wide have been waxing poetic lately on the subject of Vancouver's gastronomic blossoming. Canada's national newspaper, for example, calls Vancouver chefs "visionary" and "uninhibited." In creating their cuisine, known as Pacific Northwest, they take advantage of Vancouver's seaside location and emphasize fresh, local fish and seafood plus plenty of innovation. These days, salmon, the perennial West Coast favourite, is playing second fiddle to species like ahi tuna and delicate sablefish, also known as black cod. Vancouver's chefs also take their inspiration from the east, with plenty of Asian influences in cuisine, presentation and decor. In addition to Japanese and Chinese eateries, you'll find Indian, Malay, Italian, Greek and French cuisine, as well as seafood restaurants and fish-and-chip shops.

It has almost become cliché to refer to Vancouver's café culture. You'll find a café on nearly every street corner—including 151 Starbucks, at last count—most of which have patio seating for patrons who smoke. But those free of the caffeine addiction can also indulge in teas of every sort, including the very popular spiced East Indian chai, also available in herbal form but unfortunately often from a carton. Bubble tea, a Taiwanese invention, is also very trendy: essentially, it is a flavoured, milky tea drink served with a wide straw to suck up tapioca pearls floating on the bottom—an acquired taste (and sensation), to be sure.

Vegetarians will not be disappointed—in true West Coast style, you can get a veggie meal just about anywhere. Restaurateurs are highly conscious of the vegetarian trend and generally provide veggie options or adapt menu items on demand. Many chefs also use organic and cruelty-reduced ingredients, such as free-range eggs and chicken.

One particularly popular dining style worth mentioning is the tapas bar. While tapas have traditionally been associated with Spain, in Vancouver they come in all styles, but in the traditional size (small). They are essentially appetizer-size portions of just about anything, from soup to nuts, and make for a pleasant way to while away the cocktail hour. Also popular is brunch; a good many restaurants open for weekend brunch, when a special menu is provided.

Remember that smoking is not permitted in restaurants in Vancouver, North Vancouver or West Vancouver—hence the ubiquitous all-weather outdoor patio.

Finally, although dining out in Vancouver can be a costly affair, there are deals to be had. Some of the best ones are described in the following pages. Bon appétit!

Restaurants by Type of Cuisine

Breakfast

Cafés, tea rooms and light meals

Canadian

Vancouver

Vancouver's skyline offers an imposing background to the sailboats moored in its port.
- *C. Moreno*

The glow of a West Coast sunset with the five sails of Canada Place in the foreground.
- *Walter Bibikow*

Vancouver's Stanley Park is filled with flowering gardens, adding a splash of colour to this much-cherished green space. - *Tibor Bognàr*

Vegetarian only

Gastown and Surroundings

See map p 87.

The Old Spaghetti Factory
$-$$
53 Water St.
☎*684-1288*
With posters and photography on the walls and a cozy atmosphere, this restaurant serves up pasta at reasonable prices. Main courses come with hot sourdough bread, soup or salad, coffee or tea and ice cream.

India Village
$$
308 Water St.
☎*681-0678*
As you enjoy carefully prepared, authentic Indian cuisine, you can admire the steam-powered clock, as well as the hectic pace of the centre of Gastown.

Jewel of India
$$
52 Alexander St.
☎*687-5665*
This restaurant excels at making nan bread in its clay ovens, which perfectly accompany the popular, traditional Tandoori dishes.

Incendio Pizzeria
$$-$$$
103 Columbia St.
☎*688-8694*
(see review in "The West Side" p 218)

Water Street Cafe
$$$
300 Water St.
☎*689-2832*
The freshly baked bread that comes from the ovens of the Water Street Cafe accompanies the pasta and fish dishes. This contemporary-style restaurant has a laid-back, friendly ambiance.

Wild Rice
$$$
117 W. Pender St.
☎*642-2882*
Located on the edge of Chinatown (in more ways than one), Wild Rice is one of Vancouver's hippest, most exciting new restaurants. Abandon all preconceived notions of what Chinese cuisine looks and tastes like. Wild Rice has subdued lighting, groovy music, high ceilings and an ice-blue glow-in-the-dark resin bar—yes, it's a Chinese restaurant-cum-martini bar! The food isn't like anything you'll find in Chinatown either: you can order a selection of tapas-sized dishes *($9 and less)* or larger, main dishes *($10-$18)*. While the staples of Chinese cuisine are here, they are given a twist; even

more exciting are the many highly original menu items, such as the high-elevation-tea-smoked-duck salad on a tasty assortment of greens, or a B.C. sablefish roasted with ginger and served on a golden fried-rice paddy and sautéed moo qua—both delicious.

Raintree at the Landing
$$$$

375 Water St.

☎ *688-5570*

This restaurant offers West Coast cuisine in a beautiful, friendly dining room. Some interesting specialities are made with regional products, such as the restaurant's famous leg of lamb. Impressive wine list.

Chinatown and East Vancouver

See map p 89.

Chinatown

Gain Wah
$

218 Keefer St.

☎ *684-1740*

Treat yourself to crab, roasted chicken with tofu or the unique flavour of andouillette (a small sausage). Family-style quality cuisine.

Hon's Wun-Tun House
$

268 Keefer St.

☎ *688-0871*

This restaurant has been a Vancouver institution for more than 20 years. Its reasonably priced dishes, including traditional Chinese specialities, are all excellent. Sample some of the dishes in the noisy, jam-packed, canteen-style atmosphere. Efficient service. There is also a branch in the West End (see p 204).

Kam Gok Yuen
$

142 East Pender St.

☎ *683-3822*

This restaurant has a vast selection of mouth-watering dishes, such as Peking duck, which are often advertised in Chinese on the walls.

The Only Café
$

20 E. Hastings St.

☎ *681-6546*

A little hole in the wall in a not particularly appetizing part of the city, The Only Café is a local institution that offers some of Vancouver's best fish and chips. Takeout recommended.

Park Lock
$$

544 Main St.

☎ *688-1581*

Park Lock, which features traditional Cantonese cuisine, is a Vancouver institution. Shrimp, steak and pork chops are its specialities.

Pink Pearl Chinese Restaurant
$$
1132 E. Hastings St.
☎*253-4316*
This enormous seafood restaurant is a Vancouver institution. Dim sum is served daily and Cantonese and Szechuan cuisine are specialties.

East Vancouver

La Casa Gelato
$
1033 Venables St.
☎*251-3211*
Delicious gelato in every flavour imaginable, and then some.

Joe's Café
$
1150 Commercial Dr.
☎*255-1046*
This spot is frequented by a regular clientele of intellectuals and Sunday philosophers, among others. What brings them together, most of all, is Joe's coffee.

WaaZuBee Café
$
1622 Commercial Dr.
☎*253-5299*
The WaaZubee Café is an inexpensive treat. The innovative cuisine combined with the "natural-techno-italo-bizarre" decor are full of surprises. The pasta dishes are always interesting.

Nick's Spaghetti House
$-$$
631 Commercial Dr.
☎*254-5633*
Copious meals are served on red-and-white-checked tablecloths amidst landscape paintings of Capri and Sorrento. People are friendly here and patrons enter the restaurant through the kitchen, a reassuring element.

Sun Sui Wah Seafood Restaurant
$$
3888 Main St., at 23rd Ave.
☎*872-8822*
Authentic Chinese food, lobster, crayfish, crab, oysters and, of course, Peking duck, are served in a bright dining room. One of Vancouver's most highly rated Chinese restaurants.

Havana
$$-$$$
1212 Commercial Dr.
☎*253-9119*
This happening spot has an art gallery and performance

Vancouver

space in addition to a busy, inexpensive restaurant. Decorated with mismatched wood chairs, red velvet booths and graffiti, Havana's *nuevo Latino* menu has something for everyone, including interesting fish entrées, jambalaya, fried chicken, sandwiches, inspired salads and tapas. A good address to keep in mind.

The Cannery Seafood Restaurant
$$$
2205 Commissioner St.
☎*254-9606*
The Cannery is one of the best places in town for seafood. It is located in a renovated, century-old warehouse. The view of the sea is fantastic.

Downtown

Starbucks
$
1099 Robson St.
☎*685-1099*
1100 Robson St.
☎*685-7991*
822 Homer St.
☎*687-1187*
Vancouver has gone dotty over the green logo that marks the spot of Starbucks. At last count, 151 branches of this Seattle-based chain were scattered around Vancouver and surrounding areas. Capuccino, espresso, big, small, medium, strong, weak, decaf, with milk, cold with chocolate or nutmeg: the choice is yours. Charming terrace.

● RESTAURANTS

1. Aqua Riva
2. Bin 941 Tapas Parlour
3. CinCin
4. Da Pasta Bar
5. Dining Car
6. Diva at the Met
7. Elbow Room
8. Flying Wedge Pizza Co.
9. Gallery Café
10. Imperial Chinese Seafood
11. India Gate
12. Joe Fortes Seafood & Chop House
13. Kitto
14. L'Hermitage
15. Le Crocodile
16. Lucy Mae Brown
17. Malone's Bar & Grill
18. Olympia Seafood
19. Raku
20. Rex Rotisserie and Grill
21. Sakae Japanese Restaurant
22. Settebello
23. Starbucks
24. Subeez Café
25. Tsunami Sushi
26. White Spot

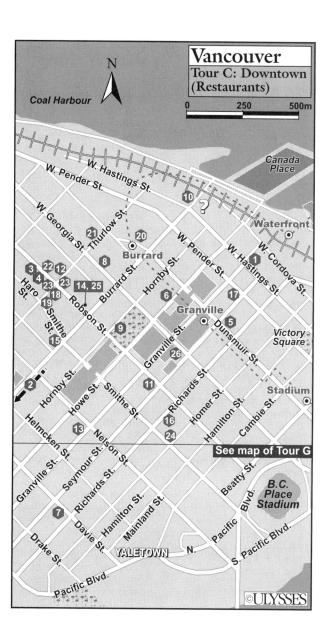

Vancouver
Tour C: Downtown (Restaurants)

0   250   500m

N

Coal Harbour

Canada Place

W. Hastings St.

W. Pender St.

W. Georgia St.

Thurlow St.

W. Pender St.

W. Hastings St.

W. Cordova St.

Waterfront

10

?

21

20

Burrard

8

Hornby St.

1

3 22 12

4 23 23 14, 25

Haro St.

19 18

Robson St.

Burrard St.

6

17

Granville

5

Smithe St.

15

9

Granville St.

Dunsmuir St.

Victory Square

26

2

Hornby St.

Howe St.

Smithe St.

11

Richards St.

Homer St.

Hamilton St.

Cambie St.

Stadium

13

Nelson St.

16

24

See map of Tour G

Helmcken St.

Seymour St.

Richards St.

Beatty St.

Pacific Blvd.

B.C. Place Stadium

Granville St.

7

Hamilton St.

Mainland St.

N.

S. Pacific Blvd.

Davie St.

Drake St.

YALETOWN

Pacific Blvd.

©ULYSSES

Dining Car

$

Mon to Fri noon to 2pm, Fri and Sat 5pm to 9pm
at the Railway Club
579 Dunsmuir St.
☎**681-1625**
A relaxing ambiance and family-style fare are served up at the Dining Car, where the clientele runs the gamut from suits to artists.

Flying Wedge Pizza Co.

$

Royal Centre, 1055 W. Georgia St.
☎**681-1233**
3499 Cambie St.
☎**732-8840**
Library Square
☎**689-7078**
These are addresses to jot down if you're looking for pizza that doesn't remind you of something you ate last week. You'll get a discount if you bring your own plate, showing that you're environmentally responsible. Also located in the West Side and the airport.

Kitto Japanese House on Granville

$

833 Granville St.
☎**687-6622**
All kinds of Japanese delicacies such as *sushi*, *robata* and *yakisoba* are available at Kitto. Reasonable prices and fast service.

Malone's Bar & Grill

$

608 West Pender St.
☎**684-9977**
You can enjoy steak, salmon, chicken, pizza or beer, all reasonably priced, while watching a hockey game on their giant screen. DJ music.

White Spot

$

580 West Georgia St.
☎**662-3066**
This restaurant belongs to the White Spot chain of restaurants established in the 1920s. A Vancouver institution, this family-style restaurant still has a great reputation and comfortable atmosphere. Its Triple O Hamburger has been and remains the all-time favourite of several generations.

Elbow Room

$

560 Davie St.
☎**685-3628**
The motto of this unique Vancouver institution is "service is our name, abuse is our game." Patrons who are brave enough to venture into the Elbow Room for all-day breakfast (try the B.C. Benny) will be mercilessly abused (read gently teased), particularly if they don't follow house rules (outlined in the menu). Single diners risk being auctioned off and those who don't finish their meals must make a donation to

charity. Among its many honours and awards, most notable is its award for "best surly and indifferent service." And if that doesn't make you feel at home, nothing will!

Gallery Café
$
8:30am to 5:30pm, Thu until 9pm
Vancouver Art Gallery, 750 Hornby St.
☎*688-2233*
Weary shoppers, downtown office workers and harried travel writers alike steal away from the crowds on Robson Street and into this lovely café, an oasis of calm in the Vancouver Art Gallery. In addition to cakes and squares at church-bake-sale prices, they also prepare sandwiches, quiches, salads and light entrées. Lovely patio.

Olympia Seafood
$
820 Thurlow St.
☎*685-0716*
Fishing for fast food like they make in the old country? Stop by this conveniently located downtown chippy for some very respectable cod, halibut or sole with chips.

Subeez Cafe
$-$$
891 Homer St.
☎*687-6107*
This enigmatic spot, a favourite casual hangout among locals, is open late

for drinks (great selection of B.C. beers, including selections from the wonderful Storm Brewery) and early enough for a late breakfast (11am) or brunch on weekends. The post-industrial decor features sky-high ceilings with suspended fans and eclectic art. All-day breakfast, interesting sandwich and salad selection, and ample vegetarian options.

Sakae Japanese Restaurant
$-$$
lunch only
745 Thurlow St.
☎*669-0067*
It is easy to walk right past this restaurant, situated in the basement of a commercial building. But the welcoming smiles and the quality of the food compensate for its location. The sushi and sashimi will literally melt in your mouth.

India Gate Restaurant
$$
616 Robson St.
☎*684-4617*
At India Gate, you can get a curry dish for as little as $5.95 at lunchtime. In the evening, this restaurant is rather deserted. The decor is not at all exotic.

Da Pasta Bar
$$
1232 Robson St.
☎*688-1288*
This Italian restaurant, located in the most refined

part of Robson Street, offers original items such as pasta with curry. Full lunches for $7.50. Pleasant decor.

Tsunami Sushi
$$
238-1025 Robson St.
☎*687-8744*

Tsunami Sushi has a revolving sushi bar, much like those in Japan, from which patrons can choose specialties at will. Excellent quality for the price. Huge, sunny terrace overlooking Robson Street.

Raku
$$
838 Thurlow St.
☎*685-8817*

A young Japanese clientele meets in this noisy bar with an open kitchen, where they prepare creative, delicious Japanese dishes, beyond what you'd get at a typical sushi bar. The grilled meats are recommende, as is the *yakisoba* (fried udon noodles).

Bin 941 Tapas Parlour
$$
closed Sun
941 Davie St.
☎*683-1246*

Tapas and tasty Pacific Northwest dishes are served in this popular spot, which is great for a late-night bite. Although long and narrow and short on leg room, the dining room is big on energy and atmosphere.

Settebello
$$
1133 Robson St.
☎*681-7377*

Settebello serves pizzas and salads with olive oil and Italian bread, in a attractive dining room and on a terrace decorated with flowers.

Imperial Chinese Seafood
$$-$$$$
355 Burrard St.
☎*688-8191*

Located in the Marine Building, an Art Deco architectural masterpiece (see p 103), this Chinese restaurant also has several Art Deco elements. It is the big windows over looking Burrard Inlet, however, that are especially fascinating. In this very elegant spot, young men in livery and discreet young women perform the *dim sum* ritual. Unlike elsewhere, there are no carts here: the various steamed dishes are brought on trays. You can also ask for a list, allowing you to choose your favourites among the 30 or so offered. The quality of the food matches the excellent reputation this restaurant has acquired.

Rex Rotisserie & Grill
$$$
1055 Dunsmuir St., Bentall Centre
☎*683-7390*

This American-style grill has a patio and a pleasant ambiance.

Aqua Riva
$$$-$$$$
200 Granville St.,
next to Canada Place
☎683-5599

Enjoy roasted and grilled meats, fish and seafood in a colourful ambiance with a magnificent view of Burrard Inlet.

🎖 L'Hermitage
$$$-$$$$
1025 Robson St.
☎689-3237

The chef-owner Hervé Martin is an artist when it comes to French cuisine. He can tell you stories from his days as the chef of the Belgian Royal Court. Wines from his native region of Burgundy accompany the finest of dishes, each prepared carefully and with panache. The decor is chic and the service exemplary. The terrace, set back from Robson, is lovely in the summertime.

🎖 Le Crocodile
$$$-$$$$
909 Burrard St., entry by Smithe St.
☎669-4298

This establishment is the beacon of French cuisine in Vancouver as much for the quality of its food as for its service, its decor and its wine list. Those who appreciate fine French cuisine will be spoiled by the choice of red meats and the delicacies from the sea. The salmon tartare is a must—

you *are* on the Pacific coast after all!

Lucy Mae Brown
$$$-$$$$ (restaurant)
$$ (lounge)
862 Richards St.
closed Mon
☎899-9199

Lucy Mae Brown may have been the keeper of a simple boarding house; she may also have been a madame with this address as her brothel. In fact, Lucy Mae has a double identity today, too: in the basement you'll find a lounge that attracts a young crowd (see p 224) while upstairs, a slightly older, more conservatively dressed crowd enjoys intimate tête-à-têtes to the strains of soft jazz from the cozy confines of circular blue-velvet booths. The much-lauded menu features simply prepared pasta and very reasonably priced, heartily prepared fillet of halibut Basquaise, free-range chicken and organic beef tenderloin. Reservations recommended.

CinCin
$$$-$$$$$
1154 Robson St.
☎688-7338

CinCin, a perennial downtown favourite, offers diners well-crafted, upscale Mediterranean and Italian food in a Tuscan-style dining room. On the menu you'll find such inspired items as pizza baked in an alderwood oven, organic pumpkin ravioli just like Mamma used to make, and local Dungeness crab risotto. Refreshingly courteous, professional service.

Diva at the Met
$$$$
Metropolitan Hotel
645 Howe St.
☎*602-7788*
Good contemporary Pacific Northwest cuisine and fine wine served up in a pleasant ambiance with elegant decor. A perennial favourite of Vancouver's jet set.

Joe Fortes Seafood and Chop House
$$$$
777 Thurlow St., at Robson
☎*669-1940*
Joe Fortes is renowned for its oysters and other seafood. With its turn-of-the-century decor and heated upstairs terrace, this bistro has an appetizing menu.

This is a popular meeting place for young professionals.

Bacchus Bar and Ristorante
$$$$$
Wedgewood Hotel
845 Hornby St.
☎*689-7777*
A lovely, intimate decor, an ambiance enhanced by piano music and a cuisine cooked up by an award-winning chef make this restaurant popular with its downtown clientele.

The West End

De Dutch Pannekoek House
$
1725 Robson St.
8am to 3pm
☎*687-7065*
De Dutch Pannekoek House is a specialist in pancake breakfasts. Big beautiful pancakes are

---

● RESTAURANTS

1. Bread Garden
2. Café Luxy
3. Ciao Espresso Bar
4. Cloud Nine Revolving Restaurant
5. De Dutch Pannekoek House
6. Flying Wedge Pizza Co.
7. Fresgo's
8. Gyoza King
9. Hamburger Mary's Diner
10. La Crêpe Bretonne
11. Le Café de Paris
12. Le Gavroche
13. Liliget Feast House
14. Miko Sushi
15. Milestone's at the Beach
16. Mondo Gelato
17. Old Bailiff
18. Raincity Grill
19. Rooster's Quarters
20. Soupspoons
21. Starbucks
22. Stepho's Souvlaki
23. Tanpopo Japanese Restaurant
24. Tapastree
25. True Confections

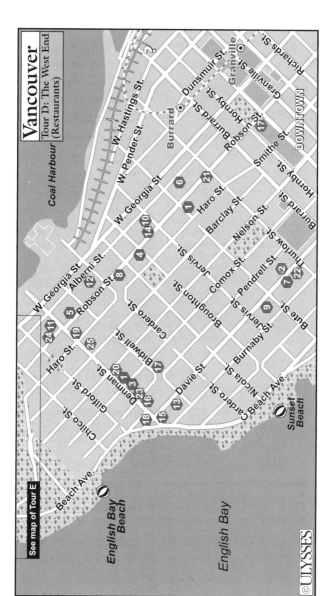

Vancouver
Tour D: The West End (Restaurants)

Coal Harbour

Burrard

Granville

DOWNTOWN

English Bay Beach

English Bay

Sunset Beach

Beach Ave.

See map of Tour E

© ULYSSES

made to order, plain or with your favourite fillings. There are several of these restaurants, in Vancouver (see p 212). The $5 Tuesday special is a great deal.

Bread Garden
$
24hrs/day
1040 Denman St.
☎*685-2996*
812 Bute St.
☎*688-3213*
These cafés sell bread, pastries and tasty prepared dishes, such as quiches, lasagnas, sandwiches, and fruit plates, to enjoy in-house or to go. Good vegetarian selections. Good service and low prices. Also located on the West Side (see p 212) and in West Vancouver (see p 208).

Ciao Espresso Bar
$
1074 Denman St.
☎*682-0112*
Folks come to this little West End establishment for the strong, dark brew and the neighbourhood atmosphere.

Fresgo's
$
1138 Davie St.
☎*689-1332*
Fresgo's is renowned for its portions and prices, and it's open late.

Hon's Wun-Tun House
$
1339 Robson St.
☎*685-0871*
See review in Chinatown and East Vancouver, p 194.

La Crêpe Bretonne
$
795 Jervis St.
☎*608-1266*
At La Crêpe Bretonne, you can enjoy a large variety of crepes—with sugar, eggs, ham or chicken—all to the sound of French songs hummed by the owner. Worth a visit. Open for breakfast.

True Confections
$
until 1am
866 Denman St.
☎*682-1292*
True Confections is a dessert place par excellence that serves huge slices of mile-high cakes that look like cartoon versions of themselves. They put those at competitor Death by Chocolate *(1001 Denman St. and other locations)* to shame. Be sure to try the divine chocolate Belgian mousse.

Mondo Gelato
$
1094 Denman St.
☎*647-6638*
Stop in at Mondo Gelato for a coffee, a sorbet or an excellent gelato in every colour of the rainbow.

Soupspoons
$
990 Denman St.
☎*328-7687*
This little café, run by a Frenchman who sings the praises of a good, simple bowl of soup, offers a number of hearty varieties in three sizes that make for a great quick lunch. Who says fast food has to be junk food?

Hamburger Mary's Diner
$-$$
1202 Davie St.
☎*687-1293*
Mary's is a popular neighbourhood joint with a 1950s-diner decor and a huge menu that includes breakfast items, burgers (organic, if you so desire), sandwiches and milkshakes. Daily specials and a few surprises to boot.

Café Luxy
$-$$
1235 Davie St.
☎*669-5899*
This simply decorated, friendly café is an excellent choice for breakfast, with five types of eggs Benedict and a half-dozen types of omelette on offer (none of which will set you back more than $8). The salmon Benny and the four-cheese Gorgonzola omelette are both winners. Also open for lunch and dinner.

Rooster's Quarters
$$
836 Denman St.
☎*689-8023*
Rooster's Quarters is where Vancouver's many Quebec-born resident head to for their fix of smoked meat, *pâté chinois* (shepherd's pie), *tourtière* (meat pie), *poutine* (fries, gravy and curd cheese) and barbecued chicken. The chicken pie is also a good bet when you're in the mood for some simple comfort food.

Stepho's Souvlaki
$$
1124 Davie St.
☎*683-2555*
This typical Greek taverna, located in the heart of Davie Village, attracts a nightly lineup of locals. Arrive early to avoid the crowds!

Gyoza King
$$
1508 Robson St.
☎*669-8278*
Interested in Japanese food but sick of sushi? Take your place in line amongst the Asian students and get ready for Japanese comfort food like ubon and ramen, served in handmade stoneware bowls, and other non-raw-fish-based staples. Oh, and don't forget the gyoza, a Japanese version of the pot stickers you'll find at Hon's (see p 194). Doughy pockets filled with meat,

seafood or veggies, they're served either pan-fried or baked. And if the menu leaves you bewildered, just point at someone else's bowl and enjoy!

🌴 Miko Sushi
$$
Mon to Sat
1335 Robson St.
☎*681-0339*
Meticulously prepared Japanese food, extremely fresh sushi and sashimi, and impeccable service are all in store at this small restaurant. Reservations recommended.

Milestone's at the Beach
$$-$$$
1210 Denman St.
☎*662-3431*
The hamburger plates, steaks and salads come in generous portions. Freshly squeezed fruit juices. Lovely terrace facing English Bay.

Tapastree Restaurant
$$-$$$
1829 Robson St.
☎*606-4680*
As the name suggests, this cozy West End establishment specializes in tapas—appetizer-size dishes, creatively concocted in the Pacific Northwest style. Tapastree is frequented by a local crowd that includes chefs on their night off—always a good sign.

Tanpopo Japanese Restaurant
$$$
1122 Denman St.
☎*681-7777*
New initiates gingerly sample and seasoned afficionados gorge themselves on all-you-can-eat sushi and sashimi at Tanpopo, a local favourite. Lunch *(11:30am to 3pm)* is around $12, while dinner *(5pm to 10pm)* is less than $20. There are also happy-hour specials and a regular menu. If you can't bare the lineup, ask for a seat at the bar.

The Old Bailiff
$$$
800 Robson St.
☎*684-7448*
At the Old Bailiff you'll find an English-style pub atmosphere with a patio and traditional British-style and Canadian fare.

Liliget Feast House
$$$-$$$$
1724 Davie St.
☎*681-7044*
Liliget is a First Nations restaurant that offers authentic Aboriginal-style food: salmon grilled on a wood fire, smoked oysters, grilled seaweed, poached black Alaskan code and wild Arctic caribou. Makes for unique dining experience on an unhurried evening.

Le Café de Paris
$$$-$$$$
751 Denman St.
☎**687-1418**
The speciality of Le Café de Paris is its *cassoulet* (a duck, sausage and bean stew originating from southwestern France). Many other dishes are inspired from different regions of France. The fries that accompany every dish are excellent. Good wine list and prompt service.

Raincity Grill
$$$$
1193 Denman St.
☎**685-7337**
The Raincity Grill specializes in grilled fish and meats in true West Coast tradition. Renowned for its selection of British Columbia wines and by-the-glass offerings.

Cloud Nine
Revolving Restaurant
$$$$
1400 Robson St.
☎**687-0511**
This restaurant-bar at the top of the 40-storey Empire Landmark Hotel (see p 182) offers an exceptional view. It takes 80min for the restaurant to rotate 360°. Sunset is particularly picturesque as the sky darkens and the city begins to glow. Unfortunately, the view is unmatched by the food.

Le Gavroche
$$$$
1616 Alberni St.
☎**685-3924**
Fine French cuisine in a Victorian house. Reservations required.

Stanley Park

See map p 117.

Prospect Point Café
$
Prospect Point
☎**669-2737**
The Prospect Point Café is located at the historic observation site on the tip of Stanley Park. You can contemplate Lions Gate Bridge at sunset and sample steaks, pasta and chicken burgers.

Teahouse Restaurant
$$$-$$$$
Ferguson Point
☎**669-3281**
During World War II, the Teahouse was a garrison and officers' mess. Today, the Teahouse Restaurant serves delicious food and offers stunning views of English Bay within a charming dining room with pale yellow walls and huge windows. Rather complicated menu hours are worth noting: brunch *($$)* is served every day until 2:30pm; high tea *($20)* as well as a simpler tea break *($12; Mon-Sat 2:30pm to 4:30pm)* are served at the

same time as a light lunch menu *($-$$; Mon-Fri)*. Full-dinner menu features seafood, lamb, steak and vegetarian dishes. Call ahead for reservations and for precise directions as it can be tricky to find. And if you're cycling, note that there is regrettably nowhere to lock your bike nearby.

The Fish House in Stanley Park
$$$$
8901 Stanley Park Dr.
☎ *681-7275*
The Fish House in Stanley Park is located in a Victorian house right in the heart of the park and just a few steps from the Seawall. Fine seafood and fish dishes are served in a lovely, opulent decor.

Burrard Inlet

See map p 123.

West Vancouver

Bean Around the World
$
1522 Marine Dr.
☎ *925-9600*
A rather laid-back crowd squeezes into this warm spot for excellent coffees and sweets, served at reasonable prices.

Bread Garden
$
24hrs/day
550 Park Royal N.
☎ *925-0181*
See review in "The West End," p 204.

Beach Side Café
$$-$$$$
1362 Marine Dr.
☎ *925-1945*
The Beach Side Café in West Vancouver is a lovely restaurant with original recipes prepared from local produce, as well as meat and fish dishes. Pub menu, bistro menu or fine dining.

The Salmon House
$$$$
2229 Folkestone Way
☎ *926-3212*
The Salmon House offers unique, creative cuisine that focuses on salmon in a superb, Canadian-cedar decor. A view of the ocean, the city and Stanley Park adds to the pleasure of the palate.

Horseshoe Bay

Boathouse Restaurant
$$
6695 Nelson Ave.
☎ *921-8188*
The Boathouse is a large glassed-in restaurant at the heart of the quaint community of Horseshoe Bay. Seafood is its specialty: oysters, halibut, salmon...

North Vancouver

Bridge House Restaurant
$$
Apr-Oct 11am to 6pm
3735 Capilano Rd.
☎*987-3388*
In a warm and intimate British-style setting, this restaurant serves traditional Canadian dishes, home-made pies and warm bread. Reservations recommended.

False Creek

See map p 131.

Maverick's
$-$$
770 Pacific Blvd, Plaza of Nations
☎*683-4436*
This grill, which features live music and a DJ on the weekends, serves up steak and beer while you watch your favourite game on the big screen.

Chateau Madrid - La Bodega
$$
Mon-Sat
1277 Howe St.
☎*684-8814*
A restaurant and tapas bar, Chateau Madrid-La Bodega serves traditional paella and sangria.

Panama Jacks Bar and Grill
$$
1080 Howe St.
☎*682-5225*
This restaurant has a terrace, colourful decor and friendly ambiance. Standard fare and pizza. Open late.

Dix Barbecue and Brewery
$$-$$$
871 Beatty St.
☎*682-2739*
Reasonably priced grills and beer are served up in a youthful, laid-back atmosphere in Yaletown.

Il Giardino
$$$
1382 Hornby St.
☎*669-2422*
This popular restaurant has a reputation for its attractive Italian-style decor, charming patio, inspired dishes with local and European accents and its vast selection of pasta. Always crowded. Warm, friendly ambiance.

Monk McQueens
$$$-$$$$
601 Stamps Landing
☎*877-1351*
This restaurant overlooks the inlet and has the decor of a small sailing club. Very pleasant inside and on the patio. Impeccable service and delicious food—specialties are fish and oysters. A jazz pianist accompanies your meal *(Thu-Sat)*.

Kettle of Fish
$$$-$$$$
900 Pacific Blvd.
☎*682-6661*
Kettle of Fish has a cozy winter-garden-style ambiance with plenty of flowers.

Vancouver

The menu includes tasty fish and fresh seafood and the wine list is excellent. Good service.

C Restaurant
$$$$
1600 Howe St.
☎**681-1164**

This "contemporary fish" restaurant, whose name evokes the sea, is the talk of the town, and for good reason. The chef has created innovative and unique recipes with a Southeast Asian influence. If you come for lunch, served at the stroke of noon, the C-style Dim Sum is a real delight. Tidbits of fish marinated in tea and a touch of caviar, vol-au-vents with chanterelles, curry shrimp with coconut milk, and the list goes on... All quite simply exquisite. Desserts are equally extraordinary. For those who dare, the crème brûlée with blue cheese is an unforgettable experience. This restaurant is an absolute must.

Yaletown

Urban Fare
$
177 Davie St.
☎**975-7550**

This yuppie food emporium is a good place to stop for lunch or a snack during your tour of Yaletown. The self-serve counter features panini, wraps and other trendy items. Brunch served weekends and holidays (*7am to 2pm*).

Yaletown Brewing Co.
$$
1111 Mainland St.
☎**681-2739**

The Yaletown Brewing Co. is a veritable yuppie temple in the post-industrial neighbourhood of Yaletown and a fun place to spend an evening. There's a cozy bar on one side (with a huge fireplace) and a restaurant on the other. Try the pizza from the wood-burning oven.

Capone's
$$
1141 Hamilton St.
☎**684-7900**

This romantic restaurant has a New Orleans–style atmosphere with a jazz orchestra. Intimate dinners by candlelight include pizza, pasta or salads, accompanied by a selection of original martinis.

Rodney's Oyster House
$$-$$$
1228 Hamilton St.
☎**609-0080**

This restaurant's boat-style decor gives it a maritime feeling. Its fish and fresh seafood soups are presented in large bowls and served up with a smile.

Provence Marinaside
$$$
1177 Marinaside Cr.
☎681-4144

The marina-side location of this new bistro-style Yaletown restaurant can't be beat, particularly when the weather is fine enough to dine outside. The seafood-centred menu features Provencal and Italian specialties (bouillabaisse and pissaladière, as well as pasta and risotto), reflecting the dual origins of the owners. There's also a takeout antipasti bar. Good value.

Brix
$$$-$$$$
1138 Homer St.
☎915-9463

This lovely restaurant features a cool and soothing decor of exposed brick, wood and tile, cream-coloured walls adorned with vivid, modern portraits, and a cozy courtyard patio. In addition to inspired lunches (including the chef's excellent daily duos: try anything with ahi tuna and/or Indian candy!) and dinners (mango-curry seared ahi tuna, porcini-dusted wild B.C. caribou), tapas are available all day. Extensive wine list, including many B.C. vintages, a good many of which are available by the glass. Reservations recommended for dinner *(Fri-Sun)*. A truly delicious choice.

Blue Water Café and Raw Bar
$$$$
1095 Hamilton St.
☎688-8078

A well-heeled Yaletown crowd keeps the Pellegrino flowing like water in this new favourite for fresh, local seafood. In addition to an oyster and a sushi bar, you'll find entrées such as smoked B.C. sablefish, Dover sole, striped marlin and albacore tuna, all fresh rather than farmed, as well as Alberta steaks. The dining room is attractively done up with terra cotta tiles, brick, exposed pipes, wood tables and leather booths, and the service is thoughtful and professional. Reservations recommended on weekends. While you're there, check out the impressive wine cellar.

Granville Island

La Baguette et L'Échalotte
$
8am to 6pm
1680 Johnston St.
☎684-1351

If you expect to be picnicking during your visit to Granville Island, here is where you will find baguettes, pastries, croissants and take-out dishes. Louise and Mario take good care of this little shop, located in the heart of busy Granville Island.

The Keg Steakhouse
$$
1499 Anderson St.
☎**685-4735**
Meat-eaters converge on The Keg for a wide selection of steaks and reasonable prices. The atmosphere is relaxed and the staff particularly friendly.

Bridges
$$-$$$$
1696 Duranleau St.
☎**687-4400**
Bridges Bistro boasts one of the loveliest patios in Vancouver, right by the water in the middle of Granville Island's pleasure-boat harbour. The food and setting are decidedly Pacific Northwestern.

Dockside Brewing Company
$$$
1253 Johnston St.
Granville Island Hotel
☎**685-7070**
You'd think that any restaurant that brews its own beer might neglect the food side of the equation—wrong! The new Dockside Brewing Company serves up surprisingly good soups and salads (the smoked-salmon chowder is a lovely surprise, as is the dockside salad) that make for good lunches, as well as rotisserie chicken and fish dishes, among other selections. Excellent heated patio on False Creek.

Pacific Institute of Culinary Arts
$$$-$$$$
1505 West Second Ave.
☎**734-4488**
The Pacific Institute of Culinary Arts offers a different gourmet menu every day prepared by its students. The dishes are exquisite and the service is excellent. The three-course fixed-price menu is available for lunch *($20)* Monday to Friday and dinner seven days a week *($30, Mon-Fri; $34, Sat and Sun)*. And there's a patio, too!

The West Side

See maps p 139 and p 215.

De Dutch Pannekoek House
$
2622 Granville St.
☎**731-0775**
3192 Oak St.
☎**732-1915**
See review under "The West End," p 202.

Bread Garden
2996 Granville St.
☎**736-6465**
1880 W. First Ave., Kitsilano
☎**738-6684**
See review under "The West End," p 204.

Flying Wedge Pizza Co.
☎**874-8284**
1937 Cornwall, Kitsilano
See review under "Downtown," p 198.

Soupspoons
$
2278 W. Fourth Ave.
See review under "The West End," p 205.

True Confections
3701 W. Broadway
☎*222-8489*
See review under "The West End," p 204.

Sophie's Cosmic Café
$
2095 W. Fourth Ave.
☎*732-6810*
This is a weekend meeting-spot for the Kitsilano crowd, who come to stuff themselves with bacon and eggs. 1950s decor, relaxed atmosphere.

Benny's Bagels
$
Sat and Sun 24hrs, Mon-Fri until 2am
2505 W. Broadway Ave.
☎*731-9730*
Benny's bagels is recommended for—wait for it—its bagels, as well as sandwiches, served in a hip, relaxed setting.

Gypsy Rose
$
2017 Fourth Ave.
☎*738-3844*
A little café situated on a shop-lined street, Gypsy Rose offers pastries, light fare and specialities from southern France. Bernard, the friendly manager, is from Marseille.

Pâtisserie Lebeau
$
1728 W. Second St.
☎*731-3528*
This little bakery is located in an unlikely spot surrounded by car dealerships. It serves up hot waffles for breakfast and scrumptious sandwiches for lunch (such as ham and cheese on a French baguette) accompanied by coffee and a lively atmosphere. Try the Liège waffles and Belgian-style pastries.

Big News Coffee Bar
$
2447 Granville St., at Broadway
☎*739-7320*
The Big News Coffee Bar, an alternative to Starbucks, is a pleasant neighbourhood café. The decor is modern and sober and they offer fast service, good coffee and a number of magazines and newspapers to leaf through while you eat.

The Vineyard
$
2296 W. Fourth Ave.
☎*733-2420*
The Vineyard serves Greek specialties until 2am as well as breakfast, a few hours later...

Ohana Sushi
$-$$
1414 W. Broadway Ave.
☎*732-0112*
This chain of Japanese restaurants offers excellent dishes at reasonable prices.

Vancouver

Service is efficient and pleasant. A fine Asian experience.

The Naam
$-$$
24hrs/day
2724 W. Fourth Ave.
☎*738-7151*
The Naam blends live music with vegetarian meals. This little restaurant, decorated with ceiling fans and wooden tables, has a warm peaceful atmosphere, friendly service, and is frequented by a young clientele. Service can be slow.

Landmark Hotpot House
$$
4023 Cambie St.
☎*872-2868*
The Landmark Hotpot House is one of the best hotpot restaurants in Vancouver. (Hotpots are meat or fish dishes sautéed in hot casseroles.) This popular restaurant is always packed. A variety of soups, such as chicken or meat, are cooked up and accompanied by vegetables and original sauces such as *satay*, the house special.

◯ ACCOMMODATIONS

1. Accommodations by Pillow Suites
2. Johnson Heritage House B&B
3. Penny Farthing Inn
4. Plaza 500 Hotel
5. Ramada Vancouver Centre

● RESTAURANTS

1. Akbar's Own
2. Amorous Oyster
3. Banana Leaf Malaysian Restaurant
4. Benny's Bagels
5. Big News Coffee Bar
6. Bread Garden
7. De Dutch Pannekoek House
8. Epicurean Caffè
9. Fiction Tapas Bar
10. Flying Wedge Pizza Co.
11. Gypsy Rose
12. Habibi's
13. Incendio West
14. Kishu Japanese Bistro
15. Landmark Hotpot House
16. Las Margaritas
17. Lumière
18. Maria's Taverna
19. Mark's Steak and Tap House
20. Naam
21. Ohana Sushi
22. Ouisi Bistro
23. Pâtisserie Lebeau
24. Primo's Mexicain Grill
25. Salade de Fruits
26. Seasons in the Park
27. Seoul House Royal Korean Restaurant
28. Smoking Dog
29. Sophie's Cosmic Café
30. Soupspoons
31. Star Anise
32. Tomato Fresh Food Café
33. Vij's
34. Vineyard
35. Wild Garlic

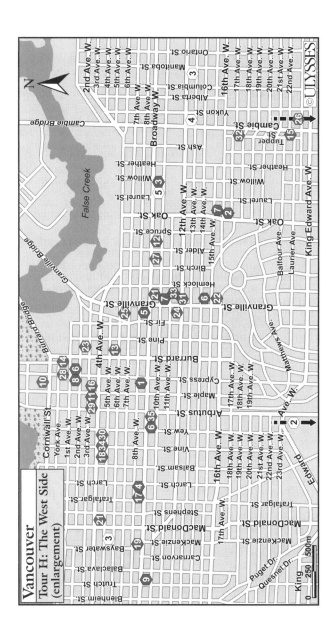

Vancouver
Tour H: The West Side (enlargement)

© ULYSSES

Akbar's Own
$$
1905 W. Broadway Ave.
☎ 736-8180
This traditional Indian res-
taurant offers a choice of
lovely aromatic dishes and
good service.

Epicurean Caffè
$$
1898 West First Ave.
corner Cypress St.
☎ 731-5370
Owners Dario and his son
Christian serve Italian-style
cuisine. Chose the dish and
the portion you desire on
the home-made menu. With
a friendly warm atmo-
sphere, this quaint little
place whips up one of the
best espressos in Vancou-
ver. Bask in the winter or
summer sun at one of the
outdoor tables. The motor-
cycles and bikes parked
along the sidewalk are a
hot topic of conversation
amongst the regulars.

Salade de Fruits
$$
closed Sun evening and Mon
1551 W. Seventh Ave.
☎ 714-5987
Located within the Maison
de la Francophonie de Van-
couver, Salade de Fruits is
not the easiest place to find
(there's no sign) but you'll
be very glad when you do!
One of Vancouver's best-
kept secrets is run by affa-
ble Frenchmen Antoine and
Pascal, who clearly take
great pride in offering

down-to-earth bistro food at
more than reasonable
prices. At lunch, the place is
packed to the rafters with
locals chowing down on
the excellent house spe-
cialty, *moules frites*, or other
dishes such as quiches and
poutine. For dinner, a
weekly table d'hôte is of-
fered, which may feature
anything from confit of
duck to *raclette savoyarde*.
All desserts (homemade by
Pascal) are only $3.99 and a
glass of wine is an astonish-
ing $3.75. Dinner reserva-
tions recommended.

Kishu Japanese Bistro
$$
1815 W. First Ave.
☎ 734-5858
Japanese Bistro Kitsilano
features an all-you-can-eat
sushi and tempura buffet.
Large patio and excellent
service.

Las Margaritas
$$
1999 W. Fourth Ave.
☎ 734-7117
Las Margaritas serves
healthy Mexican fare in a
lively setting with lots of
ambiance. A great place to
go with a group of friends.

Maria's Taverna
$$
2324 W. Fourth Ave.
☎ 731-4722
This pretty little restaurant
serves up generous portions
of authentic Greek cuisine
in a blue-and-white decor.

The roast lamb is highly recommended.

Mark's Steak and Tap House
$$
until 1am
2486 Bayswater St.
☎*734-1325*
Mark's Steak and Tap House is a yuppie hangout whose parking lot is regularly filled with Harleys. The food is Italian, with pasta and pizza, and the mood is relaxed, with jazz in the evenings.

Ouisi Bistro
$$
3014 Granville St.
☎*732-7550*
This charming little New Orleans–style restaurant features live jazz and an original, creative menu.

Primo's Mexican Grill
$$
1509 W. 12th Ave.
☎*736-9322*
Primo's Mexican Grill serves up all kinds of tasty Mexican dishes in a laid-back, friendly atmosphere. A good selection of tasty margaritas.

Seoul House
Royal Korean Restaurant
$$
1215 W. Broadway Ave.
☎*738-8285 or 739-9001*
The Royal Seoul House has a large dining room divided into compartments. Each has a table with a grill for preparing food that can

accommodate four or more people. Order your all-you-can-eat meat, fish and seafood buffet, and have fun. Everything here is good, including the service.

Habibi's
$$
closed Sun
1128 W. Broadway Ave.
☎*732-7487*
If you think Lebanese food is limited to meat shaved off a spit, think again. This cheerful, cozy restaurant lovingly offers delectable vegetarian Lebanese specialties that will put your neighbourhood kebab house to shame. Order the dinner special ($13), which allows you to choose any three dishes. Among the tasty items are the delicious smoky-flavoured *baba ganoush* (eggplant purée), *loubieh* (green beans sautéed in garlic and tomatoes) and *fathe* (chick peas with garlic-infused yogurt and pine nuts). Finish your meal with a cup of Arabic tea served in a brass *rakwy*, brought by Richard, the chef/owner, from Lebanon. A delight.

Tomato Fresh Food Café
$$-$$$
3305 Cambie St.
☎*874-6020*
Tomato's is a cheerful diner-style café boldly decorated in yellow and red. Open for three meals a day, you can start your day with

an *omelette du Pacifique*
(with wild B.C. salmon and
cream cheese), return for a
sandwich or homemade
soup at lunch, and end
your day with a *bouillabaisse
du Pacifique*, a much-raved-
about dinner offering. Reasonable wine list.

Incendio West
$$-$$$
2118 Burrard St.
☎**736-2220**
The second branch of this
popular pizzeria (the other
is in Gastown, see p 193)
offers 25 different kinds of
pizza, from an Athenian to
a volcana, fresh from a
wood-burning brick oven.
There are also a variety of
pastas, as well as some
good salads and appetizers
(the pan-seared calamari is
delicious). Ceiling fans, tile
floors and subdued lighting
make for an intimate but
casual atmosphere that
tends to get a bit loud with
the sound of friends catching up.

Fiction Tapas Bar
$$-$$$
3162 West Broadway Ave.
☎**736-7576**
Fiction is a long, New
York–style bar with a convivial atmosphere and a
menu that specializes in
tapas.

Banana Leaf Malaysian Restaurant
$$-$$$
820 W. Broadway Ave.
☎**731-6333**
If there's no Malay restaurant back home, make sure
to head out to the Banana
Leaf for a taste of some-
thing new. Malay cuisine,
which has Chinese and
Indian influences, can be
rather spicy, but you'll find
a mostly toned-down ver-
sion here. An excellent
choice is the delicious sam-
bal tiger prawns fried in
chili, garlic and dry shrimp
sauce and served with
green beans and Chinese
eggplant. The Singapore
fried chili crab also has an
extremely devoted follow-
ing. Cheerful service, reasonable prices, and pleasant, casual ambiance.

Amorous Oyster
$$$
3236 Oak St.
☎**732-5916**
This restaurant offers a
great selection of Pacific
Northwest–style dishes for
fish and seafood lovers.

The Smoking Dog
$$$
1889 W. First Ave.
☎**732-8811**
The Smoking Dog has a
warm, lively atmosphere,
lovely decor and reasonable
prices for its carefully

prepared *table d'hôte*. Exquisite steak, copious salads and creative daily specials. The *pommes frites* that accompany every dish are golden brown on the outside and tender on the inside. Jean-Claude, the owner, is a friendly Marseillais.

Wild Garlic
$$$
2120 W. Broadway Ave.
☎ *730-0880*
Wild Garlic serves up this herb every way imaginable, and also offers traditional Canadian cuisine. Meticulous, stylish setting and friendly, attentive service.

Seasons in the Park
$$$$
Queen Elizabeth Park,
Cambie and 33rd sts.
☎ *874-8008*
Seasons in the Park is a pleasant restaurant with classic, elegant decor and an unhindered view of the city. Succulent Pacific Northwest cuisine. Reservations required. Also open for lunch and weekend brunch.

Lumière
$$$$ (restaurant)
$$$ (tasting bar)
Tue-Sun
2551 W. Broadway Ave.
☎ *739-8185*
Lumière is probably the brightest light on Vancouver's burgeoning restaurant scene. Praise has been lavished on chef Rob Feenie and his lovely restaurant from far and wide, most recently by *Vancouver Magazine*, which named it Restaurant of the Year (2001). Furthermore, Lumière has recently been awarded a Relais Gourmands designation by the prestigious Relais et Chateau association. The Asian-inspired, minimalist interior allows the food to shine, and shine it does! The fresh, local ingredients used in each dish make for creative and honest, yet very refined cuisine. There are four different tasting menus—vegetarian, seafood, chef's and signature—which consist of small portions of eight to 13 courses ($80-$120). But don't let those prices scare you off: Feenie recently opened a much more accessible tasting bar adjoining his dining room, complete with a glowing Jetsons-style lime-green bar. Here, foodies with small appetites (or budgets) can sample as many as 12 appetizer-size items (such as confit of lamb shoulder, or seared marinated sablefish) each for $12. Servers will gladly tell you which are the most substantial dishes. The wine list is extensive and the service is remarkably warm and professional.

Star Anise
$$$$
Mon-Sat
1485 W. 12th Ave.
☎*737-1485*
Star Anise is a stylish, attractive restaurant frequented by patrons of the same description. Big paintings adorn the yellow walls, and lanterns illuminate the tables, where Pacific Northwest cuisine, including an assortment of vegetarian selections, is served.

Vij's
$$$$
1480 W. 11th Ave.
☎*736-6664*
One look at Vij's minimalist blue neon sign and you'll be hip to the fact that this is no ordinary Indian restaurant. Inside the spare dining room you'll find a decor unlike other East Indian restaurants in this country: instead, a 700lb Himalayan teak door from an Indian temple takes centre stage in a dark room punctuated by hanging lanterns splashing colour onto the walls. Vij doesn't take reservations so everyone—local celebrities included—is led to the bar area to comfortably await a table while drinking complimentary sweet chai and tasty hors d'oeuvres. The menu is a meeting of East and West: wine-marinated lamb popsicles in fenugreek cream curry with turmeric spinach and potatoes; tea-braised sablefish in ginger and black chick-pea curry. A glass of locally brewed IPA from the Storm Brewery is a wonderful accompaniment. Ultra-professional service.

Entertainment

The **ARTS Hotline** (☎*684-ARTS, www.allianceforarts. com*) will inform you about all the shows (dance, theatre, music, cinema and literature) in the city.

The Georgia Straight (☎*730-7000*), a weekly paper published every Thursday and distributed free throughout Vancouver, provides all the necessary information on upcoming shows and cultural events. This paper is read religiously each week by many Vancouverites and has acquired a good reputation.

For information on jazz shows in Vancouver, call the **Jazz Hotline** (☎*872-5200*).

To book tickets for cultural or sporting events, try the following:

Ticketmaster
☎*280-4444*
www.ticketmaster.ca

Bars and Nightclubs
by Type

Comedy Clubs

Rhythm and Blues Bars

Jazz Clubs

Nightclubs and Lounges

Gay and Lesbian Bars

Pool Halls

Pubs

Bars and Nightclubs

Gastown

Irish Heather
217 Carrall St.
☎*688-9779*
This casual pub has a cozy, brick-lined upstairs seating area and plenty of little nooks and crannies to hide away in, including a

Vancouver

glassed-in terrace backing onto Gaoler's Mews, site of the city's first jail. They pour a good pint of Guinness but their lack of B.C. brews is regrettable. Rather sophisticated Irish-style pub menu.

Steamworks Brewing Co
$$$
375 Water St.
☎689-2739
Conveniently located right by Waterfront Station, Steamworks is the best excuse yet for a pre- (or post-) trip sup. On hand is a wide selection of beers brewed right on site. On the main floor there's a view across Burrard Inlet, while downstairs is a super-cozy dining area, ensconced in stone and brick, next to shiny copper beer vats and spinning pizza dough. There's a full dinner menu as well as a pub menu.

Blarney Stone
216 Carrall St.
☎687-4322
The Blarney Stone is the spot for authentic Irish jigs and reels. The ambiance is frenetic, with people dancing everywhere—on the tables, on the chairs... A must-see!

The Purple Onion Cabaret
$8 weekends, $5 weekdays
15 Water St., third floor
☎602-9442
The Purple Onion is a popular two-room venue featuring live music and DJs. Wednesdays are dedicated to live music and DJ-spun funk; on Fridays and Saturdays, DJs spin R&B and hip hop in the club and electronica, house and hip hop in the lounge. A perennial favourite.

Rossini's Gastown
closed Mon in winter
162 Water St.
☎408-1300
Rossini's (see p 227) now has a second location on the busiest street in Gastown. Good beer and meals are served, accompanied by live music every evening.

Sonar
66 Water St.
☎683-6695
This very big Gastown venue offers an alternative and underground DJ format as well as some live shows. Gay-friendly.

Chinatown and East Vancouver

Hot Jazz Society
2120 Main St.
☎873-4131
The Hot Jazz Society was one of the first places in Vancouver to offer good

jazz. It's a veritable institution, where many of the big names in jazz perform. Call to find out who's playing.

Downtown

Automotive Billiards Club
1095 Homer St.
☎ **682-0040**
Very good music, excellent pool tables and great espresso. There's a small divider separating the pool-table area from the bar corner. Also, it's one of the rare pool halls that serves beer. Hip, friendly atmosphere on weekends.

Bacchus Lounge
845 Hornby St.
Wedgewood Hotel
☎ **608-5319**
This plush lounge and piano bar, lined with cherrywood panelling and decorated with rich burgundy fabrics, attracts the glitterati as well as the rest of us mere mortals seeking a romantic spot. Excellent cocktails and bar food are served while a pianist entertains.

Bar None
$5 to $8
1222 Hamilton St.
☎ **689-7000**
Bar None is the hang-out of Vancouver's trendy young set. A friendly pub atmosphere is complemented by a dance floor. Watch out for long line-ups on Friday and Saturday evenings.

Cardero's
1583 Coal Harbour Quay
☎ **669-7666**
At the end of the day, when nothing but a pint and a harbour view will do, make your way down to Coal Harbour on Burrard Inlet (at the foot of Nicola Street, by the Westin Bayshore). Baseball caps and hardhats mix with suited gentlemen and women on the wood and tan leather of this nautically themed harbour-front bar and restaurant. And if your cocktail whets your appetite, there's a casual restaurant with an open kitchen and patio adjoining.

Cascades Lounge
Pan Pacific Hotel
300-999 Canada Place Way
☎ **662-8111**
The Cascades Lounge, in the luxurious Pan Pacific Hotel, has a quiet, refined ambiance with sumptuous armchairs. Sip on wine or liqueurs as you listen to live guitar or piano music.

The Drink Nite Club
398 Richards St.
☎ **687-1307**
The Drink Nite Club's DJ plans theme nights, such as Latin night, with dance lessons for beginners. Lively ambiance.

DV8
515 Davie St.
☎ **682-4388**
This cool, sparsely lit spot is popular with a mainly

Vancouver

young, alternative crowd. DV8 hosts record launches and features an art space, which changes every few weeks. Good food, too, served (a little slowly) until late, making it a good after-hours spot.

Georgia Street Bar & Grill
801 West Georgia St.
☎602-0994
This bar is really popular with its downtown regulars, who gather here to decompress at the end of the work day. Its well-dressed clientele flocks here in the evening to guzzle down beer, nibble on grilled dishes and listen to live R&B.

Gerrard Lounge
845 Burrard St.
Sutton Place Hotel
☎682-5511
This cozy bar oozes with the atmosphere of a gentleman's club, with leather armchairs to sink into, dark wood panelling and professional service. A good place to spot celebrities and wannabees.

Ginger Sixty Two
1219 Granville St.
☎688-5494
This groovy lounge for thirty-somethings is named for Ginger, the boopsy starlet played by Tina Louise, who was shipwrecked on *Gilligan's Island*; her floor-to-ceiling portraits grace a wall in this lusciously funky,

stylish lounge with plenty of cozy seating. Good Asian-style lounge menu. Wednesdays feature house music, Thursdays are for 1960s favourites, particularly R&B, while Fridays and Saturdays feature electronica. Dress is relaxed, smart casual.

Jolly Taxpayer
828 West Hastings St.
☎681-3574
Located in the heart of the business district, this traditional-style pub is a gathering place for downtown bike couriers, among others. Shame about the lack of local brews.

Lucy Mae Brown
862 Richards St.
☎899-9199
This much-celebrated new restaurant just off Robson Street houses a basement lounge, with retro furnishings of the type that were stashed away in basements across the nation with the fading of the 1970s. Here, a young dressed-for-success crowd grooves to the latest sounds while sipping martinis, appealing appetizers and reasonably priced mains.

Luv-a-Fair
1275 Seymour St.
☎685-3288
For a heady night of techno and alternative music and dancing, check out Luv-a-

Fair. Young, gay-friendly crowd.

O'Doul's Restaurant and Bar
1300 Robson St.
☎661-1400
Located in the Listel Vancouver hotel, O'Doul's is a popular spot for live jazz, presented most summer evenings and weekends the rest of the year.

Piccadilly Pub
620 West Pender St.
☎682-3221
The best night at the Piccadilly Pub is Friday, when groovy funk gets the place hopping.

Railway Club
$3 to $8
579 Dunsmuir St.
☎681-1625
An eclectic musical menu, ranging from folk and blues to pop, punk and rockabilly, is presented in an oblong spot that brings to mind a railway car. A miniature electric train runs in a loop above customers' heads as they enjoy the live music. A popular spot for an after-work beverage.

Richard's on Richards
$10
1036 Richards St.
☎687-6794
Richard's on Richards is an institution in Vancouver. Theme nights, such as wet T-shirt contests, hip-hop and Top 40 keep the twentysomething crowd

entertained. Dress is mainly casual.

The Roxy
$4 to $8
932 Granville St.
☎331-7999
The Roxy is a boisterous rock club where the beer flows abundantly. Regulars don't seem to mind cooling their heels on the sidewalk a spell. Cruising appears to be one of the favourite pastimes here.

Shark Club
$8
180 West Georgia St., Sandman Hotel
☎687-4275
The Shark Club, where draft beer is the beverage of choice, is a modern bar with some 30 televisions beaming out hockey or football games. Dress code on weekends.

Soho Café & Billiards
1144 Homer St.
☎688-1180
Soho Café & Billiards, a block away from the Automotive Billiards Club, is very inviting with its cozy wood-and-brick decor and pool tables.

Stone Temple Cabaret
1082 Granville St.
☎488-1333
The Stone Temple Cabaret is located in a rather seedy part of town. House night on Wednesdays; cheap drinks, Top 40, house, R&B and hip-hop music on

Vancouver

Thursdays and Saturdays; and hip hop on Fridays.

Wett Bar
1320 Richards St.
☎*662-7707*
All varieties of house, plus acid jazz, R&B, hip hop, old school and Top 40 R&B radio hits.

The Yale Hotel
1300 Granville St.
☎*681-9253*
The big names in rhythm and blues regularly play at this locale—the undisputed R&B mecca of Vancouver. Great ambiance on the weekends. The cover charge varies depending on the performers.

Yaletown Brewing Co.
1111 Mainland St.
☎*681-2739*
The Yaletown Brewing Co. is a popular yuppie hang-out in Yaletown and the ideal spot for an evening of brews with some friends.

The West End

Barclay Lounge
1348 Robson St.
☎*688-8850*
The Barclay Lounge is a cabaret-style lounge. It's a quirky neighbourhood hangout with a very casual atmosphere and cheap suds.

Ciao Bella
703 Denman St.
near the entrance to Stanley Park
☎*688-5771*
Ciao Bella is a restaurant that doubles as a piano bar on Thursday, Friday and Saturday nights. Its menu includes pasta, pizza and authentic Italian cuisine.

Jolting Fish Billiards
1323 Robson St.
☎*685-8015*
This modern, colourful bar is located on the second floor, with an unobstructed view of Robson Street, and two steps away from the major downtown hotels. Young crowd, relaxed atmosphere.

False Creek

The Rage
750 Pacific Blvd. S.
☎*685-5585*
The Rage is a good bar for live music. They play all styles but it's predominantly rock. Open on Fridays *($5)* and Saturdays *($7)*.

Yuk Yuk's
750 Pacific Blvd., Plaza of Nations
☎*687-5233*
Yuk Yuk's is Vancouver's famous comedy club. Varied programme; phone for details.

The West Side

Lumière Tasting Bar
See "Lumière," in Restaurants, p 219.

Fairview Pub
898 West Broadway
☎*872-1262*
The Fairview is the place to drink wine and beer while listening to live music, which changes several times a week. Free hors-d'oeuvres.

Rossini's Pasta Palazzo
1525 Yew St.
☎*737-8080*
The small, heated outdoor terrace at Rossini's, which is always overflowing with people, faces the lively street that leads to the beach. The small dining room has a live jazz band every evening and serves up pasta dishes accompanied by good beer.

Tangerine
1685 Yew St.
☎*739-4677*
Located in the bustling Kitsilano area, this restaurant-bar, which has bamboo armchairs, offers exotic cocktails that accompany the expertly prepared and meticulously presented dishes. Enjoy lively music as you dine.

South Vancouver

Lafflines Comedy Club
26 Fourth St., New Westminster
☎*525-2262*
Located in the southeast suburbs of Vancouver, this comedy club presents local comedians as well as those from further afield. Call for details.

Gay and Lesbian Bars

In addition to the gay and lesbian bars below, many of those described above are gay friendly. Of particular note are Luv-A-Fair and Sonar.

Numbers Cabaret
$3 cover on Fri and Sat
1042 Davie St.
☎*685-4077*
This large cabaret is frequented by gay men of all ages.

Odyssey
$3-$5
1251 Howe St.
☎*689-5256*
The Odyssey is a gay dance club where young people go to meet in a fun-loving atmosphere. Theme nights and performances include retro-disco on Mondays, Hot House on Tuesdays, drag show at midnight on Wednesdays, Homo Homer with Go Go Boys on Fridays, Fallen Angel night on

Vancouver

Saturdays and female impersonators on Sundays. Straight-friendly.

Royal Hotel
1025 Granville St.
☎ 685-5335

A gay crowd packs the Royal Hotel, which boasts a "modern" decor. Monday nights feature the Diva Inc. drag show, while Tuesdays play host to a fundraising Bingo night, with all proceeds going to the Friends for Life charity. Friday nights are also very popular, when people wait in line as early as 8pm; Sunday evenings are a better bet.

The Oasis Pub
1240 Thurlow St.
☎ 685-1724

This friendly, comfortable bar is discreetly located above street level, just off Davie Street. While they have a pub-style menu, the main attraction here is the extensive list of evocatively named martinis. You and a friend can treat yourselves to an "Oasis" martini, served in a glass the size of a goldfish bowl. Live piano player Wednesday to Saturday. Rooftop patio.

The Pumpjack Pub
1167 Davie St.
☎ 685-3417

Tough on the outside, Pumpjack is warm and fuzzy on the inside (at least, the bartenders are!). The decor is spare (the gotch hanging from the ceiling is a nice touch), leather is the fabric of choice, and the pool table is front and centre. Ask about the racy in-house calendar.

Fountainhead Pub
1025 Davie St.
☎ 687-2222

The Fountainhead's lesbian and straight clientele gather in casual surroundings dominated by neon beer signs and a window-framed view of Davie Street. Inexpensive pub menu.

Cultural Activities

Theatres

Arts Club Theatre
1585 Johnston St., Granville Island
☎ 687-1644

Arts Club Theatre is a steadfast institution on the Vancouver theatre scene. Located on the waterfront on Granville Island, this theatre presents contemporary works with social themes, as well as lighter fare like musicals. Audience members often get together in the theatre's bar after the plays.

Stanley Theatre
2750 Granville St.

The younger sibling of The Arts Club Theatre Company's Granville Island stage (see above), the Stanley Theatre stages classic, mainstream plays. A movie theatre when it opened in 1930, it features a rococo design typical of the period.

Malkin Bowl
Stanley Park
☎687-0174

Theatre Under the Stars has been performing amateur Broadway musicals *(around $29)* in this open-air venue right in Stanley Park *(Jul and Aug)*, for more than 50 years.

Bard on the Beach
301-601 Cambie St.
☎737-0625 *or* 739-0559

Bard on the Beach is an annual event in honour of Shakespeare. Plays are presented, all in period costume, under two huge tents on a peninsula with a view of English Bay *(mid-Jun to end Sep)*.

Carousel Theatre Company
1411 Cartwright St.
☎669-3410

The Carousel Theatre Company is located on Granville Island. It's a small well-established theatre company with a school.

Centennial Theatre Centre
2300 Lonsdale Ave., North Vancouver
☎984-4484

The Centennial Theatre Centre is an excellent neighbourhood theatre. The auditorium seats over 700 people and has very good acoustics. All types of shows are presented here.

Firehall Arts Centre
280 East Cordova St.
☎689-0926

The Firehall Arts Centre, located in the Downtown Eastside, has a very good reputation. Like Arts Club Theatre, it presents and produces contemporary plays dealing with social themes as well as dance shows. Worth a visit, but located in a rather seedy area.

Green Thumb Theatre for Young People
1885 Venables St.
☎254-4055

The Green Thumb Theatre for Young People is a small theatre troupe that puts on plays for children. The theatre is in East Vancouver, close to the Vancouver East Cultural Centre.

Orpheum Theatre
Smithe St., at Seymour St.
☎665-3050

The Orpheum Theatre, dating back to 1927, doesn't look like much from the outside. On the inside, however, the rococo decor is a pleasant surprise. Most of the presentations here are musical; the Vancouver Symphonic Orchestra is based here.

Queen Elizabeth Theatre
Hamilton St., at Georgia St.
☎665-3050

The Queen Elizabeth Theatre, a large hall with 2,000 seats, presents musicals and

Vancouver

variety shows. It is also the main performance space for the Vancouver Opera.

Vancouver East Cultural Centre
1895 Venables St.
☎*251-1363*
"The Cultch" is an arts centre that has built a solid reputation over the years for the quality of the shows presented. Theatre, dance, singing and music all take place in this cozy, dimly lit performance space. A great experience.

Vancouver Opera
845 Cambie St.
☎*682-2871*
The Vancouver Opera performs at the Queen Elizabeth Theatre (see above) because Vancouver is one of the major cities in the world that doesn't have an opera house. The phone number here is for the administrative office, which provides program information.

Vancouver Playhouse Theatre
Hamilton St. at Dunsmuir St.
☎*873-3311*
The Vancouver Playhouse Theatre is another multidisciplinary performance space offering concerts, dance shows and plays. The shows are always of high calibre. Worth investigating.

Vogue Theatre
918 Granville St.
☎*331-7900*
The old Vogue Theatre follows the trend in Vancouver of presenting all types of shows: theatre, comedy, music and even film.

Centre culturel francophone de Vancouver
1551 W. Seventh Ave.
☎*736-9806*
www.ccfv.bc.ca
The French cultural centre of Vancouver stages a full schedule of visual and performing arts events and exhibitions representing French culture from around the world. They also organize an annual festival of music and dance *(mid-Jun)*, house a library and a good bistro (see p 216) and offer French courses.

Centre in Vancouver for the Performing Arts
777 Homer St.
☎*602-0616*
www.centreinvancouver.com
After a prolonged blackout period, the Ford Centre for the Performing Arts has recently reopened under new ownership and with a new name. This performing arts venue hosts major international productions, like Show Boat, Les Misérables and Phantom of the Opera.

Movie Theatres

CN IMAX Cinema
Second floor, Canada Place
☎*682-IMAX*
The CN IMAX Cinema con-
sists of a seven-storey-high
screen and digital, 2,000-
watt sound. The IMAX sys-
tem is an extraordinary
audiovisual experience. Call
for the schedule of 3-D
films being presented.

Capitol 6
820 Granville St.
☎*669-6000*
A large downtown theatre
showing the latest Holly-
wood productions. Dolby
digital sound.

Granville
855 Granville St.
☎*684-4000*
The Granville is located
right across from the
Capitol 6 and is also a large
theatre showing the latest
blockbuster Hollywood
productions, as well as
slightly more alternative
fare. DDSS-THX sound.

Cinemark Tinseltown
88 W. Pender St.
☎*806-0799*
This popular multi-screen
theatre screens Hollywood
blockbusters as well as
some international releases.

Hollywood Theatre
3123 W. Broadway Ave., Kitsilano
☎*738-3211*
The Hollywood Theatre is a
small neighbourhood movie
house that shows second-
run films at reasonable
prices.

Pacific Cinematheque
1131 Howe St.
☎*688-8202*
The Pacific Cinematheque is
the place to go for film
buffs. Information on their
extensive programming is
available at the Cinematheque or by phone.

Park Theatre
3440 Cambie St.
☎*876-2747*
The Park Theatre is a first-
run theatre located in a
pleasant part of town, that
always shows enticing films.

Ridge Theatre
3131 Arbutus St.
☎*738-6311*
The Ridge Theatre is a repertory theatre that's located
on the West Side. They
always offer interesting
films, including good-qual-
ity recent releases and foreign classics.

Vancouver Centre Cinemas
650 West Georgia St.
☎*669-4442*
The latest Hollywood pro-
ductions presented in modern theatres with digital
sound.

Varsity Theatre
4375 West 10th Ave.
☎*222-2235*
The Varsity Theatre, a
charming little neighbourhood theatre on the West

Vancouver

Side, shows fine first-run films.

Fifth Avenue Cinemas
2110 Burrard St.
☎734-7469
Fifth Avenue Cinemas present first-run movies as well as excellent, very recent repertory films, including many in French with English subtitles. A good spot.

Spectator Sports

Hockey

Vancouver Canucks
GM Place, 800 Griffiths Way
☎899-GOAL
The Vancouver Canucks are part of the National Hockey League. They play at GM Place Stadium from October to April (longer if they make the playoffs!).

Baseball

Vancouver Canadians
Nat Bailey Stadium, 4601 Ontario St.
☎872-5232
Vancouverites may not consider baseball their favourite sport, but the city has a professional team nonetheless. Games take place during the summer.

Football

B.C. Lions
B.C. Place Stadium, 777 Pacific Blvd.
☎669-2300
The B.C. Lions are part of the Canadian Football League (CFL). Watch for games against the Toronto Argonauts or the Montréal Alouettes.

Soccer

Vancouver Whitecaps
Swangard Stadium
Boundary Rd. and Kingsway Ave.
Burnaby
☎899-9283
Though many young people—including a large number of girls—play soccer in Canada, professional teams do not draw many people. Mainly European immigrants attend the games at Swangard Stadium to encourage players who, for that matter, are also mainly of European origin.

Casinos

Royal Diamond Casino
750 Pacific Blvd. S.
☎685-2340
If you're feeling lucky, try your hand at the Royal Diamond Casino. Casinos in British Columbia are government owned with all the winnings donated to charity. A good system!

Gateway Casinos
facing the Radisson Hotel, Burnaby
☎*436-2211*
Royal Towers Hotel, New Westminster
☎*521-3262 or 800-663-0202*
You can play blackjack, roulette or mini baccarat.

Calendar of Events

From spring to fall, Vancouver hosts a wide range of festivals. Below you will find just a sample of what's scheduled. For more details, contact Tourism Vancouver or check out the following Web site:
www.tourismvancouver.com

January

Polar Bear Swim
every year on the morning of January 1
Hundreds of people actually choose to take a dip in the frigid winter waters of English Bay. If you don't feel brave enough to challenge that icy water yourself, you can always go there and watch or see it on television.

Chinese New Year
☎*658-885*
Gung Hai Fat Choy! means "Happy New Year!" in Cantonese. The date is determined by the lunar calendar, and therefore varies every year, but celebrations are usually held around the end of January or the beginning of February. Traditional Dragon parades are organized in Chinatown and in Richmond.

February

The **Spring Home Show** is the biggest home show in Western Canada, which takes place under the BC Place Stadium dome.

April

The **Vancouver Playhouse International Wine Festival** (☎*873-3311)* is an important festival where bottles of wine are auctioned and hundreds of wine growers gather to discuss their art and offer samples.

The Vancouver Sun Run (☎*689-9441)* takes place during the third week of April, when over 10,000 people celebrate sport and spring.

May

Cloverdale Rodeo and Exhibition
☎*576-9461*
www.cloverdalerodeo.com
If you're in Vancouver and have never been to a rodeo, this is definitely the occasion. It's considered one of the most important in North America.

Vancouver

Vancouver International Marathon
☎872-2928

The Vancouver International Marathon starts at the Plaza of Nations, then goes through Stanley Park to North Vancouver, and back to Vancouver. Thousands of runners take part in this major sporting event on the first Sunday in May.

Vancouver International Children's Festival
Vanier Park
☎708-5655
www.youngarts.ca/vicf

The Vancouver International Children's Festival takes place the last week of May under red-and-white tents in beautiful Vanier Park. Drawing over 70,000 people each year, this big festival is a hit with children from all over British Columbia.

Spike & Mike's Animation Festival
Ridge Theatre
3131 Arbutus St.
☎738-6311

Held every year throughout the month of May, Spike & Mike's Animation Festival presents the best "sick and twisted" short animation films from all over the world.

June

International Dragon Boat Festival
False Creek, Concord Pacific Place and Plaza of Nations
☎688-2382

Long dug-out boats in the Chinese tradition, from all over the world, compete in these friendly races on the calm waters of False Creek.

Vancouver International Jazz Festival
☎888-GET-JAZZ

Fans can come and satisfy their hunger for jazz at this distinguished festival. Artists perform throughout the city and the surrounding area.

Bard on the Beach
Vanier Park
☎737-0625 or 739-0559
www.bardonthebeach.org

Bard on the Beach is an annual event in honour of Shakespeare. Plays are presented under two large tents against the spectacular backdrop of English Bay.

July

Benson & Hedges Symphony of Fire
English Bay
☎738-4304

The Benson & Hedges Symphony of Fire is an international fireworks festival. Two barges on English Bay serve as the staging ground from which the fireworks are launched to music. Dazzling show, guaranteed thrills.

Vancouver Chamber Music Festival
☎ *736-6034*
www.vanrecital.com/chamber
In the last week of July and the first week of August, six concerts are presented featuring talented young musicians.

Vancouver Early Music Festival
☎ *732-1610*
The music department of the University of British Columbia (UBC) hosts a series of baroque and medieval concerts performed with period instruments.

Vancouver Folk Music Festival
Jericho Beach Park
☎ *602-9798*
www.thefestival.bc.ca
The Vancouver Folk Music Festival has become a tradition in Vancouver. It takes place during the third week of July and features musicians from all over the world who play from sunrise to sunset on Jericho Beach.

Molson Indy Vancouver
Concord Pacific Place
☎ *684-4639*
www.molsonindy.com
tickets:
☎ *280-INDY*
In the heart of downtown, a course is set up where Indy racing cars (the North American equivalent of Formula 1) compete in front of hundreds of thousands of enthusiastic spectators.

Vancouver International Comedy Festival
☎ *683-0883*
www.comedyfest.com
Every year on Granville Island in late July, comics from around the world provide several days of laughs on outdoor stages.

August

Vancouver Pride Parade
☎ *687-0955*
www.vanpride.bc.ca
This colourful, popular annual event attracts more than 120,000 participants and spectators. Begins at Denman and Nelson streets in the West End.

Abbotsford International Airshow
Abbotsford
☎ *852-8511*
www.abbotsfordairshow.com
In Abbotsford, approximately 100km east of Vancouver, both young and old will be dazzled by F-16s, F-117 Stealths, and MiGs. There are also old airplanes and clothing accessories. Don't forget your aviator glasses and sunscreen.

Vancouver

Greater Vancouver Open

Northview Golf and Country Club,
Surrey
☎ *575-0324*

At the Greater Vancouver
Open, the biggest names in
golf compete on a splendid
course.

September

Terry Fox Run

from Ceperley Park to Stanley Park
☎ *888-836-9786*

The Terry Fox Run, a fundraising event for cancer
research, takes place on
foot, bicycle or in-line
skates and is from one to
10km in length. The run is
in memory of the young
athlete, Terry Fox, who
initiated it.

Vancouver Fringe Festival

☎ *257-0350*
www.vancouverfringe.com

The Vancouver Fringe Festival presents 10 days of
theatre, including original
pieces by contemporary
playwrights and performers.

Vancouver International Film Festival

☎ *685-0260*
www.viff.org

"Hollywood North" plays
host to this increasingly
significant festival which
offers film buffs up to 250
films from all over the
world.

October

Vancouver International Writers (and Readers) Festival

☎ *681-6330*

For five days during the
third week of October,
more than 90 authors from
Canada and abroad meet
with the public for conferences and readings.

Vancouver Waterfront Antique Show

Vancouver Trade & Convention Centre
☎ *800-667-0619*

This annual antique show
features furniture and *objects
d'art* from the 18th and 19th
centuries, as well as from
the beginning of the 20th.

November

Vancouver Storytelling Festival

☎ *776-2272*
www.vancouverstorytelling.org

Storytellers gather in the
West End and practice their
art in front of a captivated
audience during this three-
day event.

December

VanDusen Botanical Garden's Festival of Lights

☎ *878-9274*
www.vandusengarden.org

The VanDusen Botanical
Garden's Festival of Lights
is another festival for the
whole family. Throughout
the Christmas season, the
garden is decorated with
seasonal displays and illu-

minated with millions of twinkling lights.

Shopping

You'll surely come upon all manner of interesting shops as you explore the city. To help you discover some of the best bets in Vancouver however, read on...

Malls, Department Stores and Markets

Downtown

Pacific Centre
corner of Howe St. and W. Georgia St.
☎*688-7236*
The Pacific Centre is the largest shopping centre in the city. Approximately 300 quality boutiques offer a complete range of everything from jewellery and clothes including top-of-the-line clothing and accessories at the Hermès and Louis Vuitton boutiques in Holt Renfrew. A fitness equipment store, a Ticketmaster, The Bay and Sears, as well as Le Château, which mainly caters to a young clientele, are all here. Parking fee.

The Bay
at Granville and W. Georgia sts.
☎*681-6211*
Right downtown, this large department store offers over six floors of designer and brand-name clothing and accessories and a huge perfume department with Chanel, Lancôme, Saint-Laurent, Clinique and more. There are restaurants on various floors, and a catering service with coffee tables in the basement. They offer many promotions on Saturdays and Sundays.

Waterfront Centre
at the base of the Waterfront Hotel
900 Canada Pl. Way
☎*646-8020*
Waterfront Centre is home to souvenir shops, flowers, cigars, a tourist information counter, a hair salon, shoe repairs, a Starbucks coffeeshop, and a handful of small fast-food counters featuring various national cuisines.

East Vancouver

If you're looking for your very own sari, or simply some colourful silks from India, head to the **Punjabi Market** *(Main St., between 48th and 51st aves.)*, Vancouver's "Little India." You'll also find plenty of Indian jewellery and food stores.

West End

Robson Public Market
Robson St. at Cardero St.
Robson Market has it all and then some: vegetables; fresh fish; stands with fruit salads, meats, sausages, pastries, and other baked goods; a counter for Alsatian and German specialties; flowers and plants; vitamins and natural products; a natural medicine clinic; a hair salon; and small restaurants. The market is covered, but well lit.

Burrard Inlet

Lonsdale Quay Market
123 Carrie Cates Court
North Vancouver
at the SeaBus terminal
☎985-2191
A charming market, beautiful shops, a multitude of fast-food counters—all of it made a little more lively by artists performing on the seaside terrace.

Park Royal Shopping Centre
Marine Dr., West Vancouver
5min from Lions Gate
☎925-9576
The Park Royal Shopping Centre is the most comprehensive shopping centre in West Vancouver, comprising over 250 shops, banks, Coast Mountain and Cypress Mountain Sports

clothing stores as well as a Future Shop, which carries all brand-name electronics at the most competitive prices. Free parking.

False Creek

Granville Island Market
every day 9am to 6pm
Granville Island
☎666-5784
Granville Island Market is Vancouver's best-known and most popular market. It is an immense commercial area surrounded by water with a fairground atmosphere. Everything is available here—prepared food, organic vegetables, fresh fish and meat, wholesome breads, as well as fast-food counters and pleasant shops selling jewellery, clothing and equipment for water sports and outdoor activities. Take a day to look, sample and wander. Street parking is hard to find but there are two indoor parking (*fee*) lots nearby. Better yet, take the ferry downtown (see p 53).

West Side (Oakridge)

Oakridge Centre
Cambie St. and 41st Ave.
☎261-2511
Here, you'll find clothing boutiques, some of which feature French or British designers, such as Rodier Paris; an optical wear bou-

tique; restaurants; The Bay; and Zellers. In all, 150 shops and services. Free parking.

Accessories

Delané Boutique
130 Water St.
☎687-1782
This shop specializes in brown and beige fine leather luggage and bags made in Canada.

I Love Hats
1509 W. Broadway Ave., at Granville St.
☎739-0200
All sorts of hats in all colours. Traditional, modern or fun styles. Original sunglasses, too.

The Vancouver Pen Shop
512 W. Hastings St.
☎681-1612
This speciality pen shop has all the brand names, accessories and refills imaginable.

Antiques

Main Street, between 16th and 33rd avenues, is known as **Antique Row**. Concentrated on these blocks are shops specializing in Victorian antiques, folk art, 1950s kitsch and everything in between. A popular area for a Sunday-afternoon stroll.

Art Galleries

Gallery Row

The stretch of Granville Street leading south from the Granville Bridge until around 16th Avenue is known as **Gallery Row**. Some 20 galleries are located right on Granville or in the vicinity. Many of them specialize in the works of First Nations artists from the Northwest Coast. They offer a wonderful selection of high-quality items and probably your best chance of finding that perfect piece to take home.

Douglas Reynolds
2335 Granville St.
☎731-9292
This gallery has magnificent Aboriginal works of art, including a good collection of masks. If the totems are too heavy to take home with you, the gallery carries an excellent selection of prints by Aboriginal artists, many of which are quite affordable.

Mihrab
2229 Granville St.
☎879-6105
Mihrab sells carved doors, antique furniture, pillars, bronzes and carpets. You will find all the charm of southern Asia in this store.

Vancouver

Granville Island

A good many art galleries are concentrated on Granville Island. At the **Crafts Association of British Columbia** *(1386 Cartwright St.,* ☎*687-7270)* you'll find some gorgeous merchandise, including silver jewellery and works of glass and wood. Nearby is the **Federation of Canadian Artists** *(1241 Cartwright St.,* ☎*681-8534),* where a selection of paintings is displayed; the **Gallery of BC Ceramics** *(1359 Cartwright St.,* ☎*669-5645),* which sells original works in clay; and next to it, **Joel Berman Glassworks Ltd.** *(1244 Cartwright St.,* ☎*684-8332),* home to colourful, pricey glassworks.

The Raven and The Bear
1528 Duranleau St., Granville Island
☎*669-3990*
Excellent-quality Aboriginal works at reasonable prices. Lithographs, sculptures and natural stonework.

The Walrus & the Carpenter
1518 Duranleau St.
Granville Island Shopping Centre
☎*687-0920*
Beautiful reproductions of animals indigenous to Canada (bears, beavers, ducks).

Leona Lattimer
1590 West Second Ave.
west of Granville Island
☎*732-4556*
Leona Lattimer is a lovely gallery where you can admire some fine, expensive Aboriginal art. Quality jewellery and prints.

Other Areas

Coastal Peoples Fine Arts Gallery
1024 Mainland St.
☎*685-9298*
This lovely Yaletown shop offers an excellent selection of gold and silver jewellery, masks and totems made by the First Nations of the Pacific Northwest. Personalized service.

Marion Scott Gallery
481 Howe St.
☎*685-1934*
Marion Scott Gallery has a beautiful Aboriginal art collection, including superb sculptures.

Country Beads
2015 W. Fourth Ave.
☎*730-8056*
Country Beads has thousands of pearls and books. Workshops on Aboriginal and classic necklace and bracelet making are also offered.

Inuit Gallery of Vancouver
206 Cambie St.
☎*688-7323*
The Inuit Gallery of Vancouver sells some magnifi-

cent pieces of Aboriginal art from Canada's Far North and the Queen Charlotte Islands (Haida Gwaii).

Khot-La-Cha
270 Whonoak St., North Vancouver
☎987-3339
Beautiful sculptures by First Nation's artists, including the Coast Salish. One block from Marine Drive and McGuire Street.

Spirit Wrestler Gallery
8 Water St.
☎669-8813
Attractive sculptures and paintings by Inuit and Northwest Coast artists.

For First Nations works in silver and gold, see "Jewellery," p 247.

Birds

West Coast Tropical Bird
1679 W. Third Ave.
☎733-6246
A few friendly "hellos!" welcome clients to this

parakeet bird den. The birds will charm you with their colours and voices. Almost everything they need is sold here.

Bookstores

Duthie Books
2239 W. Fourth Ave.
☎732-5344
This independent bookstore is a favourite among Vancouverites.

Granville Book Co.
850 Granville St.
☎687-2213
Right downtown on Theatre Row, Granville Book Co. carries everything from computer manuals to science-fiction and mystery books, as well as magazines.

Hagar Books
2176 W. 41st Ave.
☎263-9412
This bookstore has been around for some 30 years.

Little Sisters Book and Art Emporium
1238 Davie St.
☎669-1753 or 800-567-1662
Little Sisters Book and Art Emporium (see box on the next page) is the only bookshop in Western Canada specializing in gay literature as well as essays on subjects such as homosexuality and feminism. It is also a vast bazaar, with products that include

Little Sisters

Little Sisters Book and Art Emporium has been engaged in a long battle with Canada Customs over the importation of books that the latter deems offensive. The store became a target of Canada Customs, which repeatedly opened, inspected and occasionally confiscated Little Sisters' shipments. Little Sisters took Canada Customs to B.C. Supreme Court, which ruled that the government agency had a right to inspect, but that its conduct infringed upon gays' and lesbians' freedom of speech rights and ultimately their equality. Little Sisters continues to fight Canada Customs' methods of detention, seizure, destruction and banning of books and magazines.

humorous greeting cards. For many years, this bookshop has been fighting Canada Customs, which arbitrarily blocks the importation of certain publications deemed to be pornographic. Books by recognized and respected authors such as Marcel Proust have been seized by Canada Customs, which has taken on the role of censor. Some of the same titles bound for regular bookshops have mysteriously escaped seizure by Canada Customs, leading to questions about discrimination.

Chapters
788 Robson St.
☎ 682-4066
In this large bookstore, readers can peruse the latest publications, magazines and specialized books.

Oscar's Art Books & Books
1533 West Broadway Ave., at Granville St.
☎ 731-0553
A large selection of fiction and books on art, cooking, nature, anatomy, travel... Wonderful books at low prices.

UBC Bookstore
6200 University Blvd.
☎ 822-BOOK
UBC Bookstore is the largest bookstore west of the

Rockies, with more than 100,000 titles. Allow enough time to park your car as the parking situation at UBC can be a problem.

Librairie Sophia Books
492 W. Hastings St. at Richards St.
☎ *684-0484*
Sophia Books specializes in multilingual books and other resources.

Barbara Jo's Books to Cook
1128 Mainland St.
☎ *688-6755*
Foodies with a penchant for cooking should check out the cookbooks in this Yaletown shop.

Clothing

After Five Fashions
545 Howe St.
☎ *899-0400*
Excellent selection of women's clothing. Complete outfits for business or for pleasure, not to mention formal evening dresses. Shoes and accessories also available.

Atomic Model
1036 Mainland St.
☎ *688-9989*
This trendy boutique imports its clothes from New York, Los Angeles, Paris and Milan.

Below the Belt
1131 Robson St.
☎ *688-6878*
Below the Belt, though a bit pricey, is a favourite with fashionable teens, but also with those for whom *look* is paramount.

Dorothy Grant
1656 W. 75th Ave.
☎ *681-0201*
Dorothy Grant makes clothing styled after that of the Haida Nation. The coats and capes are especially outstanding.

Giorgio's
1055 W. Georgia St.
☎ *682-2228*
Giorgio's is a renowned boutique that offers a lovely selection of well-known brand names, often at reasonable prices. To make you feel welcome, the staff offers you a cappuccino.

Just Cruisin' Shoppe
890 Howe St.
☎ *688-2030*
Just Cruisin' Shoppe is one of the largest bathing-suit stores in Canada. For the entire family and all sizes.

Laura Ashley
1171 Robson St.
☎ *688-8729*
Laura Ashley, is British-style women's boutique with flowered dresses and embroidered knits in pastel colours. Affordable prices.

Vancouver

Polo Ralph Lauren
375 Water St.
☎682-7656
This chic boutique has Ralph Lauren fashions for women, men and children, as well as perfumes and jewellery.

Second Suit
2036 W. Fourth Ave.
☎732-0338
Second Suit carries the best in formal menswear from Armani to Boss and Dior.

Tilley Endurables
2041 Granville St., corner Eighth Ave.
☎732-4287
From safari jackets and patch-pocket pants to vests and hats for rainy or sunny weather, this store's refined attire, made from weather-resistant material, is suitable for strolls or longer excursions.

True Value Vintage
710 Robson St.
☎685-5403
True Value Vintage is an exceptional shop that both buys and sells vintage clothing from the glory days of rockabilly and disco.

Flowers

Eden Florist
843 Davie St.
☎685-8058
Eden Florist specializes in flowers for all occasions. Personalized service and free delivery in the downtown area.

Food

Capers
1675 Robson St.
☎687-5288
2285 W. Fourth Ave., Kitsilano
☎739-6676
2496 Marine Dr., West Vancouver
☎925-3316
Capers is a natural-food store that carries fresh vegetables, meats, prepared dishes, good breads and vitamins. Somewhat expensive but practical for travellers. You can eat here, too.

Daniel's Le Chocolat Belge
1105 Robson St.
☎688-9624
One of the rare fine-chocolate shops in Vancouver, and probably the best. The dark chocolate and truffles, prepared in strict Belgian tradition, are exceptional. Small figurines, boxes and vases enhance their presentation and make lovely gifts. The prices are reasonable. There are seven branches throughout the city; call the number listed above for their locations.

Chocolate Arts
2037 W. Fourth Ave.
☎739-0475
Chocolate Arts is renowned for its high-quality chocolate as well as its elegant creations whose shapes are

inspired by West Coast Aboriginal art.

Kobayashi Shoten
1518 Robson St.
☎ *683-1019*
This Japanese store sells groceries, take-out meals and gifts as well as table settings and linens.

Leysley Stowe
1780 W. Third Ave.,
corner Burrard St.
☎ *731-3663*
Leysley Stowe is a gourmet grocer and caterer that sells cheeses and other fine products from France. The breads and cakes are always fresh.

Meinhardt Fine Foods
3002 Granville St., at 14th Ave.
☎ *732-4405*
This lovely, if pricey, shop stocks ready-made deli products, gorgeous fresh flowers and gift boxes full of sinful delicacies.

Rocky Mountain Chocolate Factory
1017 Robson St.
☎ *688-4100*
Rocky Mountain Chocolate Factory is a divine little chocolate shop. You can savour bulk chocolate with nuts and fruits, or perhaps the bitter dark chocolate, for the real connoisseur.

Gifts

Crystal Gallery
Lonsdale Quay Market
North Vancouver
☎ *986-8224*
Reasonably priced, attractive, brightly coloured crystal objects.

Jade World
by appointment only
Suite 403 - 1311 Howe St.
☎ *733-7212*
Right near Granville Island. Jade sculptures and jewellery

Rasta Wares
1505 Commercial Dr.
☎ *255-3600*
This shop offers incense and jewellery from India, Indonesia and Africa at low prices.

Wendy's Collection
2620 W. Broadway Ave.
☎ *730-8381*
The window of this shop, which sells superb statuettes and sculptures from China, catches your eye from a distance. Jewellery and gemstones at affordable prices.

Glasses and Contact Lenses

Eyes on Burrard
775 Burrard St.
☎ *688-9521*
This shop, which specializes in designer frames, also

Vancouver

has a few well-known brand names of tinted lenses.

Regency Contact Lens
607-650 West 41st Ave., Oakridge Center, entrance on Cambie St.
☎*263-0900*
Contact-lens specialists, offering quality service and competitive prices.

Yaletown Optical
1051 Mainland St.
☎*684-1243*
Yaletown Optical offers lovely frames as well as well-known brand names of trendy glasses, at premium prices.

Hairdressers

Suki's Hair Salon
3157 S. Granville St., at 16th Ave.
☎*738-7713*
Vancouver's most fashionable hair salon, frequented by the jet set. They offer a wide range of services at affordable prices.

Home Decor and Accessories

Kaya Kaya
2039 W. Fourth Ave.
☎*732-1816*
Kaya Kaya has Japanese porcelain and other Japanese accessories for the home, some of which are genuine works of art.

Kim-John
2903 Granville St., at 13th Ave.
☎*732-7311*
Articles for your house and dining-room table in fine Chinese or British porcelain (Wedgewood, Royal Doulton), Bohemian crystal or solid silver. A multitude of attractive, affordably priced objects.

The Kitchen Corner
4516 W. 10th Ave.
☎*739-4422*
Also at:
1955 W. 40th Ave.
2136 W. 40th Ave.
1684 Commercial Dr.
You'll find absolutely everything in this little store for next to nothing: anything you might need for your kitchen, for camping, a day at the beach as well as spices, candles, souvenirs...

Ming Wo Cookware
2170 W. Fourth Ave.
☎*737-2624*
You will find every kitchen utensil imaginable at this store. With their cheery, modern shapes and colours, the spoons, forks and even the garbage cans make attractive accessories. Very reasonable prices.

Paint Inspirations
2003 W. Fourth Ave.
☎*737-8558*
Paint Inspirations carries all the supplies needed to paint designs on furniture or objects. You can have a lesson on the premises or

buy some supplies and a video to watch at home.

Scandinavia Arts
648 Hornby St.
☎ **688-4744**
Scandinavia Arts specializes in high-quality Scandinavian crystal. The modern designs are elegant. Besides the well-known brand names, it also offers less expensive crystal creations.

The Spirit of Christmas
Oakridge Centre,
Cambie St. and 41st Ave.
☎ **683-2507**
The Spirit of Christmas is the largest store in Canada solely devoted to Christmas. The selection and beauty of the decorations is amazing.

Jewellery

Silver Gallery
1226 Robson St.
☎ **681-6884**
The Silver Gallery is the least expensive store for fine-quality Aboriginal jewellery and crafts. Solid silver bracelets, necklaces and rings with gold enamelling can be found at competitive prices. They also sell Indonesian objects, including masks, at affordable prices. Attentive service.

Leather

Marte's Fine Leather
134-1055 W. Georgia St., Royal Centre
☎ **684-6424**
Marte's Fine Leather is a leather shop that has luggage and overnight cases as well as briefcases and handbags.

Ocean Drive Leather
1026 Mainland St.
☎ **647-2244**
Located in the Yaletown area, Ocean Drive has fashionable leather clothing for men and women.

Lingerie

La Jolie Madame
Pacific Centre
Fourth floor in the Atrium
☎ **669-1831**
Fine lingerie and negligées for women and young ladies. Well-known brands imported from Paris.

Music

A&B Sound
556 Seymour St.
☎ **687-5837**
A&B Sound has great prices in electronics, video cassettes and compact discs. Watch out for the crowds on weekends.

Vancouver

Highlife Records & Music
1317 Commercial Dr.
☎*251-6964*
This is another spot to find music at good prices.

Long & McQuade Limited Musical Instruments
2301 Granville St.
☎*734-4886*
Long & McQuade Limited Musical Instruments has all sorts of musical instruments, both new and used, for sale or for rent for a day, month or year.

Not Just Another Music Shop
2415 Granville St.
☎*733-6526*
This shop has an excellent selection of new and used guitars. Rentals, repairs and guitar lessons.

Virgin Megastore
788 Burrard St.
☎*669-2289*
This is the only Virgin Megastore, a British CD shop, in Canada.

Natural Products

Gaia Garden Herbal Apothecary
2672 W. Broadway Ave.
☎*734-4372*
The only place in town that has everything in the way of herbal medicines. Visa cards accepted.

Finlandia
1964 W. Broadway Ave.
☎*733-5323*
This store has an excellent selection of vitamins, herbs and essential oils, as well as homeopathic products to gently cure what ails you. It's also a traditional pharmacy. Personalized, friendly service.

Tung Fong Hung
536 Main St.
☎*688-0883*
Tung Fong Hung is a traditional Chinese herbalist. Ask for Liping, who will take the time to explain the complex healing powers of these plants. The shop specializes in ginseng.

Newspapers and Magazines

Magpie Magazine Gallery
1319 Commercial Dr.
☎*253-6666*

Mayfair News
1535 W. Broadway Ave.
☎*738-8951*
Newspapers and magazines from all over the world in every language are found at these shops, sometimes a bit later than the original issue date.

Pet Supplies

Woofles
1496 Cartwright St.
☎*689-3647*
Woofles, housed in a caboose on Granville Island, profoundly believes that "dogs are kids in fur coats."

Here, you'll find organic delicacies such as peanut butter *doggotti*, hemp and veggie sticks, and, if you're lucky, flavoured bubble-blowing kits...in short, everything for the yuppy puppy.

Pharmacies

Shoppers Drug Mart
many locations throughout the city
the following two are open 24hrs/day
1125 Davie St.
☎*669-2424*
2302 West Fourth Ave.
☎*738-3138*
This national pharmacy chain has a bit of everything including, pharmacist, medicines and cosmetics.

Photocopies, Office Supplies and Internet Access

Kinko's
1900 W. Broadway Ave.
☎*734-2679*
If you need to use a computer, make some photocopies or simply buy some office supplies, this store is open 24hrs.

Websters Internet Cafe
340 Robson St.
☎*915-9327*
Conveniently located near Library

Square and a number of downtown hotels, Websters offers Internet access.

Shoes

John Fluevog
837 Granville St.
☎*688-2828*
Shoemaker to the stars (including the likes of Madonna), John Fluevog makes irresistibly funky clodhoppers. Check out the sales in January and August, when reductions of up to 60% are offered.

Stéphane de Raucourt Shoes
1067 Robson St.
☎*681-8814*
If you are looking for quality shoes that stand out from the ordinary, here is a shop to keep in mind. They are expensive, but a little window-shopping never hurt anyone.

Tallcrest Shoes
644 Hornby St.
☎*669-3738*
From sports shoes to dress shoes, this store specializes in large sizes.

Western Town Boots
2940 Main St.
☎*879-1914*
All kinds of cowboy and cowgirl boots in all sizes.

Souvenirs

Great Canadian Garment & Gift Company
213 Carrall St.
☎684-2270
Located in the Gastown area, this shop sells clothing embroidered with the colour of the Canadian flag, as well as other Canadian-made items.

Sports and the Outdoors

Altus Mountain Gear
137 West Broadway
☎876-5255
Altus Mountain Gear carries everything for mountaineering: waterproof gear and clothing, as well as tents, backpacks and more for sale or for rent.

Coast Mountain Sports
2201 W. Fourth Ave.
☎731-6181
A stop at Coast Mountain Sports is a must for mountaineers who appreciate quality equipment. Only the best is sold here; the shop is therefore quite expensive and reserved mostly for pros. The staff is very friendly and experienced.

Comor Go Play Outside
1918 Fir St.
☎731-2163
Everything for outdoor sports, especially cycling and skateboarding. Equipment, clothing, helmets, shoes and more.

Cyclepath
1421 W. Broadway Ave.
one block east of Granville St.
☎737-2344
This bike shop does repairs and sells all sorts of bicycles and accessories.

Ecomarine Granville Island
1668 Duranleau St.
☎689-7575
Ecomarine Granville Island has everything for sea-kayakers. You can even try out the kayaks before you buy.

Mountain Equipment Co-op

130 W. Broadway Ave.
☎872-7858

Mountain Equipment Co-op is a gigantic store that offers everything you need for your outdoor activities. You must be a member to make purchases, but a lifetime membership only costs $5.

Ruddik's Fly Shop

1077 Marine Dr.,
North Vancouver
☎985-5650

Ruddik's Fly Shop is a wonderful store for fly-fisheres that even inspires newcomers to the sport. There are thousands of different flies for all sorts of fish. The owner will be glad to assist you. They also sell super-light canes, state-of-the-art fishing reels, souvenir clothing as well as fishing-related sculptures and gadgets.

Nevada Bob's

88 SW Marine Dr.
☎324-1144

Nevada Bob's is one of the largest golf stores in Canada. There are a dozen locations in Vancouver. If you can't find what you want at this location, the manager will find it for you at another one.

Taiga Works

390 W. Eighth Ave.
☎875-6640

Taiga Works is a small shop with mountain sports equipment and prices that beat the competition. A good address to remember.

3 Vets

2200 Yukon St.
☎872-5475

3 Vets is a local institution. For 40 years this store has been supplying reasonably priced camping equipment to everyone from professional lumberjacks to tree planters and weekend campers.

Tea

Murchie's Teas & Coffees

Oakridge Centre,
Cambie St. and 41st Ave.
☎872-6930
970 Robson St.
☎669-0783

These two downtown locations carry a vast, unbeatable selection of teas and coffees that has given Murchie's its solid West Coast reputation. There is also a Victoria branch (see p 304).

Vancouver

Ten Ren Tea and Ginseng Company
550 Main St.
☎**684-1566**
The Ten Ren Tea and Ginseng Company is, without a doubt, the best tea shop in Canada. Big jars hold an exceptional variety of teas from around the world.

Telephones and Telecommunications

Cell City Communications
105-950 W. Broadway Ave.
☎**737-8018**
You can rent a cellular phone, a pager or obtain other services here that will put you in reach at any time of day.

Pacific Cellular
1199 West Pender St.
☎**662-3931**
If you need a cellular phone for the duration of your stay or just for a day, this store will cater to your needs.

Victoria and Surroundings

I s Victoria ★★★ really more English than England, as people often say it is? Well, with high tea, lawn bowling and cricket as local pastimes, there is no denying its characteristic English flavour.

This is still a North American city, however, and along with all the English, it has welcomed large numbers of French Canadians, Chinese, Japanese, Scots, Irish, Germans and Americans.

Located at the southern tip of Vancouver Island, Victoria is the capital of the province and has a population of nearly 300,000 scattered across a large urban area. Its harbour looks out onto the Strait of Juan de Fuca, a natural border with Washington State. Victoria is set against a series of small mountains no higher than 300m in altitude, and its waterfront stretches several kilometres.

To help you make the most of your visit to Victoria and the Saanich

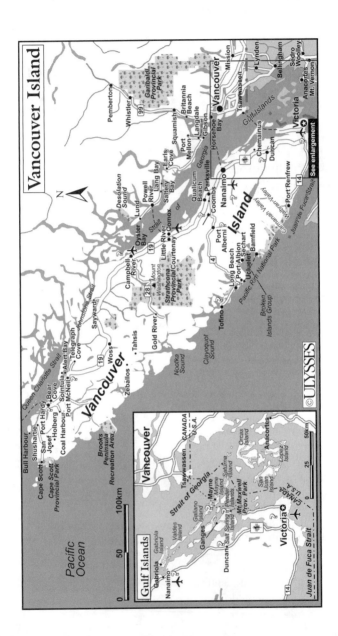

Vancouver Island

Pacific Ocean

Queen Charlotte Strait

Bull Harbour
Shushartie
Port Hardy
Cape Scott • Sart • Josef
Cape Scott • Holberg • Bear Cove
Provincial Park • Coal Harbour • Sointula • Alert Bay
Port McNeil • Telegraph Cove

Brooks
Peninsula
Recreation Area

Woss
Zeballos • Sayward

Johnstone Strait

Gold River

Tahsis

Nootka Sound

Clayoquot Sound

Vancouver Island

Pemberton
Whistler
99
Garibaldi
Provincial Park

Campbell River
Oyster Bay
Mount Washington
Little River
Strathcona Provincial
Park

Desolation Sound
Lund
Powell River
Lang Bay
Saltery Bay
Comox
Courtenay
Qualicum Beach
Parksville
Coombs

Strait of Georgia

Port Mellon
Earls Cove
Squamish
Britannia Beach
Langdale
Gibson
Horseshoe Bay

Vancouver
Mission
Lynden
Tsawwassen
Sedro Woolley

Nanaimo
Port Alberni
Sechart
Port Albion
Ucluelet • Bamfield
Long Beach
Pacific Rim National Park

Broken Islands Group

Chemainus
Duncan
Port Renfrew
Nitinat Valley
Kennan Valley

Juan de Fuca Strait

Victoria
Anacortes
Mt. Vernon
Bellingham

See enlargement

N

© ULYSSES

Gulf Islands

Vancouver

CANADA
U.S.A.
Tsawwassen

Strait of Georgia

Galiano Island
Valdes Island
Gabriola Island
Nanaimo

Ganges
Mayne Island
Saturna Island
Pender Islands
Orcas Island
Salt Spring Island
Mt. Maxwell Prov. Park
Duncan
San Juan Island
Anacortes

Victoria
14
CANADA
U.S.A.
Juan de Fuca Strait

0   25   50km

Peninsula, we have outlined five tours:

Tour A:
The Inner Harbour and Old Town ★★★

Tour B:
Scenic Marine Drive ★★

Tour C:
The Saanich Peninsula ★

Tour D:
From Victoria to the West Coast Trail ★★

The area code in this chapter is **250**, unless otherwise indicated.

Exploring

Downtown Victoria is cramped, which can make parking somewhat difficult. There are a number of public lots where you can pay to park your car.

There are city parking lots ($10/day) at the 600 block of Fisgard Street, the 700 block of Johnson Street, the 500 block of Yates Street, the 700 block of View Street and the 700 block of Broughton Street. These, as well as metred street parking, are free after 6pm, all

day on Sundays and holidays.

Tour A: The Inner Harbour and Old Town

Any tour of Victoria starts at the Inner Harbour, which was the main point of access into the city for decades. Back in the era of tall ships, the merchant marine operating on the Pacific Ocean used to stop here to pick up goods destined for England. Once the railway reached the coast, however, the merchandise was transported across Canada by train, thus reducing the amount of time required to reach the east side of the continent. From that point on, the merchant marine only provided a sea link to Asia.

Head to the **Tourism Victoria Visitor Info Centre** *(812 Wharf St.,* ☎*953-2033)*, where you can take in a general view of the Inner Harbour and the buildings alongside it, including the **Empress Hotel** ★★ (see p 286) and the **Provincial Legislature Buildings** ★ (see p 260). Tourism Victoria occupies a former gas station built in the Art Deco style in 1931. The tower above it is a miniature version of a New York–style skyscraper.

Start your tour by strolling northward along Government Street. You'll pass a series of stone buildings housing bookstores, cafés, antique shops and all sorts of other businesses. At View Street, turn left and walk down the little pedestrian street to **Bastion Square** ★. The **Bastion Square Festival of the Arts**, not so much a festival as an open-air craft market, is held here from spring to fall *(Apr Fri-Sun, May Thu-Sun, Jun to early Oct Wed-Sun and holidays 10:30am to 5:30pm)*.

Bastion Square marks the former site of Fort Victoria, constructed by the Hudson's Bay Company in 1843, with the help of hundreds of native people. Twenty years later, the fort was demolished to make way for the city. Today, the site is occupied by public buildings like the **Maritime Museum of British Columbia** *($6; every day 9:30am to 4:30pm; 28 Bastion Sq., ☎385-4222, www.mmbc.bc.ca)*, which highlights great moments in the history of sailing, from the days when tall ships sidled up alongside one another in the harbour, up until the present time.

Walk down Bastion Square, turn right on Wharf Street, then head up the north side of Johnson Street. Go into **Market Square** ★, a series of three-storey brick buildings housing shops and cafés, arranged around an inner courtyard. Built in the 1880s, it once housed hotels and saloons, as well as shops. It's a pleasant place to wander and gets very lively during the jazz, blues and theatre festivals and on the Chinese New Year.

Back on Wharf Street, turn right onto Fisgard Street, and left into the oldest **Chinatown** ★ *(west of Government Street, between Pandora and Fisgard sts.)* in Canada. Full of brightly coloured shops, its sidewalks are decorated with geometric patterns that form a Chinese character meaning "good fortune." At one time, there were over 150 businesses in Chinatown, as well as three schools, five temples, two churches and a hospital. On your way through this neighbourhood, you'll come across the Gate of Harmonious Interest, on Fisgard Street, a symbol of the spirit of cooperation between the Chinese and Canadian communities. **Fan Tan Alley** ★, which runs north-south *(south of Fisgard St.)*, is supposedly the narrowest street in Victoria. People used to come here to buy opium until 1908, when the federal government banned the sale of the drug. Here, you are in the heart of Chinatown.

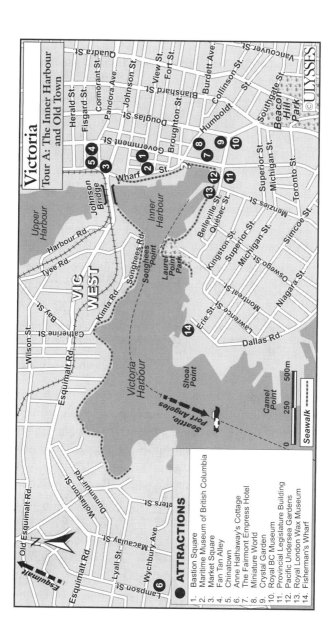

Victoria
Tour A: The Inner Harbour and Old Town

Upper Harbour

Johnson Bridge

Inner Harbour

Songhees Rd.
Songhees Point

Harbour Rd.

Tyee Rd.

VIC WEST

Kimta Rd.

Bay St.

Catherine St.

Wilson St.

Esquimalt Rd.

Laurel Point Park

Victoria Harbour

Shoal Point

Camel Point

Seattle, Port Angeles

Esquimalt

Old Esquimalt Rd.

Dunsmuir Rd.

Wollaston St.

Peters St.

Macaulay Ave.

Lyall St.

Wychbury Ave.

Lampson St.

Quadra St.

Herald St.

Cormorant St.

Fisgard St.

Pandora Ave.

Johnson St.

Government St.

Douglas St.

Wharf St.

View St.

Fort St.

Broughton St.

Blanshard St.

Humboldt St.

Burdett Ave.

Collinson St.

Southgate St.

Beacon Hill Park

Vancouver St.

Superior St.

Michigan St.

Belleville St.

Quebec St.

Menzies St.

Kingston St.

Superior St.

Michigan St.

Montreal St.

Lawrence St.

Erie St.

Oswego St.

Simcoe St.

Niagara St.

Toronto St.

Dallas Rd.

Seawalk ·········

0   250   500m

© ULYSSES

N

● ATTRACTIONS

1. Bastion Square
2. Maritime Museum of British Columbia
3. Market Square
4. Fan Tan Alley
5. Chinatown
6. Anne Hathaway's Cottage
7. The Fairmont Empress Hotel
8. Miniature World
9. Crystal Garden
10. Royal BC Museum
11. Provincial Legislature Building
12. Pacific Undersea Gardens
13. Royal London Wax Museum
14. Fisherman's Wharf

From Chinatown, turn right on Government Street, re-tracing your steps to the Inner Harbour. Or, take a short detour to **Victoria West**, home to a popular pub and a growing number of large harbour-side hotels but few attractions. It's a short walk across the Johnson Street Bridge; from there, a pleasant seawalk leads to the West Bay Marina.

The Seawalk runs alongside the houses and the water-front, offering a lovely view of the buildings downtown. Farther along, past the Victoria Harbour, you will see the Strait of Juan de Fuca. Stop in at Spinnakers Brewpub *(Catherine St.)* and wet your whistle while taking in the panoramic view.

Anne Hathaway's Cottage ★ *($10; every day 10am to 4pm; 429 Lampson St., ☎388-4353)* is located here, in Victoria West. After crossing the Johnson Street Bridge, turn left on Lampson Street after the sixth traffic light. The Munro Bus, which you can catch at the corner of Douglas and Yates streets, stops at the entrance. This little bit of England is a reconstruction of the birth-place of William Shakespeare and the home of Anne Hathaway, his wife. There are also five additional manor houses, decorated in the same style, where lodging is available (English Inn and Resort). A stroll among these buildings will take you back in time.

Fairmont Empress Hotel

West of Victoria West is **Esquimalt**, a small town known mainly for its naval military base and its **CFB Esquimalt Naval & Military Museum** *($2; Mon-Fri 10am to 3:30pm; ☎363-4312)*, which has a large collection of military equipment and retraces the history of the base.

Back at the Inner Harbour, make your way to the Fairmont Empress Hotel.

The **Fairmont Empress Hotel** ★★ *(721 Government St., ☎384-8111)* was built in 1905 for the Canadian Pacific railway company. It was designed by Francis Rattenbury in the Chateau style, just like the Chateau Frontenac in Québec City, only more modern and less romantic. Use the main entrance and cross the lobby, letting yourself be transported back to the 1920s, when the names of influential people found their way into the guest books. Above all, make sure to stop by the Empress for pricey afternoon tea (see p 297), or a curry buffet in the Raj-era Bengal lounge.

At **Miniature World** *($9; mid-May to mid-Jun every day 9am to 7pm, mid-Jun to early Sep every day 8:30am to 9pm, early Sep to mid-Jun 9am to 5pm; Fairmont Empress Hotel, 649 Humboldt St., ☎385-9731)*, you'll see what patience and meticulousness can accomplish: an operational miniature sawmill and other fascinating creations, including two buildings dating back to the end of the 19th century. A sure hit with the kids.

From Miniature World, turn right on Humboldt Street and right again on Douglas Street.

The **Crystal Garden**, by the same architect, is located behind the Empress, at Douglas and Belleville streets. A big glass canopy supported by a visible metal structure, it originally housed a saltwater swimming pool and is now home to a variety of exotic birds and endangered animals.

Kitty-corner to the Crystal Garden is the **Royal British Columbia Museum** ★★★ *($9; every day 9am to 5pm; 675 Belleville St., ☎356-7226 or 888-447-7977, http://rbcm1. rbcm.gov.bc.ca)*, where you can learn about the history of the city and the various peoples that have inhabited the province. The centrepieces of the collection are a reproduction of Captain Vancouver's ship and a Kwa-gulth First Nation house. The museum also hosts some interesting temporary exhibitions.

The spectacular First Peoples exhibit begins with some historical artifacts juxtaposed alongside some contemporary art, like that of Musqueam artist Susan Point, to demonstrate the roots and evolution of Northwest Coast art of the type you'll see in galleries, hotels and restaurants during your stay. Throughout the exhibit, there are clear distinctions between coastal and interior peoples, and pre- and post-contact periods. There is a wonderful exhibit of masks and totem poles, arranged by cultural group, with their distinctive elements identified. For example, we learn that Haida art is characterized by a carved, raised eyelid line and a concave orbit from the bridge of nose to the temple to the nostril. There are also enormous feast dishes shaped like bears and wolves; magnificent Coast Salish capes, blankets and bags woven with cedar bark; a sound-and-light show explaining the cosmology of Northwest Coast First Nations; more than 100 Haida argillite carvings and countless other items of interest.

In the Modern History exhibit, there are recreations of scenes from the last century of B.C.'s history, including a 1920s rococo-style theatre showing silent films; facades of Victorian buildings, including a hotel you can walk right into, its woodwork salvaged from a Nanaimo hotel; and a Chinatown street scene. The presentation is attractive and entertaining enough to keep children enthralled. There is also a Natural History exhibit, with models of different landscapes and ecosystems and fascinating pools of local marine animals.

The strange-looking white tower near the Provincial Legislature, at the corner of Belleville and Government streets, is the largest **carillon** in Canada, with 62 bells. Its chimes can be heard every Sunday at 3pm from April to December.

The design for the **Provincial Legislature Buildings** ★ *(free tours)* was chosen by way of a competition. The winner was architect Francis Rattenbury, who was just 25 years old at the time and went on to design many other public and privately owned buildings in British Columbia.

Return to the Inner Harbour. Across from the Legislature, the **Pacific Undersea Gardens** *($7.50; Jul and Aug every day 10am to 7pm, Sep to Jun every day 10am to 5pm, Jan and Feb closed Tue and Wed; 490 Belleville St., ☎382-5717)* highlights marine plant and animal life.

Fans of wax museums, like the fabled Madame Tussaud's, are not likely to be disappointed by the **Royal London Wax Museum** *($8.50; Jan 1 to mid-May 9:30am to 5pm, mid-May to early Sep 9am to 7:30pm, early Sep to Dec 31 9:30am to 6pm; 470 Belleville St. on the Inner Harbour, ☎388-4461).* History buffs will see everything from generations of royal families, including all six of Henry VIII's wives (looking strikingly similar), to a gory Plains of Abraham scene, with General Wolfe dying an agonizing death, to a multimedia show dedicated to famous explorers, to a Last Supper scene with the resurrection depicted in lights. In seconds, visitors are taken from the storybook land of Disney to the guillotine in the ghastly chamber of horrors, the obvious highlight of any wax museum. It's Victoria at its cheesiest!

Carry on along the Inner Harbour, past **Laurel Point Park**, where you pick up the pedestrian path. The path continues as far as the Coast Harbourside Hotel and Marina. From there, you must walk along the road *(Kingston Street)* until St. Lawrence Street, where you turn right toward **Fisherman's Wharf ★**. Here you'll find float homes belonging to local fishers, as well as an excellent fish-and-chip shop (see p 291) and a fishmonger (see p 303). The latter sells herrings at $1 a piece, which you can feed to the more socialized seals in the harbour. Just hold them out over the water until they bite.

When you—and the seals—have had your fill, wander back to the centre of town.

Tour B: Scenic Marine Drive

This tour leads you along a fabulously scenic coastal road at the bottom of the Saanich Peninsula, by way of detours to a number of important Victoria attractions, located inland. You will pass through the communities of Fairfield, Rockland and Oak Bay. Although this is definitely a driving (or better yet, cycling) tour, it is just minutes from downtown Victoria.

The tour begins at the Ogden Point Breakwater on Dallas Road, near Dock Street. From there, head out along Dallas Road for a beautiful view of wild and windy Juan de Fuca Strait. Turn left on Government Street, and continue to Simcoe Street.

Here, you are in the Carr family's neighbourhood. Built of wood, **Carr House ★** *($5.35; mid-May to mid-Oct every day 10am to 5pm; 207 Government St.,* ☎*383-5843)* was erected in 1864 for the family of Richard Carr. After the American gold rush,

the Carrs, who had been living in California, returned to England then came back to North America to set up residence in Victoria. Mr. Carr made a fortune in real estate and owned many pieces of land, both developed and undeveloped, in this residential area. He died in 1888, having outlived his wife by two years. Emily was only 17 at the time. Shortly after, she went first to San Francisco, then London and finally to Paris to study art. She returned to British Columbia around 1910 and began teaching art to the children of Vancouver. She eventually went back to Victoria and followed in her father's footsteps, entering the real-estate business. She also began travelling more along the coast in order to paint, producing her greatest works in the 1930s.

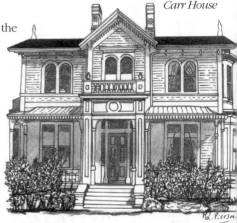

Carr House

Emily Carr and Victoria

After the American gold rush, Richard Carr and his family, who had been living in California, went home to their native England then returned to North America to set up residence in Victoria. Mr. Carr made a fortune in real estate and owned many pieces of land, both developed and undeveloped, in the James Bay area of Victoria. He died in 1888, having outlived his wife by two years. Emily was only 17 at the time. Shortly after, she went first to San Francisco, then London and finally to Paris to study art.

She returned to British Columbia around 1910 and began teaching art to the children of Vancouver. She eventually went back to Victoria and followed in her father's footsteps, entering the real-estate business. She also began travelling more along the coast in order to paint, producing her greatest works in the 1930s.

A unique painter and a reclusive woman, Emily Carr is now recognized across Canada as a great artist who left her stamp on the art world. While the Art Gallery of Greater Victoria and the Royal BC Museum have an Emily Carr collection, the Vancouver Art Gallery is home to the largest permanent exhibition of her paintings.

A unique painter and a reclusive woman, Emily Carr is now recognized across Canada as a great artist who left her stamp on the art world. Be sure to visit the Vancouver Art Gallery (see p 107) to learn more about her art, since the main focus here is her private life. The only original piece of furniture in the house is the bed in which Emily was born in 1871. The house is nevertheless furnished in a style typical

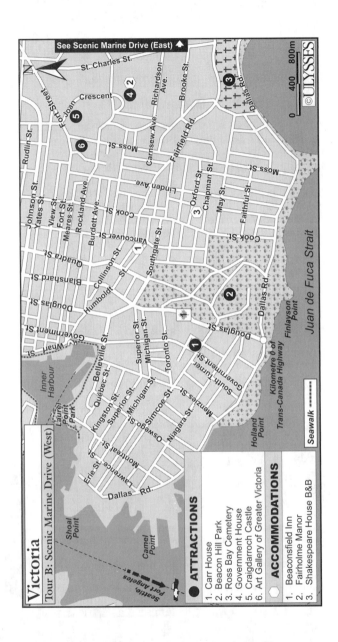

Victoria

Tour B: Scenic Marine Drive (West)

See Scenic Marine Drive (East) ▲

St. Charles St.

Crescent

Fort Street

St. Joan

Rudlin St.

Moss St.

Richardson Ave.

Brooke St.

Carnsew Ave.

Fairfield Rd.

Dallas Rd.

Johnson St.
Yates St.
View St.
Fort St.
Meares St.
Rockland Ave.
Burdett Ave.

Quadra St.
Blanshard St.
Douglas St.
Government St.
Wharf St.

Vancouver St.
Collinson St.
Humboldt St.

Southgate St.
Cook St.
Linden Ave.
Oxford St.
Chapman St.
May St.

Moss St.
Faithful St.
Cook St.

Belleville St.
Superior St.
Michigan St.

Québec St.
Kingston St.
Superior St.
Michigan St.
Simcoe St.
Niagara St.

Menzies St.
Toronto St.
South Turner St.
Government St.

Dallas Rd.

Kilometre 0 of
Trans-Canada Highway

Finlayson
Point

Holland
Point

Juan de Fuca Strait

Inner
Harbour

Laurel
Point Park

Lawrence St.
Erie St.
Montreal St.
Oswego St.

Shoal Point

Camel Point

Seattle
Port Angeles

© ULYSSES

0   400   800m

ATTRACTIONS

1. Carr House
2. Beacon Hill Park
3. Ross Bay Cemetery
4. Government House
5. Craigdarroch Castle
6. Art Gallery of Greater Victoria

ACCOMMODATIONS

1. Beaconsfield Inn
2. Fairholme Manor
3. Shakespeare House B&B

Seawalk ------

Victoria

Tour B: Scenic Marine Drive (East)

See Scenic Marine Drive (West) ►

ATTRACTIONS

1. Abkhazi Gardens
2. Oak Bay Marina
3. Oak Bay Village

ACCOMMODATIONS

1. Oak Bay Beach Hotel (R)

(R) establishment with restaurant (see description)

RESTAURANTS

1. White Heather Tea Room

0 250 500m

Victoria Golf Club

McNeill Bay

Gonzales Bay

Rose Bay

Ross Bay Cemetery

© ULYSSES

of the period. There is a small gift shop on site and a garden, animated by excerpts from Carr's writings. Carr House also distributes maps of the neighbourhood, which show where the family lived at various times.

From Carr House, turn left on Simcoe Street until Douglas Street, where Beacon Hill Park begins.

Beacon Hill Park ★ *(between Douglas and Cook sts., facing the Juan de Fuca Strait)* is a peaceful spot where Emily Carr spent many happy days drawing. A public park laid out in 1890, it features a number of trails leading through fields of wildflowers and landscaped sections. The view of the strait and the Olympic Mountains in the United States is positively magnificent from here. For a reminder of exactly where you are in relation to the rest of Canada, Km 0 of the Trans-Canada Highway lies at the south end of Douglas Street at the corner of Dallas Road (see box).

Carry on along Dallas Road until Memorial Crescent and turn right on Fairfield Road (opposite Stannard Ave.) to the entrance to **Ross Bay Cemetery**. This will take you to the oldest part of the 11ha cemetery, final resting place of many of Victoria's nota-

bles, including Emily Carr. Volunteers are often present *(every day mid-May to mid-Sep, 10am to 4pm)* and can provide short tours or self-guided brochures. Tours are regularly scheduled during the tourist season *($5; Sun 2pm Jul and Aug; tours are indicated "RBC" and start at Bagga Pasta, Fairfield Plaza, 1516 Fairfield Rd., ☎598-8870, www.oldcem. bc.ca).*

From the cemetery, turn left at Charles Street, and left again at Rockland Avenue.

Government House *(1401 Rockland Ave., ☎387-2080)* is another of Victoria's lovely attractions. The house is not open to the public, but its absolutely gorgeous 6ha garden may be visited. There is no admission charge to visit the gardens, which are open every day. If you have even a passing interest in gardens, a look at the rose and herb gardens is worth the visit.

Garden tours are arranged *($10; one or two per month Wed and/or Sun May to Sep, call for schedule; ☎356-5139).*

From the gardens on Rockland Street, head up Joan Crescent to Craigdarroch Castle.

Craigdarroch Castle ★ *($10; mid-Jun to early Sep every day 9am to 7pm; winter every day 10am to 4:30pm; 1050 Joan*

The Trans-Canada Highway

Mile/Kilometre Zero of the Trans-Canada Highway (TCH), the longest national highway in the world, is indicated by a monument at the corner of Dallas Road and Douglas Street in Victoria. The TCH ends (or begins, depending on your point of view) 7,821km east, in St. John's, in the province of Newfoundland and Labrador. In fact, in front of St. John's city hall, a sign marking the spot declares that "Canada begins right here," so the point of view on the East Coast is pretty clear!

Construction of the TCH began in the summer of 1950, and by the time it was completed in 1970 (the opening ceremonies took place in Rogers Pass, B.C. prior to completion, in 1962), it had cost $1 billion, more than three times the initial estimated cost.

In truth, the highway is neither a single entity, nor does it link the entire country. It needs some help from two ferries (to Victoria and St. John's from the mainland), doesn't quite manage to pass through every Canadian jurisdiction (the Yukon, Northwest Territories and Nunavut are left out), and is in fact two different highways for much of Ontario and Québec. West of Portage la Prairie, Manitoba, it splits into Highway 16, which heads north and ends up in Prince Rupert, B.C., and Highway 1, a southern route that ends up in Victoria.

The TCH's distinctive marker shield is a white maple leaf on a green background.

Cr., ☎592-5323) stands at the east end of the downtown area. It was built in 1890 for Robert Dunsmuir, who made a fortune in the coal-mining business. He died before it was completed, but his widow and three children went on to live here. What makes this building interesting, aside from its dimensions, is its decorative woodwork and the view from the fifth floor of the tower. This residence is indicative of the opulent lifestyle enjoyed by the wealthy a century ago.

From the castle, head back to Rockland Street, turn right, and right again on Moss Street.

Both classical and contemporary works are on view at the **Art Gallery of Greater Victoria** *($5; Mon-Sat 10am to 5pm, Thu until 9pm, Sun 1pm to 5pm; 1040 Moss St., ☎384-4101)*, the city's museum of fine arts. Visitors will find pieces by Emily Carr and by contemporary local and Asian artists. A must for all art lovers. Contact the museum to find out about on-going exhibitions and activities.

From the gallery, head back down Moss Street until Fairfield Road, and turn left if you're in the mood for another garden visit. If not, take Moss Street all the way back to Dallas Road, and carry on along the coast.

Abkhazi Garden *($7.50; Wed-Sun Mar to late Sep 1pm to 5pm; 1964 Fairfield Rd., ☎598-8096)* is a small, suburban garden created by Prince and Princess Nicholas Abkhazi in the 1940s, and tended by the latter until her death in 1994. The garden is naturalistic in style, with rhododendrons, azaleas, lilies and ponds all arranged around rocky outcroppings and trees. Since 2000, it has been run by The Land Conservancy (TLC) of British Columbia, a non-profit organization that is lovingly restoring the garden with the help of dedicated volunteers. A work in progress, the garden is quite small and provides for a very short visit, recommended for serious gardening buffs only. Consider the rather hefty admission fee a contribution to a worthwhile cause.

Take Foul Bay Road back to Marine Drive, known here as Crescent Road. Follow it past the scenic Victoria Golf Club to Oak Bay Marina, a convenient, scenic place for a stop.

From the marina, take Newport Avenue to Oak Bay Avenue. Here, between Monterey and Wilmot, is **Oak Bay Village**, the heart of the community of **Oak Bay** (pop 18,000). Also known as the "Tweed Curtain" in reference to its British heritage, Oak Bay is home to tea rooms, fish-and-chip shops and cafés galore, along with beautiful parks and gardens.

To return to downtown Victoria, take Oak Bay Avenue, which becomes Pandora Avenue, all the way there.

Tour C: The Saanich Peninsula

Victoria lies at the southern end of the Saanich Peninsula. The peninsula is first and foremost a suburb, as many people who work in Victoria live here. This region is an unavoidable part of any itinerary involving Vancouver Island and especially Victoria, since the big Swartz Bay Ferry Terminal is located in Sidney, a small town near the tip of the peninsula, 32km from Victoria, accessed via the Patricia Bay Highway.

From downtown, drive south on Douglas Street and turn left on Dallas Road, which follows the shore. This road runs through a number of residential neighbourhoods, changes name a few times (at one point it becomes Beach Drive, then Cadboro Bay Road), and offers some lovely views along the way. Notice the Tudor-style houses and lush, well-tended gardens lining Oak Bay and Cadboro Bay. Once past

Cadboro Bay, follow the shore line along Tudor Avenue. Take Arbutus, Ferndale, Barrie and Ash roads to Mount Douglas Park.

At the entrance to **Mount Douglas Park ★★**, turn left on Cedar Hill Road, then right in order to reach the lookout, which offers a 360° view of the Gulf Islands, the Strait of Georgia and Juan de Fuca Strait and the snow-capped peaks along the Canadian and U.S. coast. The colours of the sea and the mountains are most vibrant early in the morning and at the end of the day.

Upon leaving Mount Douglas Park, turn left onto Cordova Bay Road; it follows the shoreline until it becomes Royal Oak Drive, which intersects the Patricia Bay Highway (Hwy. 17) and then West Saanich Road (Hwy. 17A). These two highways access the east and west sides, respectively, of the Saanich Peninsula and then link in North Saanich by way of Wain Road. You can make this tour in a loop by reversing the order of one of the following two suggested routes, and you can take either tour from the ferry terminal in Swartz Bay by reversing its order.

West Saanich Road

The **Horticulture Centre of the Pacific** (*$5; every day Apr to Oct 8am to 8pm, Nov to Mar*

9am to 4:30pm; 505 Quayle Rd., ☎479-6162) is either a prelude or an encore to a visit to **Butchart Gardens** (see below). Attractions include a winter garden, the Takata Japanese garden and a collection of rhododendrons and dahlias.

If you like science and the stars, head over to the **Centre of the Universe** ($7; Apr 1 to Oct 31 every day 10am to 6pm, Nov 1 to April 1 Tue-Sun 10am to 6pm; Little Saanich Mountain, 16km from Victoria, ☎363-0001), which has one of the biggest telescopes in the world.

The amazing **Victoria Butterfly Gardens** ($8; mid-Feb to mid-May 9:30am to 4:30pm, mid-May to late Sep 9am to 5pm, Oct 9am to 4:30pm; 1461 Benvenuto Ave., ☎652-3822) are home to all sorts of butterflies, who flutter about freely in a tropical forest setting, accompanying you on your tour. An attractive souvenir shop and a restaurant are also on the premises.

The Butchart Gardens ★ ★
($10 to $20, depending on the season; call ahead for opening hours; Hwy. 17 N, 800

Benvenuto Ave., ☎652-4422, www.butchartgardens. com), which cover 26ha, were founded by the family of the same name in 1904. A wide array of flowers, shrubs and trees flourish in this unique space. Maps are available at the entrance. Fireworks light up the sky on Saturday nights during July and August, and outdoor concerts are held here Monday to Saturday evenings from June to September.

Patricia Bay Highway

The **Saanich Historical Artifacts Society ★** (Sep to May, every day 9:30am to 12:30pm, Jun to Aug 9:30am to 4:30pm; 7321 Lochside Dr.), located on the outskirts of Victoria, has one of the largest collections of steam engines, tractors and farming equipment in Canada. Of course, you have to be interested in that sort of thing. The museum is halfway between Sidney and Victoria and is easily accessible via Highway 17; head east on Island View Road then north on Lochside Drive and continue to the gate.

● ATTRACTIONS

Tour C: The Saanich Peninsula
1. Mount Douglas Park
2. Horticulture Centre of the Pacific
3. Dominion Astrophysical Observatory
4. Victoria Butterfly Gardens
5. Saanich Historical Artifacts Society
6. BC Aviation Museum
7. Fort Roder Hill & Fisgard Ligthouse
8. The Butchart Gardens

Tour D: From Victoria to the West Coast Trail
9. East Sooke Park

⬡ ACCOMMODATIONS

1. Guest Retreat B&B
2. Honoured Guest B&B
3. Travelodge Sidney
4. UVIC Housing and Conference Services

Victoria and Surroundings

©ULYSSES

Sidney *(Visitor Information Centre,* ☎*656-3260),* a small town near the tip of the Saanich Peninsula, has attained a certain level of importance due to the presence of the **Swartz Bay Ferry Terminal**. Among the local attractions are the pretty **Sidney Marine Museum** ★ *(admission by donation; May to Oct every day 10am to 4pm, Nov to Apr 11am to 3pm, Jan and Feb Sat and Sun 11am to 3pm; 9801 Seaport Pl.,* ☎*656-1322),* which displays some magnificent whale skeletons and explains the biology and evolution of this animal. At the same location, the **Sidney Historical Museum** *(*☎*655-6355),* meanwhile, is devoted to the history of Sidney and North Saanich.

The **BC Aviation Museum** *($5; summer every day, 10am to 4pm, winter 11am to 3pm; Victoria International Airport, the big white hangar near the control tower,* ☎*655-3300)* houses a fine collection of World War II airplanes, as well as some more recent models.

Located in the western part of the peninsula in an isolated area, the **Fort Rodd Hill & Fisgard Lighthouse** *($3; Mar 1 to Oct 31 10am to 5:30pm, Nov 1 to Feb 28 9am to 4:30pm; 603 Fort Rodd Hill Rd, follow the Trans-Canada Hwy. and take the Port Renfrew exit, 10km north of Victoria,* ☎*478-5849)* historic site will delight history buffs. You can walk along the property by the Strait of Georgia. Between 1878 and 1956, the fortifications first defended the British Empire and then independent Canada. Strategically placed, the artillery protected Victoria and Esquimalt, the gateway to Western Canada. As for the Fisgard lighthouse, located on the same site, it was the first lighthouse erected on the West Coast of Canada in the second half of the 19th century. It is still in operation.

Tour D: From Victoria to the West Coast Trail

Head north on Douglas Street, which turns into Highway 1A (Old Island Highway) and follow the signs for Sooke. At Colwood, take Highway 14, which becomes Sooke Road near Port Renfrew. You'll pass through the suburbs west of town when you get to Sooke, which lies about 30km from Victoria. At the 17 Mile House restaurant, turn left onto Gillespie Road. This will take you into **East Sooke Regional Park** ★ *(*☎*478-3344),* where hiking trails lead through the wild flora by the sea.

Victoria's Market Square, a series of three-storey Victorian brick buildings arranged around an inner courtyard, is a pleasant place to wander.
- Walter Bibikow

In winter, Whistler's majestic mountains turn into a paradise for skiiers. - *Sean O'Neill*

This is a perfect place for a family outing (see p 275).

Head back to the 14, and turn left toward Port Renfrew. The highway runs alongside beaches and bays. The farther you get from Victoria, the more twists and turns there are in the road. The terrain is mountainous, and the views are spectacular. As you continue west on the 14, you'll notice a change in the landscape; forestry has long been an important source of revenue for the province, and the large valleys in this region have been clear-cut.

Port Renfrew

Port Renfrew is one of two starting points for the **West Coast Trail** ★★★ (the other being Bamfield). This 75km trek is geared towards ex-

perienced, intrepid hikers prepared to face unstable weather conditions and widely varied terrain; in fact, it is considered one of the most difficult hiking trails in North America. For more information, contact the Gordon River Information Centre, near Port Renfrew (*647-5434).*

Excursions from Victoria: Vancouver Island

South Coast

Nature's influence is notably apparent in all forms of art on Vancouver Island including numerous sculptures and paintings by First Nations artists. By going through **Duncan**, you can visit the **Cowichan Native Village** (*250-746-8119*). The guided tour illustrates the way of life of Aboriginal people, their customs and buildings. A very beautiful film is also presented, and an art gallery and totem poles allow visitors to learn more about Aboriginal art.

Just outside the village of **Qualicum Beach**, make sure to visit the **Milner Garden and Woodland** (*250-752-6153*), a fabulous 28ha property harbouring both formal gardens and 500-year-old Douglas firs and cedars. Further north, **Campbell River** lures steelhead and salmon fishing buffs.

West Coast

On the island's west coast, the hundred-year-old temperate rain forests and beaches skirting the cliffs are frequented by amateur and professional naturalists alike. Whale-watching excursions leave from **Tofino** and **Ucluelet**. In Long Beach, waves crest as high as 8m in the winter along the spectacular 15km-long beach. Dedicated hikers will enjoy the **West Coast Trail**, in the **Pacific Rim National Park**, which takes from five to seven days to cover *(reservations required, ☎663-6000 from Vancouver)*. Other hidden ecological treasures on this island include: the **Carmanah Valley**, a forest of giant thousand-year-old trees; the wild fjords of **Clayoquot Sound** and **Walbran Valley** *(B.C. Parks: ☎250-387-5002)*; and provincial parks where old Sitka spruce trees stand almost 100m tall.

For further details, *(☎800-663-3883)* or the **Tourism Vancouver Island** *(☎250-754-3500, www.islands.bc.ca)*.

Parks and Beaches

Victoria is surrounded by a host of very different parks and beaches (city beaches, deserted beaches running alongside temperate rain forests, etc.). The West Coast boasts numerous provincial parks, which all feature sandy beaches strewn with piles of driftwood. These parks offer nature lovers a breath of fresh air.

Tour B: Scenic Marine Drive

There are two beaches in Victoria where families can enjoy a day of sand-castle building and swimming in calm waters.

Willows Beach ★ *(public bathrooms, playground; corner of Estevan Ave. and Beach Dr.)* stretches alongside the chic residential neighbourhood of Oak Bay near a marina and the Oak Bay Beach Hotel.

Cadboro Bay Beach ★ *(public bathrooms, playground; corner of Sinclair Rd. and Beach Dr.)*, a little farther east, is located in the University of Victoria neighbourhood and attracts a young crowd. It looks out onto a bay, with the Chatham Islands and Discovery Island in the distance. The ebb and flow of the tides has transformed the strand at **Beacon Hill Park** ★ (see p 266) into a pebble beach covered with pieces of driftwood.

The summit of **Mount Tolmie** ★★★ *(BC Parks, ☎391-2300)* offers sensational panoramic views of Victoria, Haro Strait, the ocean, and magnificent Mount Baker and the Cascade Range in Washington State (U.S.A.).

Tour C: The Saanich Peninsula

Mount Douglas Park *(Hwy. 17, Royal Oak Dr. Exit; BC Parks, ☎391-2300)*, which covers 10ha and offers access to the sea, is the perfect place for a picnic or a stroll (see p 269).

Tour D: From Victoria to the West Coast Trail

Goldstream Provincial Park ★★★ *(20min from Victoria by Hwy. 1; BC Parks, ☎391-2300)*, located 17km from Victoria, is one of the major parks in the Victoria area. Picture 600-year-old Douglas firs lining hiking trails leading to Mount Finlayson and past magnificent waterfalls. In November, nature lovers come here to watch coho, chinook and chum salmon make their final voyage, spawn and die in Goldstream River. The fish are easy to see, as the water is crystal clear. Not to be missed.

The end of the salmon run marks the beginning of another incredible event: the **Eagle Extravaganza**. From December to February, as many as 275 bald eagles per day will visit the estuary during low tide to feed on dead chum salmon. The estuary is off-limits to visitors, but there are viewing platforms, live video cameras and telescopes so that you can observe the feeding eagles from a safe distance. Visitors can also stop by the Nature House to obtain more information on eagles and other birds.

An immense stretch of wilderness (1,422ha), **East Sooke Regional Park** *(☎478-3344)* is sure to appeal to anyone who likes solitude and tranquility. It is laced with over 50km of trails. At Anderson Cove, you'll find the starting point of a trail leading to Babbington Hill and Mount Macguire, whose summits offer a splendid view of the region. Eagles can be seen swirling about on thermal currents.

Follow the **Galloping Goose Regional Trail** for nearly 60km by bicycle, on horseback or on foot. A former railway line, it runs through some magnificent scenery. You'll spot geese, eagles and even vultures. The trail starts in the heart of Victoria and leads beyond Sooke, and can be picked up at numerous points in between. For more information, call ☎478-3344.

On Highway 14, after Sooke, the waterfront is studded with beaches. **French Beach ★**, a stretch of pebbles and sand lined with logs, has picnicking facilities. It is also wheelchair accessible. A little farther west, still on the 14, lies **China Beach ★★**; to get there, you have to take a well laid-out trail down to the base of a cliff (about 15min). The beach is absolutely magnificent. It is not uncommon to spot a seal, a sea otter or even a grey whale or a killer whale swimming offshore. Just walk a few minutes in either direction to find yourself alone in a little bay. Surfers come here for the waves.

Botanical Beach ★★★, after Port Renfrew, is a veritable paradise for anyone interested in marine life. When the tide is out you'll discover all sorts of treasures: fish, starfish and various species of marine plant-life are left behind in little pools of water among the pebbles. To make the most of your visit to the beach, pick up a copy of the *Shore Hiker's Tide Guide*, available in Parks Canada interpretive centres.

Pacific Rim National Park *(starting in Port Renfrew)* is a marvellous green space along the ocean front. It is divided into three sections: Long Beach, the Broken Group Islands and the West Coast Trail. For more information on the latter, see p 273 and 278.

Outdoor Activities

Cycling

Cycling is a great way to explore Victoria. For information on cycling tours in the city, drop by the **Greater Victoria Cycling Coalition** *(Mon-Fri 3pm to 6pm; 1056A North Park St., off Cook St., ☎480-5155)*. You can also find information on recreational rides on their Web site: *www.gvcc.bc.ca*. Bicycles, including cute-as-a-button tandems, can be rented from the following companies:

Harbour Rentals
811 Wharf St.
☎*995-1661*

Cycle BC
747 Douglas St.
☎*385-2453*

Fishing

As far as deep-sea fishing is concerned, salmon is king. There are five kinds of Pacific salmon: coho, chinook, sockeye, pink and chum. Given this variety, fishing is possible year-round. Of course, you are likely to catch other kinds of fish, such as cod, halibut or snapper. The spawning season for coho, chum, sockeye and pink salmon lasts all summer, while chinook spawns from May to September and in winter in certain regions.

Tour A: The Inner Harbour and Old Town

Those who insist on catching their dinner, be it a sockeye salmon or a 140kg halibut, can arrange a guided fishing charter.

Cuda Marine Adventures
Hotel Grand Pacific, ground level
463 Belleville St.
☎*995-2832 or 866-995-2832*

Tour D: From Victoria to the West Coast Trail

The **Sooke Charter Boat Association** *(Sooke, ☎642-7783)* organizes fishing trips on the ocean and offers a hotel reservation service. The Sooke region is bounded by bays and coves where the rivers empty into the sea.

Sooke Charters
☎*642-3888 or 888-775-2659*
Sooke Charters provides all the necessary fishing equipment. The rates are very affordable for this sport: $180 for three people (4hrs) or $200 for four.

Golf

Tour C: The Saanich Peninsula

Golf is *the* leisure activity on the Saanich Peninsula. Golfers can try the following courses, listed in order of preference:

Ardmore Golf Course
930 Ardmore Dr., Sidney
☎*656-4621*

Cedar Hill Municipal Golf Course

1400 Derby Rd., Saanich
☎595-3103

The **Arbutus Ridge Golf Club**
*(3535 Telegraph Rd., Cobble
Hill, 35min north of Victoria,*
☎*743-5000)* has an attractive
18-hole course and rents
out equipment.

The **Cordova Bay Golf Course**
(5333 Cordova Bay Rd.,
☎*658-4075)* also has an
attractive 18-hole course
with a driving range, a restaurant, a bar and a pro
shop.

Hiking

The **Juan de Fuca Marine Trail**
(☎391-2300) stretches 47km
from the south end of
Vancouver Island (from
China Beach, west of the
little village of Jordan River)
to Botanical Beach, near
Port Renfrew. This trail,
inaugurated in 1994 on the
occasion of the Common-
wealth Games, is geared
toward experienced hikers,
and, as a safety precaution,
anyone planning to take it
is advised to leave a de-
tailed description of their
itinerary with a friend before setting out.

Note that the northern part
of this trail ends at Port
Renfrew. Those who want
to explore further can extend the hike on the 75km
of the **West Coast Trail** (see
p 273) that leads to
Bamfield. Together, the two
paths add up to 122km of
trails that require at least a
10-day expedition through
the temperate rainforest of
the West Coast.

Horseback Riding

Tour C: The Saanich Peninsula

Woodgate Stables
8129 Derrinberg Rd., Saanichton
☎652-0287
Woodgate organizes pleas-
ant outings just 20min north
of Victoria.

Sea Kayaking

Sea kayaking is a fabulous
way to take in some lovely
views of Victoria.

Victoria Kayak Tours
950 Wharf St.
☎216-5646
www.kayakvictoria.com
Victoria Kayak Tours can
take you on a paddling tour
of the Inner Harbour *($55)*,
through Finlayson Fjord to

Butchart Gardens *($169)*, or on several other tours. Guide and owner Cliff Hansen and his staff are knowledgeable about the history of Victoria and can provide plenty of amusing and interesting anecdotes to animate the tour.

Ocean River Sports *(1824 Store St., ☎381-4233 or 800-909-4233)* also arranges custom tours.

Scuba Diving

Tour C: The Saanich Peninsula

David Doubilet, a member of the Cousteau Society and a renowned photographer for *National Geographic*, describes Vancouver Island as "the best cold-water diving destination in the world." The entire coast is a maze of fjords and little islands. Veritable underwater gardens serve as a habitat for over 300 species of aquatic animals.

The Artificial Reef Society maintains some beautiful diving sites in Sidney, north of Victoria. The *Mackenzie*, a 111m de-

stroyer, was sunk so that divers could explore it, and the same was done to the *G.B. Church*, a 53m freighter. **Arrawac Marine Services** *(240 Meadowbrook Rd., ☎479-5098)* organizes dives in the area.

Whale-Watching

Tour A: The Inner Harbour and Old Town

At least four species of whales can be found in the waters around Victoria and at least 18 whale-watching companies track their every move. Visitors can go whale-watching aboard an inflatable dinghy or a yacht. Here are two good outfits to try:

Orca Spirit Adventures *(☎383-8411 or 888-672-ORCA)* offers excursions aboard the *Orca Spirit*, an elegant and extremely comfortable

The Grey Whale

The grey whale (*Eschrichtius robustus*), summers in the Arctic Ocean and the Bering Strait, where food is plentiful; some stay farther south, around Vancouver Island.

The female grey can weigh up to 40 tonnes and measure between 10 and 15m. The actual colour of the grey whale is pearl grey, but its body generally bears white scars left by the various parasites that cling to its skin.

Almost hunted to extinction in the 19th century, grey whales have been protected for over half a century and the population is no longer at risk.

Grey whales are the only bottom-feeding baleen whales. They swallow a huge quantity of water, which they expel through the baleen, bony fringes that hang in their mouths, retaining only the plankton floating in it.

Just as winter begins to take hold in the north, the whales begin their long migration south to their calving grounds in the calm bays on the Pacific coast of Baja California. They travel a distance of more than 8,000km in no more than five days, never even stopping for food. The whales take until December to arrive and stay until March.

When the migration begins, half of the females are pregnant, having mated with the males the previous winter. Because the gestation period lasts 12 months, the mother has time to return to the mating grounds to give birth.

Most whale sightings occur during the migration, particularly in March and April. The best place for whale-watching is on the west coast of Vancouver Island; Victoria also offers a great many opportunities.

15m ship equipped with large observation platforms. Transportation from your hotel is available.

Victoria Marine Adventure Centre

950 Wharf St.

☎**995-2211**

Whale-watching tours are scheduled from April or May to October. Trips are 3hrs long and cost about $75 per adult.

Windsurfing

Tour B: Scenic Marine Drive

All you have to do is park your car on Dallas Road and plunge into the sea. The scenery is magnificent and the wind, perfect.

Accommodations

Accommodations are somewhat less expensive in Victoria than in Vancouver. Believe it or not, you can actually find a very decent room in high season in Victoria for less than $150—that is, of course, if you don't mind turning your back to the harbour.

When booking your reservation, make sure you inquire whether your room will offer a harbour view; be aware that such rooms come at a premium, with rates anywhere from $30 to $100 higher per night. If you can afford it, however, it's worth the splurge, at least for part of your stay.

The Inner Harbour and Old Town

Ocean Island Backpacker's Inn

$

K, sb, ℜ

791 Pandora Ave.

☎**385-1788**

www.oceanisland.com

Ocean Island Backpacker's Inn is one of the newest youth hostels to have sprung up in Victoria. Around 100 beds are available in the dormitory and in the double rooms. There's a small, licensed restaurant on-site and Internet access is available.

Hostelling International Victoria

$

sb, K

516 Yates St.

☎**385-4511**

⇐**385-3232**

This stone-and-brick building with 108 beds, is located in Old Town, right near the Inner Harbour. Members take precedence in youth hostels, so it can be difficult for non-members to get a bed, especially during the high season. Reservations required.

Dominion Hotel
$$
ℜ
759 Yates St.
☎*384-4136 or 800-663-6101*
⇰*384-5342*
www.dominion-hotel.com
The elegant Dominion Hotel has welcomed visitors since 1876. The classic decor of its 101 rooms is sure to please. The pleasant restaurant-bar is located on the main floor.

Cherry Bank Hotel
$$$ bkfst incl.
K, ≡
825 Burdett Ave.
☎*385-5380 or 800-998-6688*
The Cherry Bank Hotel B&B is situated in a residential area two blocks from downtown. In keeping with the British ambiance of Victoria, Cherry Bank Inn is a dead ringer for a genuine Victorian English inn, with plenty of cherry-red velvet wallpaper and narrow, labyrinthine corridors sure to bring out the closet claustrophobic in you. While some might find it quaint, others will no doubt find its guestrooms downright dowdy, though a genuine attempt has clearly been made to gussy them up with plants and reasonable facsimiles of canopy beds. Service is friendly and

you can't beat the place for quirkiness or price.

Academy House B&B
$$$ bkfst incl.
ℝ
865 Academy Close
☎*388-4329 or 877-388-4339*
⇰*388-5199*
www.academyhouse.bc.ca
Academy House B&B is a peaceful establishment located on the border of wonderful Beacon Hill Park. The high ceilings and small balconies add charm.

🏨 Isabella's Guest Suites
$$$ bkfst incl.
K
537 Johnson St.
☎*381-8414*
www.isabellasbb.com
Located above Willie's Bakery (see p 292) in the heart of the Old Town, Isabella's is a real find. There are two very attractive guest suites with fully equipped kitchens, painted in deep colours, tastefully furnished with antiques and contemporary furnishings and featuring hardwood floors. Continental breakfast served at Willie's. Weekly rentals are preferred ($700).

🏨 Helm's Inn
$$$
ℜ, ℝ, *K,* ≡
600 Douglas St.
☎*385-5767 or 800-665-4356*
⇰*385-2221*
www.helmsinn.com
All things considered, Helm's Inn is probably the

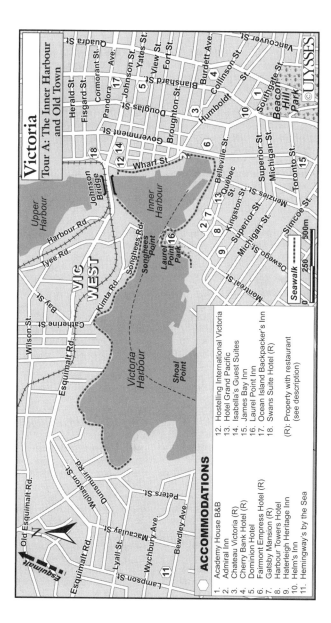

Victoria
Tour A: The Inner Harbour and Old Town

© ULYSSES

ACCOMMODATIONS

1. Academy House B&B
2. Admiral Inn
3. Chateau Victoria (R)
4. Cherry Bank Hotel (R)
5. Dominion Hotel
6. Fairmont Empress Hotel (R)
7. Gatsby Mansion (R)
8. Harbour Towers Hotel
9. Haterleigh Heritage Inn
10. Helm's Inn
11. Hemingway's by the Sea

12. Hostelling International Victoria
13. Hotel Grand Pacific
14. Isabella's Guest Suites
15. James Bay Inn
16. Laurel Point Inn
17. Ocean Island Backpacker's Inn
18. Swans Suite Hotel (R)

(R): Property with restaurant (see description)

Seawalk ·········

0   250   500m

best deal in Victoria. It is located within walking distance of downtown, the museums and the Inner Harbour and has spacious, recently upgraded and pleasantly redecorated rooms and suites, all of them with fully equipped kitchens, as well as laundry facilities. Complimentary in-room continental breakfast and afternoon tea served. A good, affordable choice.

Admiral Inn
$$$ bkfst incl.
ℝ, ⚞
257 Belleville St.
☎/⇋*388-6267*
www.admiral.bc.ca

The Admiral Inn is a quiet, family-run establishment located right downtown, a stone's throw from the Inner Harbour. The rooms are very comfortable and the rates reasonable given the central location.

Hemingway's by the Sea
$$$ bkfst incl.
ℑ
1028 Bewdley Ave. near Esquimalt
☎*384-0862 or 877-384-0862*
⇋*384-8113*

Hemingway's is a luxury facility located on the other side of the Johnson Street Bridge. The refined antique furnishings were inspired by writer Ernest Hemingway: hunting and literary themes, central to the life of the American Nobel Prize winner, were integrated into the decor.

James Bay Inn
$$$
ℜ
270 Government St.
☎*384-7151 or 800-836-2649*
⇋*385-2311*
www.jamesbayinn.bc.ca

The recently renovated James Bay Inn is a small, 48-room hotel, located a few minutes' walk from the Legislature and Beacon Hill Park. It was once a retirement home and painter Emily Carr spent the last part of her life here. The rooms are basic and simply furnished with a bed, a television and a small desk. Some of the guestrooms were recently renovated, but the rest are somewhat dowdy. Request a room with a bay window. Heavy packers are forewarned that there is no elevator.

⚘ Chateau Victoria
$$$
ℜ, =, ⊘, K, ℝ
740 Burdett Ave.
☎*382-4221 or 800-663-5891*
⇋*380-1950*
www.chateauvictoria.com

Chateau Victoria is an affordable, very pleasant budget option. It's not on the Inner Harbour, but you *can* see the Empress from some of the standard rooms! Though not huge, the rooms are cheerful enough, with duvets, desks, large TVs and armchairs, all in very good condition. All the standard rooms are located on the second, third and fourth floors, with suites (*$$$$*), all with balconies, located above. The only downside is that the hotel is located on a slight incline, with a fairly steep approach, possibly representing an access problem for guests with limited mobility. A complimentary city shuttle can help solve that problem, however, based on availability. Complimentary parking.

Harbour Towers Hotel
$$$$
ℝ, ℜ, *K*, ≈, ⌂, ⊘, 🐾
345 Quebec St.
☎*385-2405* or *800-663-5896*
⇌*385-4453*
www.harbourtowers.com
Harbour Towers is a good choice for those seeking complete comfort, obliging service and a location close to the Inner Harbour at a relatively reasonable rate. All suites have balconies and kitchenettes, while standard rooms on the eighth floor and up offer a harbour view, at a slightly higher rate; some of the latter also have refrigerators. Children are entertained in the Kid Zone, while their parents work out in the fitness centre and relax in the hot tub. Babysitting services are also available.

Swans Suite Hotel
$$$$
ℜ, *K*
506 Pandora St.
☎*361-3310* or *800-668-SWAN*
⇌*361-3491*
www.swanshotel.com
Without question, the Swans Suite Hotel is one of the best places to stay in Victoria, especially if you're travelling in a group. The rooms are actually cozy, two-storey apartments, complete with balconies, that can accommodate several people. Guests will find "real" works of art on the walls, plants, big-screen TVs and a somewhat non-descript, ski-chalet-style decor. The hotel, which dates back to 1913, is located right in the heart of Old Town, steps away from Chinatown and the Inner Harbour. A fun brew pub and a restaurant are on the ground floor.

Gatsby Mansion
$$$$$ bkfst incl.
309 Belleville St.
☎*388-9191* or *800-563-9656*
⇌*920-5651*
Under the same ownership as the Ramada Inn and situated right behind it, the Gatsby Mansion offers inn-style lodgings right on the Inner Harbour. There are 10 guestrooms in the main house and another nine in the mansion next door, each individually decorated with antiques and duvets. The location is perfect and

Victoria and Surroundings

the service is professional and polite (including house-maids dressed in black and white!) but the guestrooms, though pleasant, are not all up to scratch for the price (room number 5, with bay windows, king-side bed, balcony and Inner Harbour view, is quite lovely).

The Haterleigh Heritage Inn
$$$$$ bkfst incl.

⊛

243 Kingston St.

☎ *384-9995*

⇄ *384-1935*

www.haterleigh.com

This old house, dating from 1901, has been lovingly restored with great attention to detail. A rich past lives on in its magnificent stained-glass windows and antique furnishings. The rooms are decorated in a flowery, over-the-top Victorian style with plenty of pink and equipped with whirlpool baths and huge beds with goose-down comforters.

Hotel Grand Pacific
$$$$$-$$$$$$

🐾, ⅀, ⊛, =, ◔, △

463 Belleville St.

☎ *386-0450*

⇄ *380-4475*

www.hotelgrandpacific.com

Located right on the Inner Harbour, its facade bearing more than just a slight re-semblance to that of the Empress, the Grand Pacific was built in 1989 and ex-tensively expanded in 2001.

The lobby is elegantly done up in marble and chande-liers, and the decor in the standard rooms is rather typical of large hotels, with a nouveau-colonial style and a burgundy-and-green colour scheme. The rooms in the old wing, however, are starting to look a little dated. Each room has a balcony, individually con-trolled air conditioning, a mini-bar, a feather duvet, as well as the standard accou-trements (hair dryers, iron and coffee makers). Har-bour views generally re-quire a $30 supplement. Service is professional and courteous.

🌴 Fairmont Empress Hotel
$$$$$$

🐾, ≈, ⊛, ◔, △, ℜ

721 Government St.

☎ *384-8111 or 800-441-1414*

⇄ *389-2747*

www.fairmont.com

The Empress is located on the Inner Harbour, adjacent to the museums and the interesting public and com-mercial areas. Designed by architect Francis Rattenbury, this luxurious 475-room hotel offers a relaxing atmo-sphere and a Chateau-style setting and is commonly regarded as *the* place to stay in Victoria. A new wing has been added to the original, quintessentially Victorian building without detracting from its legendary charm. Visitors stop here for after-noon tea or simply to admire the ivy-covered facade. Its three room types, from the standard Fairmont to the slightly larger Deluxe to the harbour-side Premiere, are all lovely and done up in a cranberry, sage or pale-yellow colour scheme. Note that the Premiere rooms (about $100 more than the standard Fairmont rooms) are the only ones that offer a harbour view and that they get booked up first—reserve at least six weeks in advance for a summer stay.

Laurel Point Inn
$$$$$$
=, △, ℝ, ℜ, ≡, 🐾
680 Montreal St.
☎ *386-8721 or 800-663-7667*
www.laurelpoint.com
The Laurel Point Inn's distinctive building guards the entrance to the Inner Harbour. Its original wing, to the north, dates from 1970, and although its rooms offer the best view of the Inner Harbour, their decor is rather ordinary. The south wing, added in 1989, was designed by well-known architect Arthur Erickson, who also designed the UBC Museum of Anthropology . These spacious rooms are more luxuriously appointed and decorated in natural colours with a rather minimalist approach; those

facing the Outer Harbour offer excellent views. They come equipped with decadent marble bathrooms complete with double sinks, soaker tubs, glass walk-in showers, and even mini-TVs and telephones. The grounds are beautifully landscaped, with a pond and a harbour-side terrace. Sadly, however, despite its many attributes, the service here is not quite as professional, nor as attentive as one would expect of a hotel of this class.

Scenic Marine Drive

See map p 264.

UVic Housing, Food and Conference Services
$ bkfst incl.
May 1 to Aug 31
sb, K
Sinclair and Finnerty rds.
☎ *721-8395*
↩ *721-8930*
Located on the University of Victoria campus, UVic's 999 dorm-style rooms are open to visitors during the summer months. A number of these were built for the 1994 Commonwealth Games. The rates are based on triple occupancy, but single rooms are also available. The campus lies east of the downtown area on a hill, right near the Cadboro Bay Beach.

Victoria and Surroundings

Shakespeare House B&B
$$ bkfst incl.
1151 Oxford St.
☎/≈*388-5546*
www.shakespearehousebb.com
Situated between Beacon Park and the Straight of Juan de Fuca, Shakespeare House B&B offers comfortable rooms. The classic English architecture of the building is interesting.

The Oak Bay Beach Hotel
$$$$ bkfst incl.
ℜ, ℑ
1175 Beach Dr.
☎*598-4556 or 800-668-7758*
≈*598-6180*
www.oakbaybeachhotel.bc.ca
The Oak Bay Beach Hotel, which has 50 comfortably laid-out rooms, caters to visitors seeking English charm and a pleasant seaside atmosphere. Located on the waterfront in the residential neighbourhood of Oak Bay, it offers an interesting view.

Fairholme Manor
$$$$ bkfst incl.
⊛, ℑ, K, ℝ
638 Rockland Pl.
☎*598-3240 or 877-511-3322*
≈*598-3299*
www.fairholmemanor.com
Fairholme Manor, an Italianate mansion dating from 1885, was lovingly restored and lavishly decorated by new owners Sylvia and Ross and transformed into one of Victoria's most stunning bed and breakfasts. Its four impeccable

guestrooms, all suites, feature high ceilings and ornate moldings, walls painted in heritage colours, hardwood floors accented by Persian carpets, and plush, down-filled armchairs and loveseats; some have bay windows providing a spectacular view of the Olympic Mountains in Washington state. The gardens of Government House (see p 266) surround the place, assuring a verdant, tranquil oasis. The two garden-level suites even have small kitchens, a great idea for those who plan on a self-catering holiday. Located in Rockland, a short drive from downtown.

Beaconsfield Inn
$$$$$ bkfst incl.
ℑ, ⊛
998 Humboldt St.
☎*384-4044 or 888-884-4044*
≈*384-4052*
www.beaconsfieldinn.com
Located in the heart of Victoria, the Edwardian-era Beaconsfield Inn, listed as a historic monument, combines luxury and sophistication. Guests can enjoy complimentary afternoon tea or a glass of sherry in the library, decorated with leather sofas and Persian carpets and warmed by a gas fire, and feast on a memorable breakfast. Guestrooms are impeccably decorated with antiques and quilts, and painted in deep, rich hues or pastels;

some feature hardwood floors, others, carpeting. Expensive but British ambiance guaranteed.

The Saanich Peninsula

See map 271.

Guest Retreat Bed & Breakfast
$$ bkfst incl.
ℜ
2280 Amity Dr., Sidney
☎*656-8073*
⇄*656-8027*
www.guestretreatbb.com
This B&B is located steps away from the beach and has fully equipped apartments with private entrances and lots of closet space. The perfect place for an extended stay. Inquire about the weekly and monthly rates.

The Travelodge
$$$
K, ℝ, ≈, 🐕
2280 Beacon Ave., Sidney
☎*656-1176 or 800-578-7878*
⇄*656-7344*
This member of the Travelodge chain offers lovely, comfortable rooms at reasonable rates. The hotel is conveniently located a few minutes from Butchart Gardens, all the golf courses, the Swartz Bay BC Ferry terminal and Victoria International Airport.

 Honoured Guest Bed & Breakfast
$$$$ bkfst incl.
⊛
8155 Lochside Dr., Saanichton
☎*544-1333*
⇄*544-1330*
www.sidneybc.com/honoured
The sumptuous Honoured Guest Bed & Breakfast is located on the banks of the Cordova Channel, about 15km from Victoria via Highway 17. When the building was erected in 1994, the goal was to make the most of the landscape. The rooms have private entrances, some have whirlpool baths, and all have sweeping views of the sea and Mount Baker.

From Victoria to the West Coast Trail

Port Renfrew Hotel
$-$$$
🐕, *sb*, ℜ
at the end of Hwy. 14, Port Renfrew
☎*647-5541*
⇄*647-5594*
The Port Renfrew Hotel is located on the village pier, where hikers set out for the West Coast Trail. The rustic rooms are sure to please hikers longing for a dry place to sleep. There are laundry facilities on the premises, as well as a pub that serves hot meals.

Victoria and Surroundings

Sunny Shores Resort & Marina
$$
≈
5621 Sooke Rd., R.R. #1, Sooke
☎642-5731
⇌642-5737
Sunny Shores has modern rooms with cable television, as well as tent and RV sites. Picnic tables, laundry facilities, a large pool and miniature golf course are all provided. Open year round. Perfect for campers who like fishing. If you have a boat, you can moor it here.

The Arbutus Beach Lodge
$$ bkfst incl.
5 Queesto Dr., Port Renfrew
☎647-5458
⇌647-5552
The Arbutus Beach Lodge is a very attractive inn set on the beach, snuggled in the renowned West Coast forest. The surroundings are peaceful and the place is so comfortable that you'll feel like extending your stay. Whale-watching and fishing excursions are available upon request.

The Seascape Inn Bed & Breakfast
$$$ bkfst incl.
K, ℥
6435 Sooke Rd., Sooke
☎642-7677 or 888-516-8811
The Seascape Inn is a lovely place that looks out onto the port. The eggs Benedict are a wonderful way to start off the day, and the owner will even take

you crab or salmon fishing if you like.

The Lighthouse Retreat Bed & Breakfast
$$$ bkfst incl.
K, ℥, ℳ, ⊛
107 West Coast Rd., Sooke
☎646-2345 or 888-805-4448
www.lighthouseretreatsooke.com
Nestled in the magnificent West Coast forest, this lovely B&B offers bright, airy rooms and a private beach. Contrary to what it's name suggests, however, it is not located in lighthouse.

Arundel Manor Bed & Breakfast
$$$ bkfst incl.
980 Arundel Dr.
☎/⇌385-5442
www.arundelmanor.com
You can enjoy a quiet, comfortable stay at the Arundel Manor Bed & Breakfast, a charming house built in 1912. Its three rooms are tastefully decorated, and on the side facing the water, the view is that much more striking. To get there, head north on Highway 1.

Sooke Harbour House
$$$$$ bkfst and picnic lunch incl.
ℳ, ⊛, ℥
1528 Whiffen Spit Rd., Sooke
☎642-3421
⇌642-6988
www.sookeharbourhouse.com
Mr. and Mrs. Philip will give you a warm welcome at the Sooke Harbour House, their dream home. It's pricey, but

rest assured that staying here will make your trip to Vancouver Island a memorable one. The 28 exquisite rooms are all equipped with a fireplace and decorated with antiques and works of art. Breakfast is served in your room and lunch in the dining room (see p 299).

Restaurants

The Inner Harbour and Old Town

Paradiso di Stelle
$
10 Bastion Square, near Wharf St.
☎*920-7266*
For the best coffee in town, go to Paradiso di Stelle, where the Italian tradition is reflected in your cup. The patio, which has a view of the port, is one of the loveliest in all of Victoria.

Ali Baba Pizza
$
1011 Blanshard St.
☎*385-6666*
Ali Baba Pizza is a real treat. The generous portions are quarters of 30cm pizzas. The pesto pizza is a must!

Yuen's Mountain Restaurant
$
866 Yates St.
☎*382-8812*
Yuen's Mountain Restaurant offers the ever-popular deluxe Chinese all-you-can-eat buffet!

Green Cuisine Vegetarian Restaurant
$-$$
Market Square
560 Johnson St.
☎*385-1809*
Vegetarians should check out Green Cuisine Vegetarian Restaurant, which is 100% vegetarian (no animal or dairy products). From the salad bar to home-made baked goods to organic coffee, there's something for everyone!

Barb's Place
$-$$
Mar-Oct, 11am to dark
Erie St., Fisherman's Wharf
☎*384-6515*
What is it about being by the sea that brings on a craving for fried, battered food served in newsprint? Walk, drive, bike or bus (no. 30 from downtown) to Barb's Place for your fix of fish and chips, steamed seafood, or other such treats (veggie fare available). The halibut and chips is very good, grease and all!

Victoria and Surroundings

Willie's Bakery
$-$$
537 Johnson St.
☎381-8414
This bustling little bakery is also a little café, cozily laid out between wood floors and brick walls. In addition to muffins and other baked goods (sadly, the croissants are not up to scratch), they serve original, full breakfasts *(Mon-Fri 7am to 11:30am, Sat and Sun 7:30am to noon)*. Soup and sandwiches are served for lunch.

Gatsby Mansion
$ (breakfast/lunch)
$$ (afternoon tea)
309 Belleville St.
☎388-9191
If you've awoken with the sun in your eyes and a taste for a special breakfast, head to the Gatsby Mansion for strawberry pancakes and similar delicacies, served in a lovely sunroom, albeit cloyingly decorated with wedding portraits. You can't go wrong here for afternoon tea, either *($18.95, 2pm to 4pm)*. The scones are scrumptious.

Rebar Modern Food
$$
50 Bastion Square
☎361-9223
If you've had one too many dollops of Devon cream with your afternoon tea and feel the need to redeem yourself with some wholesome, inexpensive food,

step into Rebar. The menu at this casual, cheerful spot is vegetarian and vegan, and includes some fish and seafood. Among its popular options is the very comforting monk's curry (oyster mushrooms, Japanese eggplant, tofu in a green curry-coconut sauce) and the almond burger. Rebar has acquired such a reputation over the years that its owners have published their own cookbook! A range of fresh fruit and vegetable juices and wheatgrass drinks is available to set you back on the right track. Open for three meals a day.

Garrick's Head Pub
$$
1140 Government St.
☎384-6835
The sunny patio at Garrick's Head Pub, located on a pedestrian street, is a pleasant place to get together over a local beer. The space may be limited inside, but there is a big-screen TV for sports fans.

Swans Brewpub
$$
506 Pandora Ave.
☎361-3310
Locals claim that Swans Brewpub brews and serves the best beer in North America—visitors might not agree. Nevertheless, they make a good effort and also serve typical pub fare. A good place to meet other

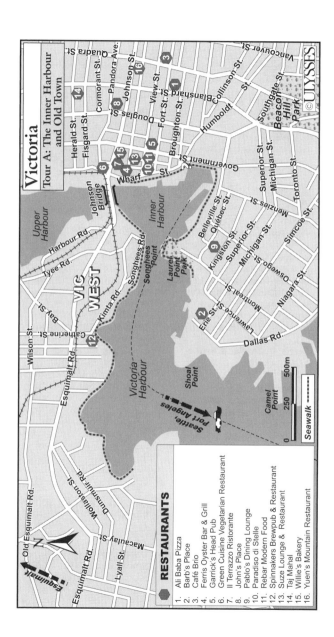

Victoria
Tour A: The Inner Harbour and Old Town

RESTAURANTS

1. Ali Baba Pizza
2. Barb's Place
3. Café Brio
4. Ferris Oyster Bar & Grill
5. Garrick's Head Pub
6. Green Cuisine Vegetarian Restaurant
7. Il Terrazzo Ristorante
8. John's Place
9. Pablo's Dining Lounge
10. Paradiso di Stelle
11. Rebar Modern Food
12. Spinnakers Brewpub & Restaurant
13. Suze Lounge & Restaurant
14. Taj Mahal
15. Willie's Bakery
16. Yuen's Mountain Restaurant

© ULYSSES

travellers. Live music Sunday to Thursday.

John's Place
$$
723 Pandora Ave.
☎389-0711
An eclectic urban crowd, made up more of locals than tourists, is drawn to the warm decor of John's Place. The copious portions of chicken, seafood and pasta, and cheap prices ensure satisfaction. This place is a must for eggs-Benedict lovers and the place is packed for breakfast on weekends. As for cheesecake, let's just say that you won't be able to resist ordering a slice—even if you're already stuffed!

Ferris' Oyster Bar & Grill
$$
536 Yates St.
☎360-1284
The pleasant Ferris' Oyster Bar & Grill serves West Coast cuisine and excellent seafood. A good atmosphere for group dining.

Suze Lounge & Restaurant
$$
515 Yates St.
☎383-2829
Suze has a terrific atmosphere. The imaginative and very reasonably priced cuisine includes tasty pizza and pasta, good fish dishes and excellent home-made desserts. The pad Thai is excellent, and a "small"

bowl is quite sufficient for most appetites! You can choose one of 18 kinds of martinis or order a Suze, the famous French apéritif for which the place is named. Simply put, the place is a site for sore eyes—highly recommended.

Vista 18
$$-$$$$
740 Burdett Ave.,
Chateau Victoria hotel
☎382-9258
You'll get a fabulous view of the Inner Harbour and the mountains beyond seated in a comfy armchair in this 18th-floor restaurant, which is open for breakfast, lunch and dinner. The menu includes pasta, steak, tuna, lamb and ostrich...in short, something for everyone. Dishes like the West Coast spinach salad with candied smoked salmon and papaya, the vodka-and-pepper-infused salmon, and the game hen and ostrich medallions testify to something creative occurring in the kitchen. Live jazz on Friday and Saturday nights.

Spinnakers Brewpub & Restaurant
$$$
308 Catherine St.
☎386-2739
Spinnakers serves beer and food in a laid-back setting, with the house specialties listed on big blackboards. The terrace is very well

positioned, beckoning guests to kick back and relax. This popular place radiates a festive, convivial atmosphere.

Taj Mahal
$$$
679 Herald St.
☎*383-4662*
The Taj Mahal, an Indian restaurant, has an eye-catching exterior. Try the house specialties—lamb biryani and tandoori chicken. An excellent vegetarian menu is also available. Highly recommended.

Pablo's Dining Lounge
$$$-$$$$
225 Quebec St.
☎*388-4255*
Contrary to what you might think, Pablo's is a French restaurant, though paella is available upon request. Located near the Inner Harbour in an elegant Victorian house. Good, but pricey.

Café Brio
$$$-$$$$
944 Fort St.
☎*383-0009*
Lovely Café Brio offers an atmosphere that is at once romantic and very welcoming, with wood tables, cozy booths and bar seating, wide-plank wood floors, subdued lighting and candlelight, and an eclectic range of framed artwork. The cuisine is Pacific Northwesr, with a strong emphasis on local ingredients where possible and a seasonally inspired menu that changes daily. Depending on the day, you might find hearts of romaine salad, pan-fried halibut cheeks (much better than they sound), seared jumbo Alaskan scallops with Jerusalem artichoke chips, and confit of duck leg with roast mushroom and red wine ragout; several pasta selections are always available and accompanying wines are suggested for every item on the menu. The extensive wine list highlights B.C. vintages and offers a selection by the glass and half bottle. A tasting menu, three courses paired with wines, is also available *($34 vegetarian, $45 carnivorous)*. Service is knowledgeable and professional. Highly recommended.

The Fairmont Empress Hotel's Bengal Lounge
$$$$
721 Government St.
☎*384-8111*
Recapturing the atmosphere of the British Empire of Queen Victoria, the very atmospheric Empress Hotel's Bengal Lounge serves a curry buffet featuring Indian specialties all week, except for Friday and Saturday, when live jazz is offered. The place is tastefully decorated with leather furniture, and guests have lots of elbow room. Stop in for a peek, at least.

Afternoon Tea in Victoria

The custom of afternoon tea is one of the many ways in which Victoria's British heritage finds expression today. While known to China for 5,000 years, tea was introduced to the English court in the 17th century but did not catch on for another two centuries or so.

The story goes that in the 1840s, Anna, the Seventh Duchess of Bedford, got too hungry by mid-afternoon to wait until the dinner hour, commonly not much earlier than 9pm. So she ordered a snack of cakes, tarts, cookies, bread and butter, and tea to be brought to her boudoir. It wasn't long before the custom made its way into the drawing rooms of London, becoming a popular Victorian social custom among women of the privileged class.

By this time, the East India Company was establishing tea planta-tions in Assam and other parts of India and Ceylon (Sri Lanka). The first shipment of Indian tea reached London in 1838.

Tea rooms as we now know them did not appear before 1864, when the enterprising manager of a bread shop near London Bridge began serving tea and snacks to her favourite clients. With that, a new custom was born!

Although there are a number of lovely tea rooms in Victoria, none has the cachet or genteel atmosphere of afternoon tea at the Empress Hotel. A pot of Empress blend tea, delicate sandwiches, fresh scones with Jersey cream and strawberry jam, and light pastries will cost you $46 ($24 in winter). If that's too rich for your budget, you can find less expensive teahouses or, you can always try making scones at home:

Fairmont Empress Scones

3 cups flour
2 cups sugar
1 cup butter
2 eggs
1 cup cream
2 tbsp. baking powder
1 cup raisins

Blend flour, sugar, butter and baking powder. Mix cream and eggs together. Add raisins, followed by cream and egg mixture, to dry ingredients, blending just enough to wet them. Roll to a thickness of about 2cm and cut into rounds. Brush with milk or egg wash and let rest for 45 minutes. Bake at 325°F for 20 to 25 minutes until golden brown.

Bowman's Rib House
$$$$
825 Burdett Ave.
☎385-5380
Bowman's Rib House offers a wide selection of exquisite meats and fresh fish. The steak here is superb and the honky-tonk piano creates a harmonious atmosphere in the dining room.

Il Terrazzo Ristorante
$$$$
555 Johnson St.
☎361-0028
Il Terazzo is a popular Italian restaurant with a menu made up mainly of pasta dishes. Creamy sauces flavoured with spices and sweet nuts make for some very interesting taste sensations. The clientele consists of young professionals and tourists. The one sour note is that the wine is kept on a mezzanine where all the heat in the room is concentrated, and is thus served at too warm a temperature.

The Fairmont Empress Hotel
$$$$
721 Government St.
☎384-8111
Tea-lovers get together in the Fairmont Empress Hotel for tea with scones served with different kinds of jam. If you've got a big appetite, stop in for afternoon tea, which comes complete with cucumber and cream-cheese sandwiches. The old wood floors, comfortable furniture, giant teapots and

courteous service make for an altogether satisfying experience. Be advized, however, it's very pricey in high season.

Scenic Marine Drive

See map p 264.

White Heather Tea Room
$-$$
Tue-Sat 9:30am to 5pmSun 10am to 4pm
1885 Oak Bay Ave.
☎595-8020
If tea at the Empress is a little rich for your blood, get thee to the White Heather Tea Room. Agnes, the delightful Scottish owner, serves afternoon tea *(1:30pm to 5pm)* as well as breakfast, Sunday brunch, and light lunches on bone china and white linen tablecloths in her small, cheerful tea room. You'll find a variety of loose-leaf teas, homemade jam and Devon cream to slather on your homemade scones, baked daily, as well as Scottish shortbread and oatcakes, pinwheel sandwiches and other goodies. At tea time, choose from "The Wee Tea" *($8.25),* "The Not So Wee Tea" *($12.75)* or "The Big Muckle Giant Tea" *(for two, $31.95).*

Reservations are recommended for both lunch and tea. Warning: Agnes's Scottish brogue is as addictive as her scones!

The Snug Pub
$$$
1175 Beach Dr.
☎598-4556
The Oak Bay Beach Hotel's pub, known as the Snug, serves local and imported beer and light meals. A quiet, well-kept place, it attracts a rather mature clientele, although a younger crowd flocks to the patio in the summer.

From Victoria to the West Coast Trail

17 Mile House
$$-$$$
5126 Sooke Rd., Sooke
☎642-5942
Located right before the entrance to Sooke Harbour Park, 17 Mile House is actually a pub, though its menu is rather more elaborate than that would suggest. The thoroughly laid-back, cozy atmosphere here makes this just the place to quench your thirst after a day of walking along the waterfront in Sooke. Sunday's seafood platter is particularly popular.

Sooke Harbour House
$$$$
1528 Whiffen Spit Rd.
☎*642-3421*
The Sooke Harbour House has been praised to the skies by people from all over the world. The Philips's gourmet cuisine has seduced thousands of palates. The hosts settle for nothing but the best and are masters when it comes to preparing local produce. The dining room, set up inside a country house, offers a view of Sooke Harbour. Enjoy the classic ambiance as you take your seat and look over the menu. The dishes, prepared in the Pacific Northwest style, reveal Japanese and French influences. Vegetarian dishes are available. See also p 290.

Entertainment

Bars and Nightclubs

Swans Brewpub
506 Pandora Ave.
☎*361-3310*
Swans Brewpub is a lively place that serves beer brewed right on the premises. A good place to meet other tourists. Live jazz, blues and Celtic music Sunday to Thursday.

Steamer's Public House
570 Yates St.
☎*381-4340*
Steamer's is a good place to have a drink and kick up your heels to an ever-changing lineup of live musical acts.

The Sticky Wicket Pub
919 Douglas St., Strathcona Hotel
☎*383-7137*
The Sticky Wicket Pub is located inside the Strathcona Hotel, just behind the Empress. This place attracts people of all ages and serves good beer. In nice weather, everyone heads up to the roof for some fun in the sun and a game of volleyball. At **Legends** nightclub, also in the Strathcona, university students dance to Top 40 hits.

Lucky Bar
517 Yates St.
☎*382-LUCK*
Located next to Suze Lounge and Restaurant (see p 294), Lucky Bar is the spot to catch live music almost every night *(cover around $5)*. It's a cozy spot, with a brick wall festooned with a collection of framed photographs. Sunday night is "Brew and View"—catch a flick, sip a beer.

Hugo's Grill and Brewhouse
619 and 625 Courtney St.
☎*920-4846*
Hugo's is a hip nightspot for a twenty- and thirtysomething crowd that

Victoria and Surroundings

congregates in its attractive post-industrial decor of wood-plank floors, exposed ceiling pipes and plenty of brick. A cozy place to sample a glass of ale or lager, brewed right on the spot.

Cultural Activities

Jazz

The **Victoria Jazz Society** (☎388-4423) can provide you with information on local jazz and blues shows. The Victoria Jazz Festival takes place from late June to mid-July.

Theatre

The **Kaleidoscope Theatre** (520 Herald St., ☎383-8124) puts on shows for young audiences.

The **McPherson Playhouse** (3 Centennial Square, ☎386-6121) presents plays and musicals.

All dance and classical-music events are held at the **Royal Theatre** (805 Broughton St., ☎386-6121).

Calendar of Events

Following are some of the major annual events taking place in Victoria and area. For a complete list and specific dates, contact Tourism Victoria.

April

Greater Victoria Performing Arts Festival (Apr and May; various venues, ☎386-9223): a variety of musical performances.

Bastion Square Festival of the Arts (Apr Fri-Sun, May Thu-Sun, Jun to early Oct Wed-Sun, as well as holidays throughout this season, 10:30am to 5:30pm; Bastion Square, Victoria, ☎413-3144): outdoor arts-and-crafts sale and music.

Victoria International Blossom Walks (mid-Apr; throughout the city; ☎380-3949, www.victoria internationalblossomwalks. com): seven different scenic walks ranging from 5 to 42km.

TerrifVic Jazz Party (mid-Apr; various venues; ☎253-2011, www.terrifvic.com): Victoria's very own jazz festival.

UNO Festival (end Apr to early May; various venues; ☎383-2663, www.victoriafringe. com): festival of one-person theatre.

Floating Boat Show (end Apr; Sidney; ☎245-8910, floating boatshow@shaw.ca)

May

Victoria Harbour Festival *(mid to late May; Inner Harbour, Victoria, ☎592-9098, www. victoriaharbourfestival.com)*: a variety of activities centred on the harbour during Victoria Day weekend and U.S. Memorial Day weekend. The annual Swiftsure International Yacht Race takes place during the festival (Juan de Fuca Strait).

Manulife Financial Literary Arts Festival *(mid-May; various Victoria venues, ☎381-1640, www.literaryartsfestival.org)*; conversations, readings and interviews with some of the world's finest writers.

Fort Rodd Hill Historical Military Encampment *(mid-May; Fort Rodd Hill National Historic Site, ☎478-5849)*: military re-enactments and artifacts reflecting a century of B.C.'s naval and military history (1850s to 1950s).

Victoria Highland Games *(mid-May; Royal Athletic Park, Victoria; ☎598-8961/1531)*: traditional Scottish games and entertainment.

Victoria Day Parade *(Victoria Day, third Mon in May; Douglas St., Victoria; ☎382-3111)*: traditional parade, complete with marching bands and floats from Victoria and beyond.

Esquimalt Lantern Festival *(end May; West Bay Walkway; ☎383-8557)* evening parade of hand-crafted lanterns followed by a dance.

Bastion Square Cycling Grand Prix *(end May; downtown Victoria, Saanich and North Saanich)*: professional cyclists compete on closed-loop circuits on city streets.

June

Oak Bay Tea Party *(early Jun; Victoria)*: where else to stage a tea party, but behind the "tweed curtain"?

Victoria Conservatory of Music's Garden Tour *(☎477-4114)* eight to 10 of Victoria's finest gardens open their gates to the public.

Summer in the Square *(Jun to Sep; Centennial Square, Victoria)*: local music and dance.

Jazzfest International *(end Jun; various venues in downtown Victoria; ☎388-4423 or 888-671-2112, www.vicjazz.bc. ca)*: more than 50 jazz, blues and world-music performances, both free and ticketed.

Folkfest *(Ship's Point, Inner Harbour, Victoria; end Jun to early Jul; ☎388-4728)*: multicultural entertainment, food and festivities.

Victoria and Surroundings

July

Victoria Symphony Summer Music Festival *(first week of Jul; Christ Church Cathedral;* ☎*385-6515)*: classical music festival.

Victoria Shakespeare Festival *(mid-Jul to early Aug; Victoria;* ☎*360-0234)*

"A Bite of Victoria" Food Festival *(Government House;* ☎*386-6368)*: Victoria's restaurants provide inexpensive samples and musicians and artists provide the entertainment.

Rootsfest Music Festival *(*☎*386-3655, www.rootsfest.com)*: a world-music festival with about 150 performers on five outdoor stages.

August

Latin Caribbean Music Festival *(Market Square, 560 Johnston St.;* ☎*361-9433 ext. 212/215, www.vircs.bc.ca)*: more than 100 performers from Latin America, the Caribbean and North America.

Victoria Fringe Theatre Festival *(383-2662 or 222-fringe2, www.victoriafringe.com)*: Your best opportunity to take in some innovative theatre performances.

Symphony Splash *(Inner Harbour, Victoria,* ☎*385-6515, www.victoriasymphony.bc.ca)*:

The Victoria Symphony performs from a barge moored in mid-harbour; a very popular event.

First People's Festival *(Royal British Columbia Museum, Victoria,* ☎*384-3211)*: a celebration of Aboriginal tradition, art and culture.

Dragon Boat Festival *(Inner Harbour, Victoria,* ☎*472-BOAT, www.victoriadragon boat.com)*: the highlight of this festival, with ancient Chinese cultural and spiritual roots, involves Dragon Boat races, where paddlers compete in a 650m sprint.

Vancouver Island Brewery Blues Bash *(Victoria,* ☎*388-4423 or 888-671-2112, www.vicjazz. bc.ca)*: blues and R&B performances staged at various locations.

September

Saanich Fall Fair *(Saanich Fairground, 1528 Stelly's X Rd., Saanich,* ☎*652-3314)*: Western Canada's oldest continuous agricultural fair.

October

Salmon Run *(mid-Oct; Goldstream Provincial Park, 2930 Trans-Canada Hwy.,* ☎*391-2300)*: see millions of Pacific salmon run upriver to spawn and die.

Ghost Bus Tours *(end Oct; Victoria,* ☎*598-8870)*: the Old Cemeteries Society organizes a tour of Victoria's favourite "haunts."

December

The Great Canadian Beer Festival *(Victoria Conference Centre;* ☎*383-2332)*: a tasty celebration of craft brewing.

Eagle Extravaganza *(mid-Dec to late Feb; Goldstream Provincial Park,* ☎*478-9414)*: hundreds of bald eagles move into the park to pick over the salmon, which have died after spawning in the Goldstream River (see "Salmon Run," Oct). Visitors can view this magnificent spectacle from an eagle-viewing platform.

Christmas at the Butchart Gardens *(Dec to Jan;* ☎*652-4422, www.butchartgardens. com)*: Victoria's most famous garden is illuminated by tens of thousands of lights and animated by carollers, children's entertainers, a brass band and food.

Shopping

The enormous **Eaton Centre** *(corner of Douglas and Fort sts.,* ☎*381-4012)* has all sorts of boutiques, shops and restaurants. It is several-storeys high and includes an entire block of buildings.

The **Market Square** *(255 Johnson St.,* ☎*386-2441)* is smaller and more intimate than the Eaton Centre. The shops are smaller and a splendid interior courtyard invites shoppers to linger a while.

With its stained-glass windows and 8m ceilings, **Munro's** *(1108 Government St.,* ☎*382-2464)* is reputed to be the most beautiful bookstore in Canada. Good selection of Canadian, English and American books.

It is worth stopping in at **Rogers' Chocolates** *(913 Government St.,* ☎*384-7021)* to see the shop's lovely early-20th-century decor and pair of Art Nouveau lamps from Italy. Victoria Creams, available in a wide variety of flavours, are the specialty of the house.

The Fish Store
Fisherman's Wharf
☎*383-6462*
Appropriately named, The Fish Store is a wharf-side spot for fresh fish, shellfish and smoked salmon, as well as herrings to feed to the seals ($1 each).

Victoria and Surroundings

Silk Road
1624 Government St.
☎704-2688
This lovely shop carries essential oils and other aromatherapy products as well as tea leaves, gorgeous tea pots and other related equipment. They also offer tea tastings and a wide range of reasonably priced workshops.

Murchie's Tea
1110 Government St.
☎383-3112
Speaking of tea, Murchie's Tea has been a B.C. institution since 1894, around the time when Grandpa Murchie made a special blend for Queen Victoria. Today you can pick up a variety of unique blends in bulk, as well as a boxes of tea bags such as the delicious, ultra-spicy chai. And of course, you can pick up tea paraphernalia and have a cuppa (or a capuccino, if that's more your style) in the adjoining capuccino bar.

If the quaint British side of Victoria stirs your passion for things antique, you might enjoy a stroll along the stretch of Fort Street between Quadra and Cook streets. Known as **Antique Row**, the area is home to a number of shops selling antiques and curios.

Hill's Indian Crafts *(1008 Government St., ☎385-3911)* sells souvenirs and Aboriginal art in different price ranges. Wide choice of art cards.

Whistler

Whistler attracts
skiers, golfers, hikers, sailors and snowboarders from all over the world.

An impressive hotel infrastructure awaits them all in the little village at the foot of Blackcomb and Whistler mountains. Other amenities at this internationally renowned resort include restaurants, shops, sports facilities and a convention centre. Whistler is popular in summer and winter alike, and each season offers its own assortment of activities.

Beautiful it is, but cheap it isn't. While those toting the relatively mighty U.S. dollar will probably be unimpressed, Canadians should expect sky-high prices on dining and accommodations, with very few exceptions.

The area code in this chapter is **604**. Note that you must use the area code, even from within the 604 area.

Exploring

In the early 1960s, a group of adventurers wanted this area to host the 1968 Winter Olympics and created

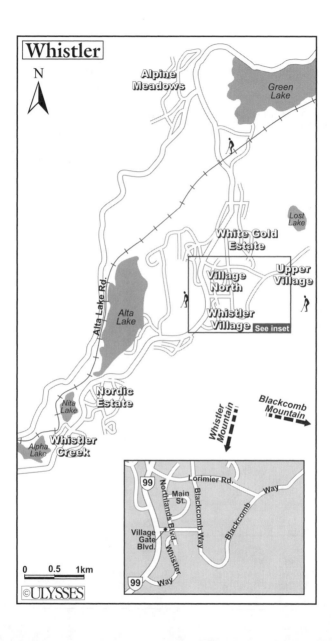

Garibaldi Park for that purpose. Although their hopes for the Olympics did not come through, they did not give up on the idea of turning the valley into a huge ski resort. The population of Whistler increased tenfold in 20 years, and by 2002, it was home to 9,000 permanent residents. More than two-million visitors make a pilgrimage to Whistler each year.

Whistler receives, on average, nearly 1000cm of snow each year, and the temperature hovers around -5°C during the winter months. For details about the host of activities available here, refer to the "Outdoor Activities" section (see p 308).

Whistler hosts all sorts of events throughout the year, including a men's World Cup downhill competition, World Cup acrobatic skiing, gay skiers' week and a jazz festival.

Should Vancouver be successful in its bid to host the 2010 Olympic Winter Games (not yet decided as of press time), Whistler would be the site of the alpine, Nordic, sliding and Paralympic events.

Take the time to walk through the hotel village at the foot of the mountains and soak up the festive, relaxed atmosphere.

Outside of the little village, at the edge of the Whistler area, lies Function Junction, a small-scale industrial centre.

Parks

Alice Lake Provincial Park (☎689-9025, *to reserve a campsite:* ☎800-689-9025) is 13km north of Squamish around the lake of the same name (Alice Lake) and has 88 campsites. It's a very popular park, especially in the middle of summer when the weather is really hot. Tourists and children flock to the beach to cool off. There are showers and many hiking trails.

Brandywine Falls Provincial Park (☎689-9025) 47km north of Squamish is a small park, with 15 campsites. The many waterfalls and vertiginous peaks make this area a photographer's paradise. Daisy Lake and the splendid mountains of Garibaldi Park are not far from here.

Vast **Garibaldi Provincial Park ★★** (*information Garibaldi/Sunshine District, Brackendale; 10km north of Squamish,* ☎898-3678), which covers 195,000ha, is extremely popular with hikers during summertime.

Highway 99 runs along the west side of the park, offering access to the various trails.

In the Whistler valley, near the village, there are five lakes where you can go swimming, windsurfing, canoeing and sailing. Here are two of them:

At little **Alpha Lake** *(at the traffic light at Whistler Creekside, turn left on Lake Placid Rd. and continue until you reach the beach)*, you can enjoy a picnic, rent a canoe or play tennis or volleyball.

Alta Lake (see p 310).

Outdoor Activities

Golf

People come to Whistler Valley from May to October to play golf in spectacular surroundings. The greens fees vary greatly from one club to the next. At the **Whistler Golf Club** *($69-$159; May to Oct; take the Village Gate Blvd., turn right at Whistler Way and go under Hwy.*

99, ☎932-3280 or 800-376-1777) you'll discover a magnificent, winding golf course set against the steep cliffs of the mountains. The **Pemberton Valley Golf and Country Club** *($48-$65; Apr to Oct; ☎894-6197 or 800-390-4653)*, in Pemberton, 23km north of Whistler, is just as beautiful as the clubs in Whistler but much less expensive.

Hiking

Except for the built-up area around Whistler, **Garibaldi Provincial Park** *(Brackendale; 10km north of Squamish, ☎898-3678)* is a huge stretch of untouched wilderness. Hiking here is a magical experience, especially when you reach Garibaldi Lake, whose turquoise waters contrast with the blue of the glacier in the background. The trails cover long distances, so you have to bring along food, as well as clothing for different temperatures.

A series of hiking trails runs all the way up **Whistler Mountain** *(☎932-3434)* and **Blackcomb Mountain** *(☎932-3141)*. From atop Whistler, you can see Black Tusk, a black sugar-loaf 2315m high.

Mountain Biking

There are plenty of mountain biking opportunities in and around the village of Whistler, as well as on the mountain itself. The **Mountain Bike Park** *($32, pass with lift ticket;* ☎*938-2769)* puts trails and guides tours at your disposal in spring and summer. Rentals are available both on the mountain and in the village.

Mountain Climbing

Mountain climbing is becoming more popular in the region. The place to go is **Stawamus Chief Mountain**. The trails leading to this granite monolith also lead to spots where you can watch the mountain climbers. For more information, contact the **Squamish & Howe Sound District Chamber of Commerce** *(*☎*892-9244).*

Downhill Skiing and Snowboarding

The Whistler ski resort is considered one of the best in North America, with an annual snowfall of 9m and a 1,600m vertical drop. There are two mountains to choose from: **Whistler Mountain** and **Blackcomb Mountain** *(*☎*932-3434 or 800-766-0449, www.whistlerblackcomb.com).* The skiing here is extraordinary, and the facilities ultramodern—but mind your budget!

Whistler and Blackcomb Mountains together make up the largest skiing area in Canada. These world-class, twin ski playgrounds are blessed with heavy snowfalls and boast enough hotels to house a city's entire population. This top-of-the-range ski metropolis

Whistler

also offers the possibility of gliding through pristine powder and, weather permitting, you will find yourself swooshing through an incredibly beautiful alpine landscape.

Whistler Mountain *($65; ☎932-3434 or 800-766-0449)* is the elder of the two resorts. Experts, powderhounds and skijumpers will all flock to Peak Chair, the chair lift that leads to the top of Whistler Mountain. From its summit, diehard skiers and snowboarders have access to a ski area composed of blue (intermediate) and expert (black-diamond and double-diamond) trails, covered in deep fleecy snow.

Blackcomb Mountain *(same price and telephone information as Whistler Mountain, above)* is the "stalwart" skiing mecca of ski buffs in North America. For years now, skiers have waged a fierce debate over which of the two mountains (Whistler or Blackcomb) is the better. One thing is certain, Blackcomb wins first place for its vertical drop of 1,609m. Check out the glacier at Blackcomb—it is truly magnificent!

If you're looking for a thrill, you can hop aboard a helicopter and set off for vast stretches of virgin powder. Contact **Whistler Heli-Skiing**

Ltd. *($630, three runs, lunch, guide; ☎932-4105 or 888-HELISKI).*

Mountain Heli Sports *(4340 Sundial Cr., ☎932-2070)* is a very versatile agency, offering not only flights over mountains and Vancouver, but heli-skiing as well.

Tyax Heli-Skiing *(☎932-7007 or 800-663-8126)* is a very well-known agency in Whistler for heli-skiing.

Windsurfing

Windsurfers come to **Squamish** *(located on Highway 99. Between Vancouver and Whistler)* for the constant winds that sweep down the sound and then head inland. For information, contact the **Squamish & Howe Sound District Chamber of Commerce** *(☎892-9244).*

Alta Lake *(north of Whistler Creekside on Hwy. 99; turn left on Alta Vista Rd. and right on Alpine Cr., then keep left until the end of the road to reach Lakeside Park)* attracts windsurfers. This little lake is located in an enchanting setting, which offers lovely panoramic views of Whistler and Blackcomb.

Accommodations

The village of Whistler is scattered with restaurants, hotels, apartments and bed & breakfasts. There is a reservation service to help you take your pick.

Whistler Resort
☎*932-4222*
Vancouver
☎*664-5625*
outside British Columbia
☎*800-944-7853*

Whistler International Hostel
$
sb, △
5678 Alta Lake Rd.
☎*932-5492*
⇄*932-4687*
www.hihostels.bc.ca
Whistler International Hostel has 32 beds and a fun vacation ambiance. Discount for Hostelling International members.

Shoestring Lodge
$
pb/sb, ℜ
1km north of the village
to the right on Nancy Greene Dr.
☎*932-3338*
☎*877-551-4954*
⇄*932-8347*
www.shoestringlodge.com
The Shoestring Lodge is one of the least expensive places to stay in Whistler. Its low rates make it very

popular, so reservations are imperative. The rooms include beds, televisions and small bathrooms; the decor is as neutral as can be. The youthful atmosphere will make you feel as if you're at a university summer camp where the students just want to have fun—and that's pretty much what this place is. The pub is known for its excellent evening entertainment (see p 315).

Stancliff House B&B
$$ bkfst incl
⊛
3333 Panorama Ridge
☎*932-2393*
⇄*932-7577*
Stancliff House B&B is one of the most reasonably priced B&Bs in the area. The view of the surrounding mountains is beautiful and the breakfasts are excellent. The home is near the centre of Whistler, but away from the hustle and bustle.

Chalet Beau Sejour
$$$ bkfst incl.
⊛
7414 Ambassador Cr.
White Gold Estate
☎*938-4966*
⇄*938-6296*
www.beausejourwhistler.com
The Chalet Beau Sejour, run by Sue and Hal, is a big, inviting house set on a mountainside. You can take in a lovely view of the valley and the mountains while eating the copious

Whistler

breakfast Sue loves to prepare. A tour guide, she
knows the region like the
back of her hand; don't
hesitate to ask her what to
see and do.

Affordable Holiday Homes in Whistler

$$$

⊛, *K*, 𝔍

2021 Karen Cr.

☎*932-0581*

☎*800-882-6991*

⇆*932-0530*

Affordable Holiday Homes
in Whistler rents five-bed-
room, four-bathroom
condominiums and studios.
Some are 5min from the
village, at the foot of the
lifts. Prices depend on the
season and the size. An
unbeatable price for Whis-
tler.

Holiday Inn

$$$$$

ℜ, ✿, ⊛, *K*, 𝔍

4295 Blackcomb Way

☎*938-0876*

☎*800-229-3188*

⇆*938-9943*

www.whistlerhi.com

The Holiday Inn is located
right near the two moun-
tains. Every room has a
fireplace and a kitchenette;
some have balconies. All
the comforts of a well-
equipped hotel are offered,
including a very sophisti-
cated fitness centre.

Listel Whistler Hotel

$$$$$$

🐾, ≈, ≡, △, ℜ

4121 Village Green

☎*932-1133*

☎*800-663-5472*

⇆*932-8383*

www.listelhotel.com

The Listel Whistler Hotel is
located in the heart of the
village, so you don't have
to look far to find some
place to eat or entertain
yourself. The simple layout
of the rooms makes for a
comfortable stay.

Tantalus Lodge

$$$$$$

≈, △, ≡, *K*, 𝔍, 🐾

4200 Whistler Way

☎*932-4146*

☎*888-633-4046*

⇆*932-2405*

www.tantaluslodge.com

Tantalus Lodge is situated
near golfing and not far
from the slopes. Its 76 con-
dominiums are spacious
and fully equipped. Tennis
and volleyball courts extend
the range of the town's
activities.

🌴 Fairmont Chateau Whistler Resort

$$$$$$

☺, 🐾, ≈, ⊛, △, ℜ, ✿, 𝔍, ≡

4599 Chateau Blvd.

☎*938-8000*

☎*800-606-8244*

☎*800-441-1414*

⇆*938-2291*

www.fairmont.com

The luxurious Fairmont
Chateau Whistler Resort lies
at the foot of the slopes of

Blackcomb Mountain. It resembles a smaller version of Whistler Village, fully equipped to meet all your dining and entertainment needs and to ensure that your stay is relaxing.

Westbrook Whistler
$$$$$$

△, ℜ, *K*, ⊛, ≡, ℑ
4340 Sundial Cr.
at the foot of the lifts
☎*932-2321*
☎*800-661-2321*
⇆*932-7152*
www.whistler.net/westbrook

The Westbrook Whistler has attractive rooms, some with kitchenettes, and beautiful suites with fireplaces. The staff even organizes receptions for newlyweds. Golf packages are available.

Blackcomb Lodge
$$$$$$

≈, *K*, △, ℜ, ⊛, ≡
4220 Gateway Dr.
☎*932-4155*
☎*888-621-1177*
⇆*932-6826*
www.blackcomblodge.com

The Blackcomb Lodge is a luxury resort whose suites are equipped with all the possible comforts, such as whirlpools and saunas. Some have balconies. Throughout the year, various packages are offered: skiing in the winter and golf in the summer. The reception is flawless. The establishment is also home

to a excellent restaurant, Araxi Restaurant and Bar (see p 314).

Pan Pacific Lodge
$$$$$$

≡, *K*, ≈, △, ❀, ℑ
4320 Sundial Cr.
☎*905-2999*
☎*(888) 905-9995*
⇆*905-2995*
www.panpac.com

The Pan Pacific Lodge is inspired by the old hotels of the Rockies, and the establishment blends in well with the countryside. Built in the middle of town at the foot of the gondolas that go to the summits of Whistler and Blackcomb, it is difficult to find a better situated or a more luxurious hotel.

Restaurants

The Roundhouse
$$

Nov to Jun 8:30am to 3pm
at the top of the Whistler Village Gondola
☎*932-3434*

If you want to be among the first to ski the slopes in the morning, head to The Roundhouse for the buffet breakfast; it is worth getting up early the day after a storm.

Whistler

Black's Pub & Restaurant
$$$
base of Whistler and Blackcomb
mountains
☎*932-6408 or 932-6945*
Black's Pub & Restaurant
serves breakfast, lunch and
dinner for the whole family
in a friendly atmosphere.
The views are exceptional
and it has one of the best
beer selections in Whistler.

Zeuski's
$$$
Town Plaza
☎*932-6009*
Zeuski's is a Greek/Medi-
terranean restaurant.
Tzatziki, hummus and souvlaki are served and the
prices are very reasonable
for Whistler.

Thai One On
$$$-$$$$
dinner only
Le Chamois hotel
base of Blackcomb Mountain
☎*932-4822*
As may be gathered by its
name, Thai One On serves
Thai food, with its wonder-
ful blend of coconut milk
and hot peppers.

Città Bistro
$$$$
Whistler Village Square
☎*932-4177*
Located in the heart of the
village, Città Bistro has an
elaborate, formal dinner
menu. This is the perfect
place to sample one of the
local beers. In both winter
and summer, a pleasant mix

of locals and tourists makes
for an extremely inviting
atmosphere.

Araxi Restaurant and Bar
$$$$
Whistler Village
☎*932-4540*
Featuring Pacific Northwest
cuisine with French and
Italian influences, Araxi is
the local Italian restaurant
of choice. It specializes in
fresh local seafood, prime
Canadian beef and locally
grown organic produce.
The wine cellar is re-
nowned as are the head
chef and pastry chef. Sum-
mer patio.

Monk's Grill
$$$$
4555 Blackcomb Way,
base of Blackcomb Mountain
☎*932-9677*
Monk's Grill is great for an
après-ski dinner. On the
menu are specialty steaks
and Alberta prime rib, as
well as fresh fish, seafood
and pasta dishes.

Trattoria di Umberto
$$$$
4417 Sundial Place, near Blackcomb
Way, Mountainside Lodge
☎*932-5858*
At the Trattoria di Umberto,
you'll find pasta, as well as
meat and fish, and a homey
atmosphere. Tuscan
chef/owner Umberto
Menghi operates a number
of restaurants in Vancouver
and Whistler, as well as a

cooking school in his native Tuscany.

La Rua
$$$$
Le Chamois hotel
base of Blackcomb Mountain
☎932-5011
Specializing in—what else—Pacific Northwest cuisine, La Rua is a local favourite. Expertly prepared entrées like fallow deer loin with oven-dried blueberries, roasted quail wrapped in bacon and drizzled in apple brandy sauce and hearty cassoulet are heaven sent after a day on the slopes. There is also a selection of good pastas, such as seafood linguine. And you can't go wrong with the mango and raspberry Napoleon for desert. The decor is rich and elegant, the service pleasant and professional. Reservations recommended.

Entertainment

Bars and Nightclubs

Boot Pub
Nancy Greene Dr., 1km north of the village
☎932-3338
Located in the Shoestring Lodge hotel, the Boot Pub offers live music, including punk bands as well as both Canadian and international acts, not to mention live, sometimes exotic, entertainment!

Tommy Africa's
Gateway Dr.
☎932-6090
Tommy Africa's hosts a medley of theme nights, including retro '80s on Mondays, soul-house on Wednesdays, disco Thursdays and funky house on Fridays and Saturdays. Lineups are common due to its popularity.

Cinnamon Bear Bar
4050 Whistler Way, Delta Hotel
☎932-1982
The relaxed atmosphere at the Cinnamon Bear Bar attracts sporty types of all ages, who come play pool or a board game, watch a game on the big screen or simply lounge by the fireplace. Live entertainment on weekends.

Calendar of Events

Following is a partial list of annual Whistler events. For more information, contact Tourism Whistler (see p 39).

January, Febuary and March

Various ski and snowboard races

Whistler

February

Altitude, Gay Ski and Snowboard Week: dance parties, performers, costumed scavenger hunts, fashion snow *(one week, early Feb; ☎888-altitude).*

April

Telus World Ski and Snowboard Festival: ski and snowboarding competitions, outdoor music, film, sports celebrities *(10 days).*

July

Canada Day: parade and festivities *(Jul 1).*

August

Whistler's Celebration of Aboriginal Culture: music, art, dance, workshops, traditional ceremonies *(mid-Aug, one week; Weetama; ☎932-2394).*

September

Whistler Comedy Festival: *(mid-Sep, 5 days).*

June to August

Whistler Daily Street Entertainment: clowns, cowgirls, world music, etc *(late Jun to early Aug).*

June to October

Whistler Farmer's Market: Upper Village, near Chateau Whistler Hotel, *(mid-Jun mid-Oct, Sun 11am to 4pm).*

October

Oktoberfest: beer, bratwurst, beer, oom-pah-pah, beer *(mid-Oct, 3 days).*

November

Cornucopia Whistler's food and wine celebration: wineries and chefs host wine and food tastings, seminars, etc. *(early Nov, 5 days).*

December

Western Film Festival: mountain and adventure films, workshops, seminars *(early Dec; ☎938-3200).*

Nokia Snowboard FIS World Cup: *(mid-Dec).*

First Night Celebration: a family New Year's Eve party *(Dec 31).*

Shopping

Just south of the little village, on the outskirts of Whistler, lies Function Junction, a small commercial and light industrial area of sorts—not just *any* industries, however!

Blackcomb Cold Beer & Wine Store *(in the Glacier Lodge, across from Fairmont Chateau Whistler Resort, ☎932-9795)* has a large selection of B.C. wines. Helpful, courteous staff.

The Wright Choice Catering Co. *(12-1370 Alpha Lake Rd., ☎905-0444)* will make supper for you. Every day you can pick up something different such as focaccia, pizza, grilled vegetables and chicken. They also prepare complete picnics, ready to take out.

Little Mountain Bakery *(7-1212 Alpha Lake Rd., Function Junction, ☎932-4220)* sells bread, pastries and sweets.

Whistler Bloom *(Market Place, ☎932-2599)* has a wonderful selection of fresh flowers and bouquets for special occasions. You can also have flowers sent anywhere in the world.

Whistler Sailing and Water Sports Centre *(Lakeside & Wayside Parks Alta Lake, ☎932-7245)* has all the necessities for sailing and water sports.

Adele-Campbell Fine Art Gallery *(4050 Whistler Way, close to the entrance of the Delta Whistler Resort, ☎938-0887)* exhibits works by renowned artists from B.C. and throughout Canada.

The Plaza Galleries *(22-4314 Main St., ☎938-6233)* present works by both local and international artists.

The Grove Gallery *(Delta Whistler Resort, ☎932-3517)* specializes in contemporary art, including landscapes of Whistler and the mountains.

Whistler Inuit Gallery *(Fairmont Chateau Whistler Resort, ☎938-3366)* exhibits very attractive wood, bone, marble and bronze pieces by Aboriginal sculptors.

Index

Index

Index

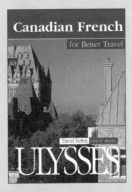

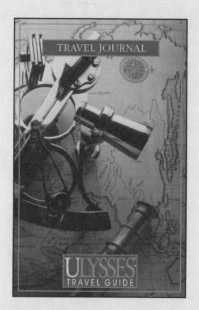

Order Form

Ulysses Travel Guides

☐ Acapulco	$14.95 CAN	$9.95 US
☐ Alberta's Best Hotels and Restaurants	$14.95 CAN	$12.95 US
☐ Arizona–Grand Canyon	$24.95 CAN	$17.95 US
☐ Atlantic Canada	$24.95 CAN	$17.95 US
☐ Beaches of Maine	$12.95 CAN	$9.95 US
☐ Bed and Breakfasts in Ontario	$17.95 CAN	$12.95 US
☐ Belize	$16.95 CAN	$12.95 US
☐ Boston	$17.95 CAN	$12.95 US
☐ British Columbia's Best Hotels and Restaurants	$14.95 CAN	$12.95 US
☐ Calgary	$17.95 CAN	$12.95 US
☐ California	$29.95 CAN	$21.95 US
☐ Canada	$29.95 CAN	$21.95 US
☐ Cancún & Riviera Maya	$19.95 CAN	$14.95 US
☐ Cape Cod, Nantucket and Martha's Vineyard	$24.95 CAN	$17.95 US
☐ Cartagena (Colombia)	$12.95 CAN	$9.95 US
☐ Chicago	$19.95 CAN	$14.95 US
☐ Chile	$27.95 CAN	$17.95 US
☐ Colombia	$29.95 CAN	$21.95 US
☐ Costa Rica	$27.95 CAN	$19.95 US
☐ Cuba	$24.95 CAN	$17.95 US
☐ Dominican Republic	$24.95 CAN	$17.95 US
☐ Ecuador and Galápagos Islands	$24.95 CAN	$17.95 US
☐ El Salvador	$22.95 CAN	$14.95 US
☐ Guadalajara	$17.95 CAN	$12.95 US
☐ Guadeloupe	$24.95 CAN	$17.95 US
☐ Guatemala	$24.95 CAN	$17.95 US
☐ Havana	$16.95 CAN	$12.95 US
☐ Hawaii	$29.95 CAN	$21.95 US
☐ Honduras	$24.95 CAN	$17.95 US
☐ Huatulco–Puerto Escondido	$17.95 CAN	$12.95 US
☐ Inns and Bed & Breakfasts in Québec	$14.95 CAN	$10.95 US
☐ Islands of the Bahamas	$24.95 CAN	$17.95 US
☐ Las Vegas	$17.95 CAN	$12.95 US
☐ Lisbon	$18.95 CAN	$13.95 US
☐ Los Angeles	$19.95 CAN	$14.95 US
☐ Los Cabos and La Paz	$14.95 CAN	$10.95 US
☐ Louisiana	$29.95 CAN	$21.95 US
☐ Martinique	$24.95 CAN	$17.95 US
☐ Miami	$9.95 CAN	$12.95 US
☐ Montréal	$19.95 CAN	$14.95 US

Ulysses Travel Guides *(continued)*

☐ New England	$29.95 CAN	$21.95 US
☐ New Orleans	$17.95 CAN	$12.95 US
☐ New York City	$19.95 CAN	$14.95 US
☐ Nicaragua	$24.95 CAN	$16.95 US
☐ Ontario	$27.95 CAN	$19.95 US
☐ Ontario's Best Hotels and Restaurants	$27.95 CAN	$19.95 US
☐ Ottawa–Hull	$17.95 CAN	$12.95 US
☐ Panamá	$27.95 CAN	$17.95 US
☐ Peru	$27.95 CAN	$19.95 US
☐ Phoenix	$16.95 CAN	$12.95 US
☐ Portugal	$24.95 CAN	$16.95 US
☐ Provence & the Côte d'Azur	$29.95 CAN	$21.95 US
☐ Puerto Plata–Sosua	$14.95 CAN	$9.95 US
☐ Puerto Rico	$24.95 CAN	$17.95 US
☐ Puerto Vallarta	$14.95 CAN	$10.95 US
☐ Québec	$29.95 CAN	$21.95 US
☐ Québec City	$17.95 CAN	$12.95 US
☐ San Diego	$17.95 CAN	$12.95 US
☐ San Francisco	$17.95 CAN	$12.95 US
☐ Seattle	$17.95 CAN	$12.95 US
☐ St. Lucia	$17.95 CAN	$12.95 US
☐ St. Martin–St. Barts	$17.95 CAN	$12.95 US
☐ Toronto	$19.95 CAN	$14.95 US
☐ Tunisia	$27.95 CAN	$19.95 US
☐ Vancouver	$17.95 CAN	$12.95 US
☐ Washington D.C.	$18.95 CAN	$13.95 US
☐ Western Canada	$29.95 CAN	$21.95 US

Ulysses Green Escapes

☐ Cross-Country Skiing and Snowshoeing in Ontario	$22.95 CAN	$16.95 US
☐ Cycling in France	$22.95 CAN	$16.95 US
☐ Cycling in Ontario	$22.95 CAN	$16.95 US
☐ Hiking in the Northeastern U.S.	$19.95 CAN	$13.95 US
☐ Hiking in Québec	$22.95 CAN	$16.95 US
☐ Hiking in Ontario	$22.95 CAN	$16.95 US
☐ Ontario's Bike Paths and Rail Trails	$19.95 CAN	$14.95 US

Ulysses Conversation Guides

☐ French for Better Travel	$9.95 CAN	$6.95 US
☐ Italian for Better Travel	$9.95 CAN	$6.95 US
☐ Portuguese for Better Travel	$9.95 CAN	$6.95 US
☐ Spanish for Better Travel in Latin America	$9.95 CAN	$6.95 US
☐ Spanish for Better Travel in Spain	$9.95 CAN	$6.95 US

Ulysses Travel Journals

☐ Ulysses Travel Journal (80 Days)	$14.95 CAN	$9.95 US
☐ Ulysses Travel Journal (Quill, Lighthouse)	$12.95 CAN	$9.95 US

budget●zone

☐ Central America	$14.95 CAN	$10.95 US
☐ Western Canada	$14.95 CAN	$10.95 US

Title	Qty	Price	Total

Name:	Subtotal	
	Shipping	$4.75 CAN $5.75 US
Address:	Subtotal	
	GST in Canada 7%	
	Total	

Tel: Fax:

E-mail:

Payment: ☐ Cheque ☐ Visa ☐ MasterCard

Card number_____ Expiry date_____

Signature_____

Ulysses Travel Guides

4176 St. Denis Street,
Montréal, Québec, H2W 2M5

305 Madison Avenue,
Suite 1166,
New York, NY 10165

Toll-free: 1-877-542-7247
☎(514) 843-9447
Fax : (514) 843-9448
Info@ulysses.ca
www.ulyssesguides.com

DENMARK

COMMUNICATIONS

Denmark includes 100 inhabited islands, and an efficient system of boat and ferry connections links these with the mainland. Daily air services operate between the main parts and the Danish State Railways cover most of the country with a criss-cross network.

SOME PLACES TO VISIT

1. Voergard Manor
2. Lindholm Høje, excavated Viking settlement
3. Spøttrup Manor
4. Viborg Cathedral
5. Gammel Estrup Manor
6. Vorbasse, Wild-West Camp for children
7. Koldinghus Castle
8. Ribe Cathedral
9. Haderslev Cathedral
10. Gråsten Castle
11. Odense, Birthplace of Hans Christian Andersen
12. The Viking Ship at Ladby
13. Nyborg Castle
14. Egeskov Castle
15. Brahetrolleborg Manor
16. Tranekær Manor
17. Kronborg Castle at Helsingore
18. Frederiksborg Castle, Museum
19. Fredensborg Palace
20. Roskilde Cathedral
21. Vordingborg, The 'Goose Tower'
22. Maribo Cathedral
23. Østerlars Round Church

Roads ———
Railways +—+—+
Places of interest ①

0 10 20 30 40 50 Km

SKAGER

Thisted
Nykøbing
Lemvig ③
Struer Sk
Holstebro
Ringkøbing Hernin
J L
Skjern Brande
Grindsted
Varde
Esbjerg
Ribe ⑧
Tøn